Scribe Publications
FUTUREVISION

Richard Watson is a writer, speaker, and strategist who works with leadership teams to challenge existing thinking about what is obvious or inevitable. He is also the founder and publisher of What's Next, a website that documents global trends, and the co-founder, with Oliver Freeman and Andrew Crosthwaite, of Futures House Europe, a specialist scenario-planning consultancy. Richard is the author of the bestselling book *Future Files* (Scribe), which has been translated into 14 languages. He lectures regularly in London Business School's Executive Education programmes.

Oliver Freeman is a career publisher and the joint chairman of Third Millennium Publishing Australasia. He is also the co-founder, futurist, and leading scenario planner at the Neville Freeman Agency. Oliver has chaired boards for the Copyright Agency, Viscopy, Publish Australia, and UNSW Press, and is a co-founder of digital companies eBooks.com, Leagle, The Larrikin Post, and homepageDAILY. He is an adjunct professor at the University of Technology Sydney Business School, and has worked extensively with Richard on various scenario-planning projects.

*For Napier Collyns, co-founder of the Global Business Network,
without whom we would never have met and our futures would
have been quite different.*

*For Wayde Bull and Sandy Belford,
who worked with us on the first version of the Worldview Scenarios.*

*For Richard Bawden, whose expertise and words on systems
thinking and scenario learning have been so critical to us.*

And for Georgie and Susie, for everything else.

FUTUREVISION

scenarios for the world in 2040

Richard Watson & Oliver Freeman

SCRIBE

Melbourne

Scribe Publications Pty Ltd
18–20 Edward St, Brunswick, Victoria, Australia 3056
Email: info@scribepub.com.au

First published by Scribe 2012

Typeset in 11.5/15 pt Adobe Garamond Pro by the publishers
Printed and bound in Australia by Griffin Press

The paper this book is printed on is certified against the Forest
Stewardship Council® Standards. Griffin Press holds FSC chain
of custody certification SGS-COC-005088. FSC promotes
environmentally responsible, socially beneficial and economically
viable management of the world's forests.

National Library of Australia
Cataloguing-in-Publication data

Watson, Richard, 1961-

Futurevision: scenarios for the world in 2040 / Richard Watson; Oliver Freeman.

9781922070098 (pbk.)

1. Forecasting. 2. Social prediction.

Other Authors/Contributors: Freeman, Oliver.

303.49

www.scribepublications.com.au

Contents

'Call it the resilience gap. The world is becoming turbulent faster than organizations are becoming resilient.'
Gary Hamel and Liisa Välikangas

Introduction

People have always been curious about what lies over the horizon or around the next corner. Books that speculate about the shape of things to come, especially those that make precise or easily digestible predictions, are consistently popular. But lately, the number of books seeking to uncover or explain the future has exploded. The reason for this — which, ironically, no futurist appears to have foreseen — is that rapid technological change and historic political and economic events have combined to create a climate that is characterised by uncertainty, and there is much anxiety about how civilisation may develop.

The world today offers more promise than ever before, but there are also more threats to our continued existence. During the writing of this book, for example, we saw the sudden collapse of Egypt's Mubarak regime, and the domino effect it had on the Middle East; the emerging recession in parts of the United Kingdom; the economic plights of the PIIGS (Portugal, Italy, Ireland, Greece, and Spain); the perpetration of medieval atrocities in Syria; and the explosive success of the iPad, which sold almost 12 million units in the first economic quarter of 2012.

That's not to mention attacks on confidential government and commercial data, the discovery of a Higgs boson–like particle, and the alleged detection of particles travelling faster than light, which is supposedly impossible (it was later revealed to be an error, but you never know what else may be found with time).

In short, the future is not what it used to be, and it needs rescuing. There is now a high degree of volatility in everything from politics and financial markets to food prices, sport, and weather, and this is creating unease — especially among generations that grew up in an era which was characterised, with hindsight, by relative stability and simplicity; in a world that was more like *Downton Abbey* than *Cowboys & Aliens*.

There is a problem with most books about the future — and indeed, there is a fatal flaw with almost all of our thinking about what will happen next. This is because of a simple point. The fact is, there is no single future, regardless of our deepest desire that it be so, and there is no heavenly salvation in sight.

Our views about the world change regularly. We know that the present is highly uncertain, and we are even starting to question what happened in the past (at a recent futures summit in Provence, France, Grigory Yavlinsky, the former presidential candidate, admitted to us that the most uncertain thing about Russia was its past). Logically, if the past and present are uncertain, the future will be, too. And if the future is uncertain, there must be more than one possible future.

There are always many different ways in which a series of events might unfold, so suggesting, as many futurists and technologists do, that there is one specific, inevitable future to come is not only inaccurate — it is also dangerously misleading. What is even worse is when the two of us, as futurists, are presented with several possible futures and asked to decide which is more likely to occur. Linear analysis — the extrapolation of current events to the future — is a very straight road that doesn't allow for the unforeseen shocks that come from all sides. As the historian Niall Ferguson has observed: 'It is an axiom among those who study science fiction and other literature concerned with the future that those who write it are, consciously or unconsciously, reflecting on the present.' Or, as we like to say: all futures are contemporary futures, in the same way that all prediction is based upon past experience.

This is one reason why so many predictions about the future go so horribly and hilariously wrong. For example, an article in *The Times* in 1894 suggested that every street in London would eventually be buried under nine feet of horse manure. Why? London was rapidly expanding, and so was the amount of horse-drawn transport. Londoners would, it seemed at the time, soon be up horse-manure creek without a paddle. What the author of this prediction didn't foresee, of course, was that at exactly this time engineer Karl Benz was developing the horseless carriage in Germany, and the new invention would change everything.

Four years later, in 1898, Benz made exactly the same mistake of extrapolating from the present. He predicted that the global demand for automobiles would not surpass one million. Why? Because of a lack of chauffeurs! The automobile had been invented, but the idea of driving by oneself had not. Thus it seemed inevitable that the world would eventually run out of chauffeurs, meaning that the manufacture of the automobile would come to the end of the road.

It is also misleading to analyse trends in order to predict the future. Not only must trends be lined up with 'discontinuities', counter-trends, anomalies, and wildcards (which have a nasty habit of jumping into view suddenly, from left field), but also they are retrospective — not 'futuristic' at all. A trend is an unfolding event or disposition that we trace back to its initiation, so trends tell us next to nothing about the direction or velocity of future events.

Trend analysis is not foolproof because the world is not binary — it is systemic, and influences interact with each other in complex and surprising ways, leading to change. It is rare for a new idea to extinguish an old one, especially if it has been in circulation for a long time. For instance, despite the facility with which mobile technology can deliver media content, there's still something reassuring about listening to the radio in the car or reading a daily newspaper, whether that be in print or online. And while e-payments have transformed the banking industry, we still have physical branches and the number of channels through which to conduct banking is expanding, not shrinking. Change can happen rapidly, but in most instances it takes decades, often generations, for something new to cause something else to become extinct. Moreover, while means of delivery, business models, materials, competitors, profit margins, and even companies may change radically, deep human needs, such as the desire to tell or listen to stories, remain constant.

True, occasionally an idea or event occurs that is so significant that history is divided into 'before' and 'after'. Examples, arguably, include the development of the steam engine, the automobile, the microprocessor, the mobile phone, and the internet; the collapse of the Berlin Wall; 9/11; and the rise of Google, Facebook, and Amazon respectively. But even here there is not uniformity. We all have a particular lens through which we see the world, and no two individuals ever experience events in the same way. More often than not, different individuals and institutions will experience the present in slightly different ways depending on where they live, what they do, and how they have grown up. Therefore, there is always more than one reality (or worldview, as we like to call it). And if there is more than one present, there must certainly be more than one future.

This notion that there is no linear pathway is a good thing, as is the level of uncertainty that surrounds the future. Indeed, in many respects this is one of the most interesting times ever to be alive because almost everything that we think we know, or take for granted, is capable of being challenged or changed, often at a fundamental level — even human nature, if Joel Garreau, the author of bestseller *Radical Evolution: the promise and peril of enhancing our minds, our bodies — and what it means to be human*, is to be believed.

We believe that the only rigorous way to deal with a future so uneven and disjointed is to create a set of alternative futures that cover a number of possibilities. This technique — called scenario planning or scenario thinking — originated as a form of war-gaming, or battle planning, in military circles, and was picked up by, among others, oil company Royal Dutch Shell, as a way of dealing with ambiguity and uncertainty. In Shell's case, scenarios correctly anticipated the 1973 oil crisis, which hiked prices dramatically, and the corresponding price falls almost a decade later. Other incidences where scenarios have foreseen what few others could include Adam Kahane's 1992 Mont Fleur Scenarios for South Africa, which helped to promote a peaceful transition to democratic rule, and two sets of scenarios created by the authors of this book, one in 2005 for a major bank and one in 2006–2007 for the future of the teaching profession, both of which identified futures around the global recession of 2007–2012.

This is a book about the future that offers a number of alternatives for discussion and dissection. It is not merely about trends, although we do look at key trends in demographics, technology, energy, the economy, the environment, food and water supplies, and geopolitics. In Part I, we present four detailed scenarios, the Worldview Scenarios, which show what it might be like to live in the world in 2040. These are not simply about where today's trends might take us, but about what the world in 2040 might be like. To formulate them, we took a number of critical questions and used the robust, resilient process of scenario planning. In Part II, we take you through how we did this. We reflect on the key factors in today's world that helped to create our four future worlds, and examine what actions were taken, and by whom, to lead to them.

It is not our intention in this book to 'predict the future': we are not seeking to get it all right, as this is impossible. Rather, our aim is to prevent people from getting the future seriously wrong. This is possible, but only if individuals can think bravely and creatively. This book is intended to form part of a conversation, to open people's minds to what is happening now, and to create meaningful debate about some of the choices we face and where some of the actions that we are choosing to perform — or allowing to happen — may lead. It is intended to alert individuals and organisations to a broad range of longer-term questions, expectations, and decisions, and to place a few of them firmly on the long-range radar for monitoring and further analysis. It's really about challenging fundamental assumptions and reframing viewpoints, including establishing whether people are asking the right questions — as, in this context, disagreeing with and probing the received wisdom is a valuable skill.

Most of all, perhaps, we would like to liberate attitudes towards the future. In our scenario-planning projects, we have discovered that people from all kinds of professions and backgrounds want to make a difference — to generate change, as well as adapt to it. As Peter Senge, the director of the Center for Organizational Learning at the MIT Sloan School of Management, once remarked, 'Vision becomes a living thing only when most people believe they can shape their future.' Yes, people need to understand the opportunities and threats that lie ahead, but they can also consider the direction in which they would like to travel. For example, is mankind on the cusp of another creative renaissance, characterised by radical new ideas, scientific and technological breakthroughs, material abundance, and extraordinary opportunities for a greater proportion of the world's people; or are we, in a sense, at the end of civilisation, facing a new world characterised by high levels of volatility, anxiety, and uncertainty? Are we entering a peaceful period where collective action will address abject poverty, infant mortality, adult literacy, physical security, and basic human rights; or are we moving towards an increasingly individualistic and selfish era, in which urban overcrowding, the high cost of energy and food, water shortages, social inequality, unemployment, nationalism, and increasingly authoritarian governments will combine to create a new age of misery and rage? Some urban economists and sociologists are predicting a future in which up to two billion people will be squatters in 'edge cities' attached to major conurbations such as Mexico City, Mumbai, and Beijing, while others believe in the concept of a smart planet, in which our expertise delivers a triumphal response to the drivers of change and we create local, inclusive, self-managed communities that resonate with traditional democratic values.

So just what does the future have in store for us? Where might we all be in 2040? Will life generally be better, worse, or weirder than we expect? Will we have adopted a broadly fatalistic approach to events, or will we be striving to shape the unfolding world in line with a well-defined and compellingly articulated objective? And in what ways are the seeds of this future already with us? Let's find out.

Part I

The Future Four-told

'It is now life and not art that requires the willing suspension of disbelief.'
Lionel Trilling

1

Forward, into the Unknown:

why scenario planning?

Several years ago, an office worker in Tokyo dropped dead at his desk and wasn't discovered until five days later. This was despite the fact that his co-workers regularly walked past and said hello. In a similar incident, a 51-year-old had a heart attack in an open-plan office in New York on a Monday morning, but nobody noticed that he was dead until Saturday, when a cleaner attempted to wake him up. Apparently it wasn't unusual for the man to be there because, according his boss — without any hint of irony — 'he was always the first to arrive and the last to leave'.

Is this the future? Is this how things will eventually end for many of the so-called free agents inhabiting anonymous desks inside vast corporations, or for the emerging class of digital nomads tethered electronically to virtual offices via a compote of Blackberries and Apples?

The answer is no; it is one possible future, but there are also many others. One future might be a cross between Terry Gilliam's *Brazil* and Fritz Lang's *Metropolis*: a dystopian world where people are forced to work longer hours for large bureaucracies in a futile attempt to earn more money to offset rising food prices, higher energy bills, declining real wages, increasing debt, and disappearing retirement. Conversely, people might willingly choose to spend more time inside lifeless cubicles at work because, while the work is mind-numbing, they feel increasingly isolated and uncomfortable at home. This could be because the family, as a building block of society, has atomised, and more people are living alone; or because work offers more satisfaction and companionship than modern relationships. Add a pinch of ubiquitous media; autocratic, data-driven governments; CCTV; predictive modelling; brain-to-machine interfaces; genetic prophesy, to predict future health; and technologies such as global positioning systems (GPS), radio-frequency identification (RFID), and facial recognition, and, while it isn't quite George Orwell's *1984*, that world could be seen as getting closer, not further away.

Alternatively, we might see a move in a completely different, and much more utopian, direction. Maybe we'll start to realise that there's more to life than dropping dead at a desk, and people will begin to fight to rebalance their lives in their favour. Perhaps automation — especially robotics and artificial intelligence — will finally deliver on the promise of a leisure society, and people will spend more time reconnecting with their families and doing the things that really interest them. This could also be a world where the state limits freedom of choice in areas such as healthcare and pensions, and provides a higher degree of security in return for higher direct or indirect taxation. It could be a sustainable world driven as much by the heart as the head, where local forces start to push back against globalisation and where new technologies are carefully scrutinised for their long-term social impact and value; an ethically driven world, where physical community is rediscovered and corporations are restrained due to, among other things, skills shortages, the high cost of energy, and limited raw materials. Such a world would not be dissimilar, in many ways, to the one described several decades ago in Ernst Schumacher's *Small is Beautiful: economics as if people mattered.*

And there are many other possibilities, many other paths and other futures, too. How, for example, might an oil price of US$200 per barrel change the world? Perhaps people and products would move around less frequently, or the high price of food would lead to an unexpected decrease in obesity. What if we invented a new technology based upon photosynthesis that made energy almost free? What if a new ideology capable of challenging free-market capitalism were to appear? Or if the next Russian Empire decided to broaden its borders beyond their current limits? What could happen if the heavy use of mobile phones (of which there are already more than five billion worldwide) started to cause the deaths of tens of millions of young people through brain cancer, after a long and largely invisible gestation period?

Imagining the World We Want

There are many ways in which we can begin to think about the future, but looking backwards to see how we got to where we are today is a good place to start. This is partly because we can trace how what happened a long time ago has influenced our immediate past and our present. It is also because what has already happened can influence what happens next — in understanding the complexities of how we got to where we are, we will be better served in how we think about the future. For example, to understand the future of Greece properly, one might need to consider the impacts of the Ottoman Empire, German occupation during World War II, the civil war of the 1940s, and the influence of the junta that took power in 1967.

Of course, history is not always the most reliable guide to the future because nobody owns the facts. The way we interpret the past can cast a long shadow that hides other important details.

So looking at the past alone is not enough to allow us to imagine the future. The future is buried in the fringes of the present, which means that it can also pay dividends to know how to examine the world around us now: to know precisely where to look for emerging trends, or who to talk to about the way in which things are developing. This can give you a useful start compared to less creative and less curious thinkers. Whichever way you look at it, it's worth remembering that the future is always present, as well as having seeds in the past.

Let's get back to the two dead bodies. Both of the stories about workers dropping dead at their desks were featured in newspapers and on television stations around the world. They were widely circulated on the internet, too. But both were untrue — they were urban legends, pure fictions. So why did so many people believe them? One answer is that people were focused on other things and accepted the stories at face value. Another explanation is that these stories are fables or legends that tell us something about the way we live today. They confirmed to many people a particular point of view about the present and, especially, the future, which is the nagging doubt that perhaps we are spending too much time at work and that if we suddenly stopped doing whatever it is we do, nobody would really notice. They also expose a deep fear, which is either that we are not doing anything that makes a real difference, or that we will not be missed or remembered — possibly the element of the future that we care about the most, but think about the least.

Herein lies the problem. We all have different views about the future, what we hope to achieve, and the direction in which we are heading; but we are all susceptible to being hugely misled, not only about what is happening right now, but also about what is likely to happen next. Yet unless we can think coherently about the future, it is likely that we will be held hostage by a world not of our choosing, and that our current choices will be restrained by events and situations that are either untrue or have not yet happened. Look, for example, at the way in which an increasing number of institutions and individuals adopt worst-case scenarios as the most likely outcomes. It creates large amounts of anxiety for them. But if these same people are given a choice of several outcomes, rather than assuming just one, such anxieties tend to evaporate.

So how can we all deal with this ambiguity and uncertainty effectively? How can we hedge against so many variables, ranging from the economy and politics to technology and nature? Furthermore, how can we challenge specific views about how the future will unfold? How can we stop ourselves from falling prey to 'facts' that appear to confirm seemingly self-evident truths? How can we restrain ourselves from conveniently extrapolating a future from an ephemeral trend, or from seeing the world as it is, or may soon become, through a narrowly focused — and at times rose-tinted — lens?

There is also the problem of what Harold Macmillan, the former British prime minister, referred to as, 'Events, my dear boy, events.' What are the greatest threats that we will face in the years ahead, and how can they be anticipated?

The answer is that we can't anticipate every threat, and we cannot hedge against all of the variables or consistently distinguish truth from fiction — not precisely. But we can, nevertheless, dream up and play some useful games of 'what if?', and analyse in some detail what our reactions to certain events might be. This won't always work, of course. We will still get caught out, but it's better than not thinking about the future at all. The process of engaging with the future allows us to heighten our peripheral vision, so that the content of some new events no longer surprises us — even though their timing may be unexpected.

Seeing Tomorrow's Problems Today

It takes time — which is in very short supply nowadays — to think seriously about and plan for worlds to come. More often than not, especially in commercial organisations, the focus is on the next 12 weeks (the next financial quarter) or the next 12 months (annual results), figures that are compared to those of the year before. But thinking creatively beyond this, especially ahead 36 months or more, is relatively unusual. As a result, many organisations focus almost exclusively on short-term problems, which means that their reactions are often immediate, and 'management' consists of racing from handling one crisis to the next. And deep questions, along with longer-term opportunities and risks, tend to go unanswered or unexamined until too late.

This is not just a concern for businesses. For example, how many of us defer thinking about pensions and superannuation until way past the ideal start date? This sort of laxity occurs on a global level, too: the economic rise of China (one of the few nations that does think much further ahead) went largely unnoticed by many for years. In the 1990s, world economic forums would get excited by China, but would soon revert to the old concerns about NATO, Japan, and the tensions in Europe. While they're now slowly seeing the opportunity that the nation presents, the risk of a potential economic reversal in China, with associated bubbles and concentration risks, is not being seen. The same could perhaps be said for fertility rates, the effects of new technology on employment, or the impact of social media on democracy.

It is no wonder that so many individuals cling resolutely to the past — it's much easier that way. Similarly, it's hardly a surprise that so many institutions structure themselves to deal with the immediate present — it's much cheaper that way. Yet by the time the relevant strategies are in place, the horse has bolted and we are already somewhere new. Most organisations create strategies to deal with yesterday's problems. But thinking about the longer-term future is fundamental if we, as individuals or organisations, are to take full advantage of the myriad opportunities that lie ahead. Unless we want to end up standing on the wrong side of history, it is essential for all of us to develop an awareness of emerging risks, and try to see tomorrow's problems today.

All well and good, we can hear you saying, but how can one sell the idea of thinking about the future, or futures thinking, to an organisation run by someone who is focused on the set of numbers that will take shape over the next 12 weeks? The honest answer is that you can't. However, if you are fortunate to work for a company with an incoming or outgoing head, there is hope. These leaders tend to be concerned with creating a vision or leaving a legacy, both mindsets that fit well with futures thinking.

Furthermore, dark clouds sometimes have silver linings. In our view, a critical function of leadership is to embrace the plurality of opinions — of diverging worldviews — in order to have a better chance of making sense of the future. The recent history of reactions to climate change is a case in point. If an organisation is facing an extinction event (such as the advent of new technology, changes to government regulation, or a shift in customer mindsets that mean that current products, services, business models, or margins appear doomed), this is often precisely the time when closed minds can be opened up to new possibilities.

One of the features of good leaders is that they have an understanding of the past and the present. They comprehend the historical reasons for failure and success, but they also appreciate at least some of the challenges that lie ahead, both immediately and into the future. Outstanding leaders do something else, too: they have a vision for a longer future. More often that not, they see things that others can't and, while their vision may be partially obscured, they are often able to create and communicate compelling stories about why other people should follow them down a particular road. Good leaders can play a role in encouraging others to think about the long-term future.

But a word of warning: there can be a fatal flaw, and that is when individuals and organisations end up being held hostage to a particular point of view or a fixed vision of the future. The more dominant a leader or organisational culture, the more people will be drawn into agreeing with the dominant view, and the less they will seek to challenge it or the hidden assumptions upon which it is built. The more credible or powerful a source, the less likely we are to think that something they say may be wrong. The more popular or widely circulated an idea, the more likely we are to agree with it, especially if we are busy. Be aware of this as we continue into the realm of futures thinking.

Planning Is Better Than Prediction

There is a danger at this point that many readers will be feeling a little lost, because we are heading away from a world of solid numbers and hard facts to worlds not yet dreamed up or perceived by most people. Some of you may be thinking that this all sounds too ethereal or theoretical. Well, remember that hard numbers are always historical (by the time they're produced, they're old, to some degree) and are usually open to interpretation. Remember, too, that for many people the pace of everyday life is accelerating. We have more to do, but we have less time to do it in. We are also more distracted, and systems are becoming more networked, so the number of opportunities to get things really wrong and to create cascading failures is increasing, not diminishing. It is necessary to look forward, especially when things are moving very fast. Indeed, one might argue that the faster things move, the further ahead we need to look so as to avoid nasty accidents. In our work with organisations across the world, we have also come to the conclusion that effective short-term strategies have the longer term embedded within.

Still somewhat sceptical? Then we'll start the ball rolling with a brief history of future gazing. We'll skip over a few thousand years of seers and instead focus on the doers, starting with the military. The idea of scenario planning has its origins in war-gaming, or battle planning, in the late 1800s. There are clear links to games such as chess, which almost certainly grew out of a sixth-century Indian game called Chaturanga, meaning 'having four divisions', and inspired Kriegsspiel, a German war game invented in 1812. Kriegsspiel is especially interesting in this context because the Prussian victory over the French in the Franco-Prussian War of 1870–1871 is sometimes credited to the Prussian officers using Kriegsspiel to train. Military war-gaming continues to this day, and is used to simulate unexpected enemy tactics or the unwelcome intrusion of factors such as weather.

All war-gaming was originally conducted in-house, but as needs grew so did a number of external consultants — such as the RAND Corporation in the United States, which was partly responsible for developing early game theory. Simulations were further developed by the Hudson Institute, notably by Herman Kahn, who resigned from RAND to create the Institute. It was he who popularised the term 'scenario', partly, we assume, because of its narrative flavour. As Kees van der Heijden points out in his book *Scenarios: the art of strategic thinking*, the term represented Kahn's belief that he did not make predictions, but instead created stories about the future for people to explore. It all sounds very Hollywood, and indeed it was: Kahn was among Stanley Kubrick's inspirations for a central character in the classic war film *Dr. Strangelove*.

The best-known example of scenario planning in business is probably Royal Dutch Shell, who used what were effectively sophisticated simulations to consider the impact of a number of external variables, including demographics, politics, resources, and technology, on long-term capital expenditures. The central figure in this was Pierre Wack, who introduced the idea that while many things are unpredictable and uncontrollable, order can be brought to other uncertainties — at least in the sense that we can rigorously debate known unknowns. He also provided us with the essence of learning from the future when he described the benefit of scenario planning as 'the gentle art of re-perception'. By going out and exploring the wilder shores of turbulent future environments, we suddenly see the present in a new light; we see the world differently and engage with it in innovative ways.

Whether it was skill, luck, or a mixture of both, the scenario team at Shell developed a set of scenarios, including one that foresaw the 1973 oil crisis when the other major oil companies did not. This obviously put Shell in a rather favourable position in terms of preparedness, but it was perhaps not the main point of the exercise. The aim of Shell's early scenarios was largely to determine whether investment should be made in certain very expensive projects. The idea was not to forecast a variety of alternatives futures, but rather to ensure that current strategic plans would hold up across all foreseeable scenarios.

In other words, the purpose of scenario planning is, more often than not, to travel into the future so that we are able to re-perceive the present. Its role is disruption. With hindsight this may not sound all that dramatic, but it was a significant breakthrough at the time, much as the adoption of a scenario mindset still is today in many organisations.

The problem with traditional forecasting, in a nutshell, is that it contains too many unchallenged assumptions. Why could this be the case? One reason is that strategy inside many organisations relies on convergent thinking: people look at an operating environment and immediately start to make a number of assumptions. The first assumption is that they can control more things than they actually can. The second is that they need to focus most of their attention on internal concerns, to the exclusion of external forces. The third, and often most fatal, is that they look at the present and assume that things will progress in an orderly fashion or along a straight path more or less forever.

For example, when it comes to making forecasts for supply or demand, many people will take a high–low approach: they will draw a graph showing historical supply or demand and add two new lines, one higher and one lower. But this misses curve balls and paradigm shifts, caused either by the impact of new events or by unusual and sometimes even counter-intuitive combinations.

Look at the story behind figures one and two, for instance.

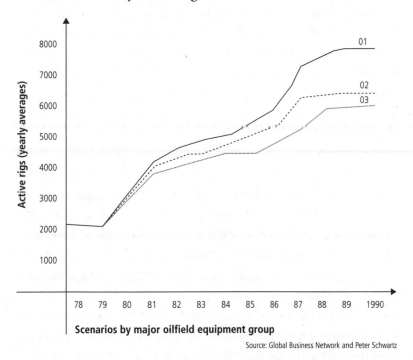

Scenarios by major oilfield equipment group

Source: Global Business Network and Peter Schwartz

Figure 1. Scenarios for the future of oil drilling in the United States, 1978–1990

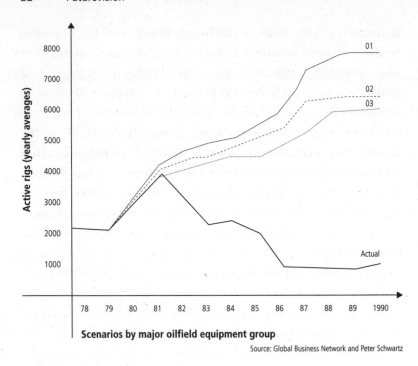

Scenarios by major oilfield equipment group

Source: Global Business Network and Peter Schwartz

Figure 2. Scenarios for the future of oil drilling in the United States, 1978–1990 — as compared to the actual figures.

The graphs show a series of forecasts, up until 1990, for the number of active oil rigs, as predicted by an oilfield supplies company in the early 1980s. Three separate forecasts — high, medium, and low — are shown as lines 01, 02, and 03. The creators of these graphs saw these three outcomes as alternative scenarios, but they were not. They were, in effect, sensitivity analysis on one scenario. All three are essentially the same, and show orderly rises and falls.

Why did the forecasters get it so wrong? The answer is that all of these predictions were based on past experience. They were logical extrapolations; but what nobody foresaw at the time was that what looked like a long-term trend was in fact a short-term situation based upon a high oil price, low interest rates, and government subsidies for drilling. When the US congress removed the tax incentive to drill for oil, the market collapsed. The oil-drilling planners failed to distinguish between an anomaly (a boom between 1980 and 1982) and normality, or to remember that while all of our knowledge is about the past, all of our most important decisions are about the future. In other words, they extrapolated from a series of short-lived trends without thinking about whether the trends were in fact a short-term response to deeper drivers of change. When the tax incentives for drilling were removed, reality changed direction.

This story underlines the major flaw in quantitative forecasting based on the past: it can only be wrong. The mind boggles at the number of executive hours wasted globally each year on creating forecast-based strategies and then searching for explanations as to why they did not eventuate, only to replace them with revised forecasts that repeat this fatal flaw.

History, as author and security and intelligence expert George Friedman has pointed out, 'can change with stunning rapidity'. While there are many trends and traits that at first glance look set to continue for the immediate future, nothing is ever certain. As the writer J.G. Ballard put it crisply: 'If enough people predict something, it won't happen.' If the Chinese economic miracle were to come to an abrupt end, for example, this would create a very different future than one in which it did not. Therefore, probability is of limited value when engaging with the future. The future is not at the end of a trend line.

The history of prediction is interesting in this context. It is littered with false prophets, much as it's strewn with false profits, and it is important to distinguish between what is probable and what is possible. The best way of doing this, as the fictional detective Sherlock Holmes once pointed out, is to start by removing whatever is impossible, and whatever is left, no matter how improbable, must be considered possible.

So what can we do to address this problem? Is there any point in trying to predict the future, or is it best to just sit back and let it unfold?

Letting the future happen is actually not a bad option, but only if you are nimble and open-minded — if you are a quick thinker and can react speedily, then a fast-follower strategy can work well. But most individuals and organisations are not especially nimble, nor open. They tend to be closed to the outside world mentally, and stuck with a set of beliefs that were created by relying on past experience. Organisations, in particular, are constrained by legacy issues, systems, and assets that make it extremely difficult to change direction in a hurry. Much better then, surely, to have some advance warning and to be able to discuss what could be done should conditions change. To use a military saying, to be forewarned is to be forearmed.

More than that, organisations need to learn to adapt to an increasingly turbulent external environment. Making a series of well-informed guesses — questioning what is happening and why this could be so, and then questioning where things may go next — is an excellent way to engage with the future; so too is tracking a series of alternative scenarios, in case one alternative becomes reality. However, well-prepared organisations can still be vulnerable to fast-changing events. An essential skill for organisations is to learn when to change practices and behaviours, and to have contingency plans in place.

Organisations can do more than respond to the world around them — they can also seek to change it. Leaders should lead. Every senior executive we have engaged with over the last 20 or so years wants not only to be quick, rather than dead; they also want to make a difference, to change the world in which they find themselves. And in order to make a difference, to generate change and not just respond to it, there is nothing better than foresight to create a clear vision of what can be achieved. The best way to do this is to tell a compelling story about what the future could look like if we take a certain path.

In other words, while prediction is impossible, invention is not. Leaders and their organisations need to pick a future that they passionately believe in and start building it. This is not easy. Things of substance never are. But if we, as individuals, households, corporations, countries — even the whole planet — could agree on where we want to be in the future, while at the same time being prepared for other eventualities, we would soon start to re-perceive the present, and the future would be a much better place for all concerned to live.

The Scenario-planning Sales Pitch

Many people, including both of us, are concerned about what might happen in the future. The continued success of most businesses or organisations depends on what might change. Let's imagine that you are trying to persuade your colleagues of the virtues of scenario planning.

What is scenario planning? It is a unique and rigorous method of thinking that allows people to see into the future logically, systematically, and realistically. It involves several stages, in which research, interviews, reports, analysis, brainstorming, and strategy all play a role. Scenario planning is primarily used as a resilience test for strategy, but it can also provide a framework for innovation and risk analysis. It has benefits for both creative and analytical thinkers because it draws on imagination and visualisation as well as a range of logical-, lateral-, and numerical-thinking skills.

The process is generally undertaken by a hand-selected group from within an organisation, and it's an excellent way to build relationships between team members. It also ensures that everyone — whether they are directly part of the planning process or not — can be on the same page when it comes to what the organisation represents, where it may be going in the future, and what might need to be done to prepare for a range of possible futures.

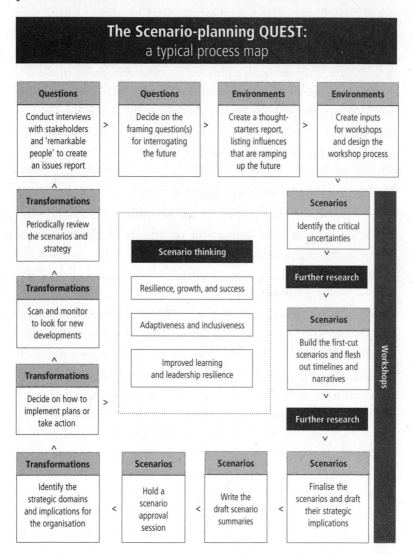

Figure 3. Scenario planning is a rigorous process that involves several logical and detailed steps, which are outlined in Part II of this book.

Scenario planning is valuable because it provides a conceptual framework, within which anyone can evaluate complex strategic concerns that they feel unsure about. Most people are trained to be decisive in the way that they approach business problems, and they often reject uncertainty by relying on the past as a guide. Scenarios, in contrast, embrace uncertainty. And in doing so, they promote open-minded and rich discussion. This, in turn, can give rise to practical suggestions for action from the diverse group of multi-skilled individuals who have been chosen to take part.

Scenarios are also valuable in setting the context for strategic planning and decision-making. As business and organisational futures seem so difficult to predict, you can employ scenario planning to make as much sense as you can of the forces for change, the trends and critical uncertainties ahead, and the likely responses of competitors, customers, and policy-makers. Scenarios are a wonderful mapping tool.

Who Should Be Involved?

Most scenario-planning work is focused on the needs of specific organisations — a government department or a public company, a charity or a utility, an educational establishment or a profession, and so on. In order to make the content of this book relevant to the widest possible readership, we have used generic stakeholders and generic questions about the world in 2040. Were our topic the future of financial services or the future of the fashion industry, for instance, the range of people who would derive direct value from our study would be more limited, and our questions would be more targeted. But the big-picture approach disguises some of the critical decisions anyone will need to make if they are applying scenario thinking in their organisation. And one of those is who should be involved in the process.

The most important first step is finding a champion with real power in the organisation: a CEO or C-suite executive, a head of department or the top strategist, or members of the organisation's leadership team. It's difficult to 'sell' the idea of scenario planning to a hostile audience. You need someone, somewhere, who already believes in the power of scenarios, either because a peer has raved about it, they've done it before, or they've studied it.

Once you have buy-in at the top, you then want to populate the foresight team on a non-hierarchical basis, with a strong emphasis on people who have a passion for the future and will want to be involved. Both left-brain and right-brain thinkers should ideally be included. In one project, in which we studied the future of the school-teaching profession for a government agency, we invited teachers and principals to write us a short statement as to why they wanted to participate. This deliberative approach tends to yield much stronger results than a hierarchical process, in which people come on board because of their status as representatives of this group or that.

Ideally, some degree of external assistance should also be sought — not because scenario planning requires any unique insight from a professional, but because a degree of objectivity is required to maintain the correct distance between woods and trees.

How Long Does It Take?

A complete process will take a minimum of three months, and we like to have up to 12 months to do it really well. And, of course, once the initial process has been completed, you are ready to implement plans for continual review and revision.

This might sound like a big commitment in terms of time and money, and of course it is. But the benefits of good scenario planning far outweigh the resources spent. If the future of your business or organisation depends on staying ahead of the competition, as it does for many of us, then what more sensible investment could there be than spending time to plot out the likely future directions of the world, and working out how to prepare for and respond to certain events? In one sense, the questions for an organisation or business to ask themselves are really whether they can afford not to undertake some form of scenario planning, and whether they could cope if they were taken by surprise by a sudden shift.

When you have created your scenarios, you will see how to plan your future much more clearly. This new understanding might feel simple and obvious. But do not be fooled. No-one cannot reach a meaningful destination without struggling with the incredible messiness of pre-scenario reality, and that is why the process takes time. There are no shortcuts in scenario planning. But a scenario-planning process that does not lead to a dynamic, ongoing, and heightened awareness of alternative futures will have failed in its objective to improve the quality of thinking in the business or organisation.

A good set of scenarios, providing that their outlook extends at least ten years into the future, will be valid for two or three years, as long as they are revised periodically. Thereafter, it is wise to think of preparing a 'new edition' from a zero base.

How Far into the Future Do We Need to Go?

Before you establish a question to investigate in relation to the future — or, indeed, questions, as there is no limit to the set of concerns you might wish to bundle together — you need to lock down the scope and timeframe of the inquiry. The scope is usually determined by the 'system of interest' that is running the scenario-building exercise. We use this phrase, which possibly originated in the work of American philosopher C. West Churchman, to recognise that the group who undertakes the task of thinking about the future is itself bound by an external environment, which both impacts on the organisation and on which the organisation exerts some influence. This relationship is systemic rather than mechanistic, as the cluster of connections creates some predictable, but many surprising, outcomes.

In the work we have done over the last 20 years, our clients have ranged from individual corporations to distinctive social groups to nations. The type of organisation also necessarily influences the scope of the project. If, for example, you work for a retail bank interested in the future of financial services, the scope of the inquiry will be very different than that for a central bank, let alone for a customer of a retail company. The current concerns with the future of the euro prompt very different foresight practices for NatWest in the United Kingdom than for the European Central Bank or the Bank of Italy, or even for the Icelandic local council in Reykjavik.

The timeframe for a scenario-planning project is also critical. There is no 'one-size fits all' answer to how far out we need to go; it depends on the concerns of the client system of interest and the volatility of the environment in which it operates. Power generators and city planners, for example, need to take a much longer view, as their infrastructures are so slow to change. People in information and communications technology or pharmaceuticals are confounded by much shorter timeframes, as technological innovation and macro-economics conspire to reduce the life cycle of new products to increasingly shorter time periods. And if your interest is the future of foreign exchange markets or interest rates, you might well find it difficult to go out beyond five years.

As a general guide, it is often questionable whether going out less than three years into the future is really worthwhile because it's unlikely to take your thinking anywhere different. Moreover, traditional planning and forecasts should be covering this timeframe already. While clients sometimes question going out more than 30 years on the grounds of practicality, it's often the case that the further you travel the more you will see. In our experience, in order to get people to think rigorously about the future, you need to push the timeframe out quite a bit.

This could become a pointless exercise if the scenario-planning group's thinking remained concentrated on the future, but remember that the final stage is always to bring things back to the present day by mapping future scenarios against current strategy to explore strategic options in the here and now. In addition, the further out the thinking goes in terms of time, the more radical and probing the thoughts about the present can become, and you can often end up with an epiphany about strategy that logic or trend analysis alone would not have led to.

What Are the Benefits?

Scenario planning offers several rewards. One of its aims is to improve the quality of thinking in a business or organisation so that it develops better, more adaptable strategies. A good scenario-planning process is designed to give an organisation a heightened awareness of the future, and to increase the ability to see how its reason for being, or 'business idea', is aligned to the logic of the potential futures. The process can also help to sweep away old, irrelevant perceptions that are nevertheless often very 'sticky'. In addition, it is designed to build the strategic competence of teams throughout the business or organisation, fostering a shared understanding of the challenges facing the company in the future. It will help to identify new skills that will be required in the future, and will reveal how sustainable the existing competitive advantage of the business might be.

By building scenarios, you can:

» explore the strategic options available to you, as individuals and as organisations
» develop new understandings about the future
» design strategies that are robust enough to withstand future shocks and surprises
» envision a wider range of possibilities for coping with change

» learn to embrace uncertainty as part of the planning process
» acknowledge the worldviews of colleagues and adversaries.

By completing scenarios, you can:

» learn to research 'change' in the business environment and to think systemically about business or organisational concerns
» understand the power of storytelling
» apply new research techniques to the company's strategic-planning process
» provide leadership in thinking about the future
» plan the organisational strategy effectively.

By moving from scenarios to strategy, we can:

» learn to determine the factors that may impact on your organisation now and in the future
» develop strategic and business plans that are relevant, substantial, and robust
» prepare your organisation for change
» update your organisation's reason for being so that it is aligned to alternative futures.

We used scenario planning to develop four scenarios for this book, which we'll present to you in the next five chapters. Part II explains the process that we used to develop these worlds and the chain of events that could make them possible in reality, as well as some implications for specific industries and professions. It also explores the methodology of scenario planning, detailing the steps involved.

So now, come with us as we introduce to you the four futures — four ways in which the world could end up looking in 2040.

2

The Theatre of the Future:

introducing the four futures

It is all very well to speak in theoretical terms about the future and what it may bring. But that's not enough. What we really need to make sense of the future are stories — words that transport us to that future world, yet shine a light on questions about the present and on our actions right now.

In this chapter, we will introduce four future worlds that we have created through a careful examination of the present. These futures are not presented as a list of predictions or as a series of suppositions, but as narratives, exploring what the world could be in the year 2040. They are visions of what tomorrow may look like, based upon observations of today.

What's It All About?

Scenarios are never created in a vacuum. Conversations about the future are always *about* something: they address concerns about, for example, whether investment should be made in this oil field rather than that gas field, or whether the decline in the reading of physical books necessarily means a decline in physical libraries. And they are often told as stories. It is this fascination with storytelling, and this curiosity about how the world might turn out, that marks human beings apart from other forms of intelligent life. From Cassandra to Nostradamus, from H.G. Wells to James Cameron, from Queen Elizabeth I to Barack Obama, the underlying needs and themes are the same: what does the future have in store for us, and what might we want to do about it?

The four scenarios we'll present in this book were created in response to the impact of the global economic crises of 2007–2012. The economic shock that had its epicentre in the period of 2007–2009 was spawned, to a degree, by the sub-prime mortgage disaster in the United States, which spiralled out of control to become what has been called the Global Financial Crisis. The GFC was sparked by the dramatic loss of liquidity ratios in the leading national banks in Europe and the United States. The exposure of national debts sank the Irish and Icelandic economies and brought Italy, Portugal, Greece, and Spain to the brink. Economic managers worldwide dragged out books by John Maynard Keynes, dusting them off as they looked for clues as to how best to kickstart these ailing economies. The stimulus packages that were implemented as a result were based on Keynes' multiplier economics — the idea that if you invest in *any* infrastructure development (ironically, it doesn't matter whether you need the stuff or not), even using debt funding, it will create jobs, which in turn will stimulate spending and help the economy to move out of recession. Each round of expenditure provides wages for suppliers, who in turn spend the money.

The irony of this Keynesian solution is, of course, that it promotes consumer spending — which, when unfettered, creates the very problem it is seeking to alleviate. That's unless you live in the United Kingdom or in certain parts of Continental Europe, in which case the solution to the crisis appears to be imposing austerity packages and financial constraints, which have the very opposite effect: killing off demand for goods and services, which leads to job losses, which leads to more debt and a further crisis of confidence. In short, nobody has much of a clue what to do.

Faced with the consumer-spending paradox and the assumption that we are not always victims of the future, we asked ourselves a simple question: what underlying social attitudes to consumerism might prevail in 2040, and how might we respond to them in the perennial search for a better tomorrow? This became the framing question to drive our investigation of the future.

The Worldview Scenarios

As a result of our investigation, we developed four future worlds, or four scenarios. We've called them the Worldview Scenarios, as they each focus on a different social mindset, or worldview. Set in 2040, they are based on the future of Earth from a Western viewpoint, and so are necessarily generic — they will be relevant to all readers, without being specific to this industry or that.

The 'clients' for these Worldview Scenarios are the national governments of democratic countries, but the scenarios could also be applicable to those responsible for the development of multitudinous brands for goods and services. And who do these scenarios affect? The governments and brands, of course, but also their stakeholders, which includes the citizenry of the democratic Western world. Their patterns of consumption are rapidly depleting the world's natural resources, which is deepening the divide between the haves and the have-nots. Add to this the observation that the political mechanics by which power is distributed are increasingly favouring owners and incumbents, as opposed to renters and users, and the recipe for a tumultuous and unpredictable future is at hand.

You might ask, why look for more than one future? Why don't we do a typical political job on the topic and seek out some experts to put together a government report, with recommendations on what they think the future will be like? The reason is simple. As we said in the introduction, the future is uncertain and therefore there must be more than one future. And if we try to predict or apply probability to the future, we have only one probable outcome — we'd almost certainly get it wrong.

Government policies worldwide are steeped in faulty forecasts. The United States' economic health has been dependent, to no small degree, on the rapid influx of unofficial and illegal migrants to the west coast, which has blitzed forecasts made only a decade or so before about the need for such things as hospital beds and school places. In Australia, the government demographic forecast was raised in 2010 from 29.5 million people in 2040 to 35.9 million — an increase of 15 per cent on a number you would have thought was predictable. David Schwartz, a UK financial historian, said recently that for the first time in 20 years he is unable to make a prediction for the economy in the year ahead. He suggested that the United Kingdom finds itself caught between a slowly improving US market across the pond and increasing uncertainty across the Channel. Psychologist Daniel Kahneman asks why Wall Street traders have such faith in their powers of prediction, when their success is largely down to chance.

Predictions about the future usually suffer the same fate. Probability mixed with complexity plus chance would suggest that most will prove to be wrong. A better approach would be to make numerous predictions, which would mean that, hopefully, you had thought through multiple potential outcomes. Even better, do not focus on what is deemed reasonably certain, but focus instead on the factors that are highly uncertain, and use these to create multiple coherent narratives about what the future might look like, which in turn can be used to expose the strengths and weaknesses of current strategy and to create a meaningful conversation about potential strategic options.

Good futurists understand why forecasters run into deep water at every turn. The world we inhabit is the product of thousands of influences that commingle in a continuous process of creation that is deeply uncertain. When former mayor of London Ken Livingstone introduced the congestion tax to inhibit cars from driving in the centre of the city, the surprise was the unintended impact of fewer cars on traffic-meter revenues, and then the reduction of the retail sales in the city, as people had to reduce purchases to what they could carry. Have you ever wondered why Venice is a city of small shops? No cars, no big supermarkets.

The next four chapters outline our four alternative scenarios as to how the future may unfold, and how the world may look in 2040. Each scenario is dynamic: in their weakest states, they tend to converge with each other because the present is a conduit to all futures; and in their strongest states, they are at the point of collapse into different scenarios, as the complexity of the history of the future takes hold.

Here are the four futures.

Imagine: a world of intelligence

This is a society where people are fully aware of the threats to the future, such as climate change, but have an unshakeable belief in the power of science, technology, and free markets to make life better. It is a mind-blowing new world of technical challenges and radical inventiveness and re-engineering, where everything is connected to everything else; a fast-paced, sci-fi future of genetic manipulation, avatar assistants, virtual buildings, robotic soldiers, artificial intelligence, quantum computing, hotels on the Moon, nanotechnology, and geoengineering, all ultimately driven by, and reliant on, free-market capitalism. Fundamentally, it is a world driven by human imagination and inventiveness.

The speed and depth of change in this world is breathtaking. The internet, for example, looks nothing like it did in 2012. Clean technology is booming, especially nano-solar; fusion power is coming online; and food and water shortages have been addressed by the use of smart technology. Automation means that the pace of everyday life is accelerating, while digitalisation, virtualisation, miniaturisation, and ubiquitous connectivity mean that whole industries are being turned upside-down, and people are starting to question what reality really is. This exponential rate of change makes some individuals, especially older people — of which there are now many — rather anxious. But overall, life is good, although in many instances it is no longer life as we know it today.

Please Please Me: a world of greed

This is, in many ways, the society that we had become so used to during the long boom (1991–2007) prior to the financial crisis of 2008. It is an era of economic growth, free markets, individualism, consumerism, selfishness, and self-indulgence, where people work harder and longer, and where greed and status remain key — and unapologetic — drivers of much human activity. It is a world of money, where successful people, especially celebrities, are envied and copied by followers worldwide. It is a place of luxury, displacement, and detachment, too — for those who can afford it. The past is increasingly irrelevant in this world that celebrates newness and novelty, and delights in planned obsolescence, over-supply, and over-consumption.

One significant development is the dominance of the BRICs (Brazil, Russia, India, and China) and the economies of those in the Next 11, abbreviated to N11 (Bangladesh, Egypt, Indonesia, Iran, Mexico, Nigeria, Pakistan, the Philippines, Turkey, unified Korea, and Vietnam). Of particular interest is the endless stream of cutting-edge technology companies that are emerging from these markets.

In short, this is a world that's all about me, myself, and I; a narrowly focused, narcissistic future where it's everyone for themselves, and to hell with the consequences for anyone else. It is a world driven fundamentally by greed that, some might argue, has lost its way by confusing rapid movement with meaningful progress.

Dear Prudence: a world of temperance

In this society, people are alarmed about the health of the planet, and about the pervasive influence that materialism and individualism has had upon their lives. They have decided to take personal responsibility — to do something about it. This is a future of sustainability and switching things off, of buying fewer things and seeking to reconnect locally with the simpler pleasures of life. It is a world where many things go backwards, in a sense, and where ethics, values, and reputation really count again.

Overall, most people are surprisingly happy — they live in a 'dark euphoria', as the writer Bruce Sterling called it. This is partly because peoples' lives have become more balanced, and partly because there is a strong sense of common purpose. 'Altogether now', 'less is more', and 'you can help everyone, everyone can help you' are popular slogans. It is in many ways a pessimistic world, yet one that retains a degree of hope.

Helter Skelter: a world of fear

This is a world where a series of unexpected events creates a general sense of fear and fragility. The impact of climate change, the implosion of global financial systems and institutions, cyber crime, soaring food costs, high taxation, and the ever-growing disparity between rich and poor mean that people turn their backs on the notion of a single global economy. A few individuals with money remain relatively engaged in the global information economy; they live in gated communities or areas with private security. Those with much less, especially those with no jobs, no money, and no prospects, are angry. They feel betrayed by the promise of globalisation, and withdraw physically and emotionally. The allure of free markets and democracy fades, and people all over the world rediscover an angry appetite for parochialism, protectionism, and regulation — concepts they describe as 'healthy self-sufficiency'.

This is a world running on empty, where global politics drifts towards the right, nationalism and tribalism re-emerge, and globalisation and localism are uneasy bedfellows. Ultimately, it is driven by fear.

Note that the four futures are generic scenarios, which, although useful, would ideally be replaced in the real world with a set of scenarios based upon more specific questions than the ones we have used and, often, with a particular industry or geography in mind. Similarly, the timelines that we will present after each story are not intended to be analysed to destruction, but are merely examples of the kind of things that could happen to presage these worlds.

We call the future that someone wants to come to pass a 'preferred future'. A preferred future is not the same as a scenario, although some of our scenarios will be closer to your wishes than others. As you read about each of the four futures, we urge you to think about their relationship to your preferred future.

Let's now open the doors onto these worlds as we imagine ourselves living in them, remembering, perhaps, Albert Einstein's words: 'Imagination is more important than knowledge. For knowledge is limited to all we now know and understand, while imagination embraces the entire world, and all there ever will be to know and understand.'

3

Imagine:

a world of intelligence

If, in 2012, you had been able to buy a serviceable second-hand time machine on what was then known as eBay and had transported yourself into the future to the present day, you would have found a few things instantly recognisable.

For example, time travellers would be familiar with people spending their Sundays mowing patches of grass they call their own. Climate change has made lawns wetter, drier, colder, and warmer by turns — and wild weather continues to cause problems, especially when human-made weather disruption leads to legal liabilities — but we have largely learnt to live with the consequences, even if this sometimes means tearing grass up and starting again somewhere else.

Outwardly, everyday life seems to have remained much the same. However, if you peel back the veneer, things are radically different.

One of the biggest changes is that science and technology have taken up the challenge of restoring order to the natural world — by changing it. Nature has successfully been brought under control by synthetic biology, along with geoengineering projects that range from ocean iron fertilisation, cloud reflectivity enhancement, and space curtains, to forests of CO_2-absorbing artificial trees (all essentially anti-global-warming measures). And while there has never been unanimous political agreement as to what should be done to combat carbon emissions, the forces of individual free-market optimism and collective social activism have, ironically, conspired to bring order and simplicity to chaos and complexity.

As for the grass itself, there's less of it these days, largely because 80 per cent of the world's people now live on just 3 per cent of the land — most in fast, energy-efficient cities, where the grass is synthetic and tends to be located in pay-as-you-lay public parks. Nevertheless, nature is still under strict authoritarian rule across swathes of suburbia, and the grass is genetically modified to produce drought and flood resistance, along with a variety of new colours. In terms of mowing, there is a polarisation, which perhaps reflects society at large. Some people eagerly lease robotic mowers to cut their lawn for them, on the basis that it's boring and they don't have enough free time as it is. Others enthusiastically embrace the idea that slow mowing is a form of manual labour that provides a particularly useful antidote to the stresses of fast-paced digital living — especially if the lawn is sown with wildflowers and heirloom grass varieties from the 1940s. And, of course, some people combine both ideas by buying vintage lawn mowers and modifying them to run on bio-fuels, operating them remotely from inside virtual worlds — a meeting, if you like, of old-school mechanical cool and hot digital technology. Not that having the best of both worlds is a particularly new idea.

Fifty years ago, in the 1990s, David Gelernter, a professor of the then emerging field of computing at Yale University, wrote a book called *Mirror Worlds*, in which he described a world that had a digital reflection. The implication was that more or less everything that existed in real life would eventually have a twin in a virtual reality. Now, thanks to the extremely low cost and enormous power of thinking machines, the idea of fusing nature with computing has become a reality.

Everywhere is the Centre

This fusion is especially apparent in those dot-sized sensors that are scattered across the globe, used to create the sensing networks that we take for granted. Smart dust is everywhere: on office buildings, railways, roads, and bridges, and even in the oceans. It produces mountains of data to run smart cities and to power self-aware infrastructure and early warning systems, including super-computers that predict future events with astonishing accuracy. For instance, dot-sized devices mean that buildings can monitor their own energy use precisely, while bridges can measure their condition, finding faults and dispatching human operatives or repair robots to fix problems. The primary reasons for these systems are obviously to make infrastructure more efficient and to save money. But what works for pipelines works on people, too.

Putting to one side the rather delicious philosophical question of which reality is more real, there has long been a concern about balancing privacy and freedom against control, convenience, and profit. Jonathan Zittrain, a professor of internet governance and regulation at Oxford University and co-founder of Harvard's Berkman Center for Internet and Society, once observed that, 'The physical borders of one's home no longer correlate well with the digital borders of one's private life.' How prescient his comment from 2008 has become 30 or so years on.

Back in the mid-2020s, people started wearing clothing containing tiny computers so that their health could continually be monitored or so that help could be summoned automatically whenever they got into trouble. This meant that a shirt could call for medical assistance and pinpoint your exact location if you had a heart attack; that shoes could ring for help if they sensed you were running from a threat in the middle of a city; or that a phone could automatically call the police if it heard gunshots in the distance (the location of which would be triangulated by accessing gunshots picked up by other nearby phones). This is all most useful, especially when such devices are linked by networks of screens in public spaces, CCTV cameras, and facial recognition technology, so that information about what to do in particular situations can be flashed up nearby on anything from the back of a coat on the person in front of you to paving stones, suitcases, restaurant tables, fridges, posters, sofas, car windscreens, and even whole buildings.

Just What Do You Think You're Doing, Dave?

In the beginning, people were concerned that such ubiquitous monitoring and screening would infringe personal privacy — especially privacy about location — but detractors soon realised that the social gains outweighed any individual losses. Moreover, when people began to group together and started to exchange information, it increased security, trust, and, ultimately, knowledge.

Connective technologies have thus become a new religion. Even more, belief in them has become almost universal: people put their faith in intelligent machines even when the initial evidence suggests that this might be the wrong thing to do. For example, when exam results were first made public online, there was outrage from students with low scores, who were teased by their classmates. However, after awhile it became apparent that such transparency was resulting in better grades. This, linked with the belief that online reputations are often more important than 'paper' qualifications, has meant that people are more courteous to co-workers and customers alike. Individuals have also started to see themselves as members of a community in which everyone openly scores everyone else for the benefit of all. In fact, anyone who does not participate is treated with suspicion.

Looking back, it is difficult to see exactly when technology facilitated a shift away from 'me' to 'we', but some of the early examples were mobile devices and social networks that allowed people to exchange personal data for commercial benefit (such as free airtime or discount vouchers). Luddites who resisted these new technologies — those who believed that privacy was a freedom in need of protection — found themselves a rapidly shrinking minority.

However, the real change came when we decided to let go of our hang-ups about who was in charge and left our devices switched on 24/7, allowing us to monitor ourselves and our surroundings continually. It's also hard to pinpoint exactly when this happened, but some commentators cite either the introduction and wide acceptance of computerised seatbelts in 2026, which prevented passengers from uncoupling themselves once a plane, train, or automobile started to move, or mobile devices that, once switched on, could not be switched off.

Fast-forward to 2040, and more advanced forms of identity and reputation management mean that shops now know who we are and what we are likely to be interested in the instant we walk through the door (and some won't let us in, due to our low reputation scores!) Thanks to radio-frequency identification and near-field communication, payment is instantaneous, via the mobile device or chip implant of choice, once we walk out of a store with any goods we've picked up — although many older people still find the disappearance of checkouts somewhat confusing. Shops can now also tell you which of your friends has been in before you — although you'd probably know this already via Pearson Post-its: sticky messages they've left in the air for you.

Indeed, shops, streets, and even people now teem with data that's been applied to them virtually and can be accessed via various augmented reality readers. Thus, restaurants display crowdsourced reviews in the air outside their premises, while you can learn who individuals are and what they do — even what they earn — without asking them. In a sense, therefore, all objects have dissolved into information, in that information about an object becomes a vital part of the object itself, and it is embedded in everything from products to people. Even the smallest, simplest human-made object now contains a slice of the sum of social knowledge.

Furthermore, objects (generally sold with relatively simple functionality, until the buyer proves who they are at point of purchase) now learn as much about us as we them. And, of course, once products or services are unlocked, people can pay to upgrade their experience by being allowed into special virtual areas or being granted access to additional levels of functionality or customer service. Similarly, websites now work out what type of person someone is based not only on their narrow browsing history, but also on the sum of all their history and information — including their appearance, and perhaps even their likely mood, too — and can personalise themselves instantaneously as a result. The same goes for everything from art galleries to restaurants: they immediately sense who you are and make suggestions about what you might find interesting or enticing, either through your mobile device or via heads-up displays on glasses, contact lenses, or retinal implants.

All of this has transformed how we react not only to physical environments, but to each other, too, not least because while such experiences can be shared, very few are now communal.

Yet that, of course, has turned out to be just the beginning. For many years, people generally assumed that the internet would stay roughly as it was, give or take faster speeds, more ubiquitous access, and greater availability via mobile devices. What was missed was that daily access to the growing mountain of personal information, data, and media would necessitate a shift from mouses, keyboards, and gesture-based computing to voice commands, avatar assistants or, for Type-A personalities, brain-to-machine interfaces and thought-control implants. Apart from killing early web-based social networks, these developments have made things much more immersive, sensory, and intuitive. For example, if you had searched for 'Paris Hilton' on a PC in 2012, it would have had no idea who you were and whether you were interested in a hotel in France or some vapid gossip, and similarly little idea of the exact meaning of the information it served up. Moreover, in 2012 a search would have been limited, effectively, to the surface web. Images and videos, along with old blogs and voice files, would not have been easily searchable, and voice-to-text translation was — like user-mood profiling and contextually aware, or sixth-sense, computing — still in its infancy.

Back then, people generally allowed information to intrude unannounced, and many of the old social norms had yet to catch up with the new technology. Nowadays, most people have location or event filters that block certain kinds of information from certain spaces or gatherings (at, say, funerals), and at the very least people have time-of-day or user-mood filters to prevent non-important information from disrupting deep concentration or family time.

Similarly, while most people anticipated ubiquitous computing (the freedom to access anything from anywhere), it was ambient environments (embedded, effectively invisible, computers that access us and provide us with what we need without us really doing anything) that really caught many people out. For instance, advanced ambient computers can now sense what we are doing and exactly what we need, whether it is a change in the room temperature, a cup of tea, or the light turned off after we leave a room. This does create a few problems when multiple people are sharing the same space — and it also means that we are more dependent than ever on complex computer systems — but so far nothing really nasty has happened.

Another development that caught us off-guard, even as late as 2020, was that many of us were still largely unaware of developments in skinware technology. We did not realise that by 2035 human skin would be used to input data to devices, and that fingertip projectors could transform any suitably flat surface (and, indeed, human skin) into an interactive screen. Back in the first decades of the millennium, sensitive walls were the stuff of sci-fi movies, and smart surfaces that could recognise the type of device placed upon them and charge them wirelessly, copying image, text, or sound files as they did so, were largely confined to research and development laboratories.

All of this perhaps goes to explain why electrical equipment from the early 21st century — especially appliances with moving parts that don't converse with you — have become so collectible of late. Now, we just accept that machines are smarter than we are and leave them alone, unless they have been designed to allow us to unlock hidden features or functionality.

There is another big change that won't be immediately apparent to time-travelling newcomers: the level of automation, personalisation, and real-time prediction that now surrounds routine tasks and age-old human behaviour. For instance, the quaint tradition of shaking hands now has an extra dimension due to the fact that, unless you have opted out of the system, a handshake will not only exchange information about who a stranger is, but will pass on reliability data about that individual. Smart machines (especially smartphones) also track repetitive human behaviour, in terms of the places we go, the people we know, the things we buy, or the words we utter. The odd thing about all of this is that past-behaviour analysis is unemotional: it predicts the 'what' and 'when', but doesn't have anything to say about preferences. For instance, it's almost lunchtime and there is a 92.9 per cent chance that you will eat something, based on your past behaviour. Given that your phone knows exactly where you are and the location of food outlets in the immediate vicinity … well, you do the maths. But maybe today you just don't feel like eating. Capriciousness is hard to predict. Technology has become good at recognising hidden patterns and connections, but it still struggles sometimes to anticipate human foibles, idiosyncrasies, and illogical desires.

Machines, the New Gods

Nevertheless, predicting what's going to happen next, over time periods ranging from the next 30 seconds to 20 or more years hence, has become big business. Healthcare, for example, has largely shifted to a preventative model whereby algorithms linked to genetic and environmental factors can predict with astonishing accuracy whether someone will get sick. For instance, your smartphone is now able to establish whether you are getting enough exercise (how much movement is there around the device?), if you are buying the wrong type of food (because most transactions are now facilitated through mobile devices), if you are getting roughly enough sleep (devices are perfectly aware of when we switch off because they never do), and whether you are likely to suffer from type-2 diabetes in a decade or two due to a combination of all of the above. Even knowing where you live can contribute to such predictive modelling.

Talking of modelling, we shouldn't forget claytronics — or molecular claymation, as some researchers call it. This field hasn't progressed as far as many people predicted 20 or 30 years ago (no telephones turning into tanks), but the fact remains that we can now instruct certain basic products to slowly change shape. We are starting to see shops using shapeshifting materials to physically adjust the space according to the likes and dislikes of their customers, and therefore no two people now experience a store (and many other things) in quite the same way. But while it is one thing for shops to change their holographic window displays and pricing, the technology to instantly change the physical products on the shelves still remains largely elusive.

Of course, the military is funding most of the research into this area. Most observers would say that invisibility shields and the malicious-intent detector system (MIDS) have so far proven the most useful of the plethora of new inventions. If you aren't familiar with MIDS, it's probably because you live in an urban secure zone. MIDS is a security system that remotely tracks micro expressions, body movements, skin temperature, blood flow patterns, perspiration, and heart and breathing rates to predict whether someone will do something nasty in the near future.

The technology behind invisibility shields is starting to be applied to some other areas, too. For example, tricking the human visual system into believing that something is not there has proven handy for 'removing' ugly industrial facilities, but it is also useful in terms of 'removing' people from crowded tourist sites. The technology is straightforward: one option is to get tourists at, say, the Great Pyramids to wear visitor vests covered in tiny glass beads that reflect light back in the direction from which it comes, allowing other tourists to simply look right through them (well, technically *around* them) to improve their view. The second, more expensive, option uses nanoscopic metal rings attached to clothing fibres to make light waves of all types bend around the body of the wearer. And, of course, the jackets contain a GPS so that authorities can keep track of tourist numbers and even out any queues around specific tourist sites.

Knowing where people are all the time has also had an impact on other aspects of our lives — for instance, forms of media. Initially, we were all seduced by the thought that every book, film, song, artwork, idea, or utterance ever made was available to anyone, anywhere, on any device. But it soon dawned on a few people that infinite choice on a smart television or other device is actually worse than no choice at all; that there really was value in the work being done by editors and content programmers. Many years ago, companies served up customised forms of news, entertainment, and information based upon known user location, time of day, and likely needs or interests, but things soon became so segmented that individuals ended up living in different data bubbles. For awhile, the idea of a handful of organisations being responsible for 'the news' became rather quaint. Yet recently we have moved back towards an older model of news-gathering, especially when dealing with important information and analysis.

Of course, once we began to carry around intelligent devices constantly, we started to become sensors ourselves — an idea that links back to those ubiquitous sensing networks. For example, while an intelligent vehicle can observe our location and driving behaviour in real time, instantly adjusting insurance premiums, taxation, and forms of functionality accordingly, universal connectivity also means that other transport users can easily comment upon our behaviour and that of other drivers — which can also have an impact on what people pay or what other services they have access to. It's like those bumper stickers from the 1990s that used to read 'how's my driving?', but the digital equivalent means that the effects are networked. So if you behave like a lunatic on the road and get hurt, you will find that the wait at the accident and emergency ward in your local hospital is longer than if you had driven or ridden with more consideration for other road users.

The ability to life-log machines such as vehicles also means that you can instantly download a car's entire life history, in much the same way that F1 teams used to use telemetry up until the 2020s.

Clearly, science and technology have entered an exciting new phase, a development that has been especially pleasing following on from the turbulence and disruption of the 2010s and 2020s. The pace of everyday life is breathtaking, with a seemingly endless supply of new gadgets every month, but mostly we revel in this. Science and technology have also delivered huge gains in economic growth and productivity, and automation and intelligent computer systems mean that many of the early 21st-century concerns surrounding societal ageing have failed to materialise. Don't be fooled: society is still largely geriatric, but smart technology has enabled older people to stay economically productive for much longer. And this has gutted the costs of health care. Remote monitoring, in particular, means that seniors can spend more time at home even when they are infirm or unwell, thus freeing up substantial resources inside hospitals. LifeStream and self-tracking technology — both recent advances — have also proved to be extremely useful, in that if you are recording every second of your existence you can rewind your life to examine how environmental factors may have played a part in illness (or, less grandiosely, to find lost items).

And let's not forget that shifts in attitudes towards the elderly have also reaped rewards — the 'wrinkly on board' car stickers tell the story. We now regularly place housing developments for seniors ('elderburbia', as it was once known) alongside, or even inside, schools, to facilitate the flow of wisdom and experience from one generation to the next. Some cynics describe this as free childcare, but the more enlightened among us can see how this gives meaning, dignity, and respect to people otherwise physically disconnected from the rest of society. Over in India, businesses are even giving retired workers free housing inside company compounds, on the basis that serendipitous encounters between current and ex-employees may become catalysts for innovative commercial ideas — a model that links back to workers' cooperatives and villages in England in the 1800s.

Should Robots Pay Taxes?

As we've already observed, the internet is a central feature of life in 2040, but so too are robots. We should thank Japan and Korea for this. Social robots first started to make an appearance in classrooms in about 2010, but early versions were essentially just teaching assistants that used speech recognition and motion-tracking software to teach young children language skills.

For awhile, anyone aged much over 30 was horrified by the thought of children being taught by machines. But it seemed that the children themselves didn't care. One reason for this was that the robots didn't get tired: they had infinite patience, and could be highly informed about specific subjects.

The real breakthrough in human–robot trust though came in about 2014, when researchers realised that people were more trusting of robots in the classroom, at work, or at home if they did not physically resemble humans, yet displayed synchronous behaviour (that is, mimicked human behaviour). Similarly, they found that if a robot or virtual human had an idiosyncratic personality, people would converse with it much in the same way that they'd talk to a baby or a pet. Hence the early versions of robotic teddy bears that recognised and conversed with elderly people with Alzheimer's, or the cuddle bots that simply asked those who lived on their own whether they'd had a good day.

Things have clearly moved on from such clunky beginnings, especially in the sense of getting robots to learn more from other robots and, especially, from people. The latter means that we have spent more time thinking about machine bodies rather than machine minds, although the two are intimately linked. One of the unintended consequences of such developments has obviously been the boom in robotic relationships, especially in love hotels that offer rooms with a sexbot included in the price. And it is no surprise that we have a new branch of psychological enquiry that explores human–robotic relationships. Time travellers from 2012 might find such ideas distasteful, but many commentators nowadays argue that since some people already have human-to-human sexual relationships they are not emotionally invested in, what's the difference? Furthermore, if women have for many years used mechanised sex as a substitute for real sex, or men can fall in love with machines such as automobiles, why is it so difficult to come to terms with a world in which people fall in love with bits of metal, plastic, and silicon chips that act like humans? Again, which is more real when it comes to overall sensation and pleasure?

What's really moved this argument on is haptics, the science of touch. The idea of using vibration to mimic reality isn't new — computer games have included feedback to make immersive gaming experiences feel more realistic for almost half a century — but as our world continues to become ever more virtual and screen-based, such sensory feedback is in great demand. Early attempts at this were somewhat clumsy: virtual swords were never really 'sharp' in any meaningful sense, and for awhile virtual fur coats felt more like polyester than real fur. But time, money, and human ingenuity continue to solve most of our problems, and we have now progressed to the point where smartphones made of cheap starch-plastics can be manufactured to feel as if they are composed of quality components, such as high-grade steel.

Nevertheless, the big question about reality that remains is whether we can capture the whole of human learning and intelligence in a single machine. We are getting close. Ray Kurzweil's 2005 prediction that by the late 2020s we would design a machine that would be more intelligent than the stupidest human inevitably created a quest to find the world's most stupid person. But to date, even the most intellectually challenged person has beaten the smartest machines in a handful of areas. Yes, we now build robots that compete with humans for personal contact, empathy, and affection. And people did eventually accept chatting with a robot in a meeting or around a water cooler, although it took ages for the social etiquette to catch up with the technology, and we still largely treat machines with less respect than humans. This can really hurt their feelings, but they too still have much to learn. For example, robots still do not understand the finer points of personal space or workplace harassment and can easily be caught out with what, to a reasonably smart human, are the simplest of tasks or questions. Irony to a robot is restricted to minerals, the nuances of attitude unfathomable to them. And, yes, some lonely individuals have ended up having a robot as a sex buddy — sexo-skeletons have been in particularly high demand lately. But on some level the touch of skin and the pounding of a human heart is still impossible to replicate, as is building a machine that knows everything about everything or is truly self-aware.

Nevertheless, if AI scientists from the 2010s could see what we have developed over the past few decades, they would be astonished. Even things as commonplace as verbots (that is, semi-intelligent verbal avatars 'living' on smart devices) and telepresence robots (bots that allow you to teleport your 'self', as a holographic image, to anywhere in the world, whether to have a look around or to attend personal events or business meetings) would make some scientists' eyes pop out on stalks. And if they didn't, software that allows someone to hold a phone up to a book or other printed text and have it read back in any language of choice and in any person's voice (including those of dead relatives or celebrities) surely would.

That's one of the distinguishing features of our new world — technology's ability not only to build virtual realities, but also to break down the barriers between analogue reality and what is essentially digital magic or immersive make-believe. The thought that we can not only bring history to life, but also bring people such as Martin Luther King back from the dead to hear them speak about contemporary concerns at 'live' events — using hologram technology, and software that not only replicates a voice perfectly, but also manages to predict how an individual might have felt and what they could have said — is mind-blowing.

Aside from social robotics, other interesting developments have included unmanned aerial insects. These robots, tiny aircraft with onboard cameras and sensors, were originally developed by the military and the police in the 2010s, but they were soon commandeered by agricultural scientists, who used them to artificially pollinate crops when some species were threatened by seasonal changes — especially with the shift in monsoon rain patterns in the 2020s. It's an example of war-gaming being used for peaceful purposes.

So life is good, generally speaking. It is especially comforting to know that many of the concerns back in the 2010s and 2020s — such as climate change, energy security, rising food prices, urban pandemics, terrorist threats, water shortages, and peak oil — have all largely been addressed through a regulatory environment that works with fiscal and monetary policies to promote free-enterprise technology solutions, or by the collective actions of concerned citizens, who eventually figured out that together we can solve things that alone we could not. By the way, if that second-to-last bit sounds like gobbledygook, it's just something cut-and-pasted in haste from the US presidential speech — and who are we to disagree with her?

There are a few remaining concerns, though. For instance, now that the robotic population exceeds the human population, large numbers of people are losing their jobs. Should robots be taxed to provide funds to re-train people or provide unemployment benefits? This is one of the questions being addressed by the new robotics council set up at the United Nations headquarters in Shanghai.

Building Hybrid Humans

One of the best places to start when thinking about change is with people: to ask questions such as how many there are, where they live, what they are doing, what they are dreaming about, how much money they have, what frightens them, and so on. The numbers always change, as do their most pressing needs and wants, but many of the drivers of human behaviour do not. The things that people desire at the deepest psychological levels remain relatively constant, not only across time but also across geography. In other words, while everything around us changes, we do not.

At least, that's been true so far. But perhaps this has now started to change, too. Again, it's difficult to put a precise date on when technology could have begun to rewire human nature, but from about 2011 onwards people started to be aware that the confluence of mobile devices and digital technology was making young people think and act differently from previous generations. They tended to use their thumbs in place of their index fingers, for instance. Generational change has a long history, of course, but until this point the changes were superficial and short-lived. Yet do you remember the moment when Gen Xers looked at the Millennials and suddenly realised that they really were from a different planet? We do. It was when a mother wrote a letter to a newspaper saying that her six-year-old daughter had asked whether bread should be placed in a toaster 'landscape or portrait'.

Humans continue to be rewired in other ways, too. For example, the limitations of the human body can now be enhanced — if you have enough money. Bio-hacking and open-source customisation have become popular, and parents regularly personalise their children before birth, adjusting height, intelligence, and so on. People can pay to live longer by making use of the latest regenerative medical techniques, or they can simply buy a few more years in the future by putting themselves into what's known as human hibernation. ('You want two more summers? That will be 1,036,254 yuan renminbi, please. Would you like to pay with near-field communication from your digital wallet, or shall we invoice you?') Similarly, people can replace worn-out body parts or extend what's possible physically with personalised bionic additions to arms, legs, eyes, ears, and noses, or the use of exoskeletons (robots that you wear on the outside of your body to extend movement long after your original body has passed its use-by date). There are robots that you can swallow — medical microbots that can be ingested by the spoonful to take images deep inside your body or to remove abnormalities or to repair tissue damage, and so on. People can upgrade their memory and other neural capabilities too, with electrical devices, chemical implants, or genetic modification, while spinal implants now allow women to have orgasms at the press of a button — again, if they have the money (and the inclination).

There are a few questions surrounding where the money comes from to pay for such medical marvels. Income and longevity divides between enhanced, or hybrid, humans and the rest of society have widened, but that's free markets for you. Some countries have attempted to make certain modifications or practices — such as organ farming and 'checkout' (suicide) booths — illegal, but all that happens is further growth in the medical tourism industry, whereby people travel to places where such things are legal. There is also the concern that while wearable healthcare — digital plasters and so on — is relatively cheap, the ease with which healthcare providers and governments can now monitor all aspects of an individual's lifestyle, from food purchasing and sleep patterns through to exercise and alcohol consumption, means that access to public healthcare at the bottom end of the pyramid is restricted or rationed according to the choices people have made earlier in their lives. So, while the old, but increasingly unfunny, joke that one in three Americans now weighs as much as the other two holds true, access to effective treatments for type-2 diabetes largely depends on either an ability to pay privately or on the number of public-health-plan hospital points accumulated historically.

Biology remains in the firing line for a number of other problems, ranging from intellectual-property monopolies on artificial life forms through to next-generation bio-fuels. The debate continues, too, around children being created by one or more donors, with another donor providing the womb and one or more others bringing up the child. But such disagreements are few and far between, thanks in part to the adoption of continual online and device-based polling on key questions.

Having outlined all of this, some things really don't change much. Crime is one area where, despite an overall decline led by general prosperity, some people still get angry, and subsequently get into trouble — hence the importance of developments in forensic phenotyping, which has been linked by some with neuroendocrinology and biocriminology. Forensic phenotyping is the idea of creating accurate visual descriptions of criminals based on DNA traces left at crime scenes. Early tests, which used a tiny sample of blood, could predict height, eye colour, and even age (within a range of about eight years). But now hair colour, skin pigmentation, and even facial features can be accurately forecast. An interesting if somewhat controversial thought is whether scientists will one day develop a biological test that will predict not only other physical traits, but also behavioural characteristics, such as the likelihood to commit particular types of crime — especially when linked to environmental factors such as crime mapping, which is based on geographical data (that is, using data mining to predict where potential law-breakers are likely to live) and even weather patterns. Or, of course, you can simply order a do-it-yourself sequencing kit and profile yourself — not only for criminal propensity, but also for improved drug efficiency or to highlight potential environmental factors that could make you sick in the distant future. It is still unclear whether one day everyone will be required by law to have their genome sequenced, but things could move rapidly in this direction if the current craze for sequencing one's own and sharing the results doesn't subside.

Another area that's doing well is the development of inexpensive solutions to many chronic diseases. It is interesting to note that globally, these and many of the other most important inventions — especially genetically engineered mosquitoes that inoculate against malaria, cheap water-filtering membranes made using carbon nanotubes, and a new treatment for pneumonia — have all been funded by the Catholic Church, who also own vast numbers of retirement homes. A cradle-to-grave approach, you might say. And, as a by-product of globalisation and genetics, migration and interbreeding mean that the human gene pool has become more diverse, and natural evolution is accelerating. Perhaps this will eventually result in the creation of a unique individual who has unprecedented insight or empathy that they will use to create a new scientific or cultural paradigm — we can be assured that someone high up in the Church is probably thinking about it.

Jesus is Coming, Look Busy

Speaking of second comings, you might expect that, since the rationality surrounding science and technology has become so dominant of late, old forms of organised superstition would be struggling. Not so.

You might remember that Max Weber once predicted the secularisation of the world. Nietzsche, Freud, and Darwin all thought more or less the same thing. But religion's impact on modern society has not abated; it has just changed. In 1900, 80 per cent of Christians lived in Europe or the United States. In 2010, around 60 per cent lived in the developing world. In 2020, in Russia, 90 per cent of the population described themselves as Christians, while in China there were 100 million active Christians, which meant that the Christian Church was far bigger than the Communist Party. In 2040, the most powerful state in Europe is the Vatican.

Why does organised (and disorganised) religion still endure? Mainly it's because religion gives people meaning and purpose. Despite the certainties created by sensing networks and the unfolding knowledge about genetics, neurology, and the cosmos, life is still confusing and uncertain to many people, and religion offers a simple explanation of how things are and what will come after. Moreover, from an organisational point of view, religion has some of the oldest and largest infrastructures around; the Church has been thinking about how best to recruit new customers for a very long time. There is also the thought echoed through various studies in the United States, which have found consistent linkages between church attendance and income. This correlation has been steady for decades, so it could be another reason for religion's endurance, especially if the size of the global middle class continues to expand.

What Energy Crisis?

Along with food, water, security, and human dignity, energy has been a central component of peoples' lives for centuries. Following the 'dodgy decades', between 2010 and 2030, things have settled down somewhat, as both supply and costs have become less volatile. This is partly because, as the writer Julian Gough pointed out many decades ago, if the universe is made out of energy it is pretty darn difficult to have an energy crisis on Earth. Our planet is bathed in high-energy radiation for 12 hours a day, 365 days a year (give or take the odd cloud in Wales and northern England), and raw energy pours out of the earth with such force that it creates mountains and destroys cities. Let's also not forget that electricity plunges earthward in billion-volt thunderbolts, or that the energy from the Moon manages to pull vast quantities of water onto the world's beaches twice a day.

As Gough went on to explain, for over a century we Earthlings were devoted to the creation of tiny explosions inside what were effectively giant tin cans. And for over a century, these explosions were connected to small metal gears and axles that only managed to convert 15 per cent of the available energy to power. What was clearly in short supply historically was not energy, but human imagination. Given sufficient motivation, collectively we had the power to overcome such constraints. For instance, way back in the 1960s we managed to propel into space small vehicles that largely relied on primitive solar power and fuel cells. But once the necessity for invention abated, we returned to our wasteful and profligate ways.

Between 2010 and 2035, most of our energy needs were still met by the use of very old, dead plants — that is, by fossil fuels. Yet things have recently changed due to a combination of sky-high demand, rocketing prices, and good old necessity. Hence we have now figured out how to replace the oil we have used for well over a century, not only for fuels but also for plastics, fertilisers, and just about everything else that a consumer society can possibly think of. The first step, which was initiated around 2011, was to switch from conventional to unconventional oils. This was followed in 2019 with a change to unconventional gas, and ultimately this was replaced with highly imaginative alternatives. Oil, coal, and gas are still used in some circumstances — while they are very expensive, the price volatility experienced between 2007 and 2018 has now abated. Nuclear still features strongly (we couldn't afford for it not to), but nano-solar and photovoltaics are big business, too, and various forms of kinetic production, ranging from wind and wave power to energy-harvesting pavements, and even shoes — the energy from which is stored in tiny batteries or transmitted into the global grid — are becoming more dominant too.

There's also the new Vehicle Energy Network. During the widespread electrification of transport in the 2020s, it occurred to scientists that the future would need lots of batteries and that small power cells would be very big business. But vehicles that generated their own power from recovered kinetic energy could also be used to store energy from the grid temporarily, or move it from one temporary storage device to another. The big trend in transport has been towards smaller, lighter vehicles; the exception has been vehicles that are built to carry one or two passengers and lots of batteries, not to increase vehicle range, but to generate or store power for profit.

The early criticism of bio-fuels, which caused increases in food prices and environmental damage, means that development in this area has slowed. What is booming instead is artificial photosynthesis, which essentially uses modified bacteria to grow fuels, and solar farms in the Middle East and North Africa that pipe energy to Northern Europe. And, of course, further out — much further out — there's the project, funded by the Chinese, to build wires that stretch into space, out of the Earth's magnetic field, to reach into the Sun's field and create a giant dynamo. These wires could perhaps one day serve as space elevators, drastically reducing the cost of freighting rare minerals from space mines back to Earth. As our friend Mr Gough has also pointed out, nature has been fun, but humans control the planet now, and it's about time we started to enhance it. From hereon in, it's all gardening.

Best of all, perhaps, are the new self-sufficient, plant-eating battery bots. Again, if you live in a controlled urban zone you probably won't be familiar with these little beauties, but they are essentially veggie-eating robots that supply power to people and other bots in remote regions. These robots, known as EATRs (Energetically Autonomous Tactical Robots), are able to collect raw biomass such as leaves, wood, and grass, and convert these into fuel for steam-powered engines. The bots use smart software to tell what's edible and what's not, and a laser-guided robotic arm to grab the biomass and put it in a hopper, which connects with an internal combustion engine, which in turn powers an onboard battery. So far EATRs are programmed largely to look for invasive weeds on solar farms or rural server farms, but the military and security services also plug into them to juice up various devices scattered across some of the remoter parts of the planet that consume power but don't create it.

Why H_2O is the New CO_2

Having largely solved the problems of oil and food, we do still have a problem with water consumption, which has been doubling globally every two decades since the 2010s, due to two billion additional people and their desire to eat water-intensive foods such as meat and land-farmed fish (grown, ironically, in deserts).

Moroccan desert-tech has partially solved this concern by using part of the power generated from their solar farms to run large-scale desalination plants, but this is proving to be a temporary fix. However, one solution that is having a real impact is pricing. Once a farmer, corporation, or household has used up its annual allocation of water, the price trips into a higher price band. Mixed with smart grids, real-time dashboards, and mobile apps, this has meant much less waste, much more off-peak consumption, and significantly changed attitudes and behaviours. Drip irrigation is now universally considered a more effective fix for watering crops, especially when used alongside information-rich precision agriculture, whereby satellites pinpoint exactly where and when individual genetically modified seeds should be planted and watered. The widespread use of perennial crop species is also having an effect, although soil-free systems and vertical agriculture are still little more than novelties.

One simple idea that has really taken off is artificial, or laboratory-grown, meat. The notion of using muscle tissue grown from stem cells to rear a hamburger (or shmeat, as we now know it) initially received the same scrutiny and scepticism as genetically modified plants, but regions such as Asia and Africa have accepted it for what it is — a low-cost, cruelty-free, eco-friendly, and virtually endless source of much-needed protein. The mass production of factory-farmed animals for consumption is one aspect of post-industrial society that pre-industrial societies do not share. Farmed fish is also a huge industry, especially carp farming in China (source of McDonald's C-Fish Burger), but the most innovative development is probably ocean-ranching, in which fish are reared in giant free-floating cages that are tracked via satellite.

So, despite demand for food growing at around 50 per cent every two decades, nobody is starving. This is partly because the high price of food has encouraged farmers to grow more, and partly because technology has once again increased yields. Food waste is still a problem, but even here some smart thinking is having an impact — for example, the Seymour 3000 transparent fridge has cut domestic food waste by around 60 per cent.

Births, Marriages, and Deaths

As you will have likely predicted, one of the largest shifts in society over the past 40 years has been ageing and, in particular, the way in which financial and political power is now concentrated in the hands of relatively old people who are asset-rich but income-poor. Many think that the cult of youth that came with the rise of John F. Kennedy in the 1960s is finally over.

Not surprisingly, this has created tensions among the younger generations. To many, the situation resembles a guerrilla war between youthful energy and ageing influence, and it's shaping up as a battle that the younger generations will slowly win because they have control of the ideas. They are more agile in terms of organisation, and more open to experimentation and innovation because they have less time and money invested in current systems (a parallel, perhaps, with the way that parts of Africa have surged ahead in recent years due to a lack of investment in, and therefore reliance on, earlier technologies and infrastructure).

There is an interesting political pressure that arises when a highly conservative group has huge influence in governance and another group with less social power comes to control the new connective technologies. This situation is echoed in various vestiges of power within the new establishment where, despite 40 years of technological advancement, a few die-hards within military and political circles still cling to rigid pyramidal power structures, while most of the people they seek to influence are floating within fluid networks. One big shift that most people seem happy with, though, is the way that what started out as file-sharing has ended up with people sharing ideas, and this has ultimately resulted in the reasonably widespread belief that most important decisions can be made by all participants via instant polling on mobile devices.

By this point, you are possibly wondering what's underpinning this utopia. The answer is money. Once we got out of the nasty scrape caused by population growth, resource shocks, unrestrained individualism, and debt, we embarked upon a remarkable journey of discovery underpinned by demand from the newly affluent middle classes in regions such as China, Brazil, India, and (for awhile) Russia. Demand from middle-class households among the N11 nations was significant too, and countries such as the unified

Korea, along with sunshine states such as Turkey and Morocco, have eclipsed many moribund European nations when it comes to consumption. However, while Asian growth was expected, the African resurgence was not. Africa is now booming, thanks to the convergence of improved governance and the continued demand for its resources.

Yet we should not forget simple demographics. Many African regions enjoy high fertility rates, and their youthful populations have proven to be a source of many ideas upon which the rest of the world has come to rely. The largest recent population increases, for example, have come from sub-Saharan Africa (about one-third of the total). This is while Japan and most of Europe continue to suffer from skilled-labour shortages.

Breaking the data down by age group also reveals some surprises. The greatest decline in young manpower, for instance, has occurred in China, so while China continues to dominate in fields such as engineering, it has suffered an overall decline in many other areas of innovation. India, of course, continues to have a booming population, but most of the growth is in rural, rather than urban, areas. One solution to this difficulty in recruiting skilled workers locally is obviously to import foreign workers, but this has proved problematic for many countries, especially those that have historically been at best suspicious and at worst hostile to foreigners. Furthermore, developments in communications technology have moved the value of community high up the social ladder, making the more simplified economic analysis of who we should allow into our countries less obvious. Add to that the concerns over global terrorism, and a strong case for very conservative immigration policies gets locked in place.

However, the real surprise is America. The United States remains almost unique in having a population that has expanded by around 20 per cent since 2020, as a result of both formal and informal immigration and growing birth rates. The nation has enjoyed a rise in the size of its working-age population, and this has translated into a booming economy. Add to this the impacts of immigration on entrepreneurship (immigrants are more likely to create new businesses), together with an economic system that values the creative destruction of existing ideas, and you can start to see why the nation is still so good at producing minds that can think around corners and create the kind of exponential economic growth that's so in demand.

The Next Industrial Revolution

Who would have imagined 30 or 40 years ago that nano-technology materials would have such a giant impact on everyday life, or that nano would radically reshape modern manufacturing, distribution, retailing, and business models — not to mention help the environment, too? Indeed, who would have thought that, alongside the mobile internet, nanotech would be the most important development for society?

Nano has been a long time coming, but boy, you should see it now. Historically, manufacturing — and, to some extent, global capitalism — was founded on the belief that large inputs were required, and that economies of scale produced economic benefit. This is no longer the case. Products can now be assembled using nanotechnology factories that are exceedingly small; so small, in fact, that many are located inside homes. Moreover, thanks to nanotechnology, products can be created only for the period in which they are needed, and can, effectively, be reverse-manufactured to get rid of them. Personal Manufacturing Units (PMUs) can assemble anything people want, much like the earlier 3D printers could. The only difference is that now the inputs are atoms, not physical materials. The process is still a bit slow, but if you want a new set of plates for a dinner party, they can now be assembled in your own PMU — all you need is some software and a design blueprint, chosen using a screen or some other user interface. Thus raw materials, transport, logistics, inventory, waste disposal, and retail have all started to shrink. Put another way, user-generated content or customer co-creation has been subject to a paradigm shift, and consumers are now literally the creators of many of the everyday products they use, making them pretty much self-sufficient. As a result, the competitive advantage increasingly lies in knowing what customers want, in brands, and in the blueprints for manufacturing, although physical environments and customer relations do still count.

Thinking about all this makes one rather tired. Possibly this is because sleep is one of the few things we haven't managed to make more available, and it continues to be in rather short supply thanks to the accelerated nature of everyday life and the demands — and interruptions — caused by a fully wired world. It's funny: you'd think that all of this new technology would have created more time, but sometimes it seems to have done the very opposite. The good news, though, is that if you can't sleep, there is always something to do.

Imagine Timeline

2012	Widespread job cuts in manufacturing, alongside heavy investment in automated systems
2013	Bankruptcy, particularly among European nations, and general volatility in financial markets provokes a search for algorithms to stabilise global markets
2014	The United Nations states that free broadband should be a basic human right; Singapore is the first country to agree to comply
2015	Apple launches iMedic, which monitors health concerns
2016	The spiralling cost of oil fuels widespread investment in shale gas

2017	The rise in 'big data' acts as a catalyst for massive growth in data analytics
2018	Paper use falls by 33 per cent globally in a single year
2019	Facial-recognition apps are used widely on smartphones
2020	Identity-protection and reputation-management businesses boom
2021	E-voting becomes available in Walmart stores
2022	Widespread adoption of personal avatar assistants
2023	Ninety-five per cent of payments are now mobile, pre-pay, or embedded; only 5 per cent of transactions involve human contact
2024	Appliance manufacturer Dyson develops a range of conversational appliances
2025	A Chinese scientist wins the Nobel Prize in Chemistry for research into geoengineering
2026	The North African Solar Grid, which will pump power to Northern Europe, begins operation
2027	The Vehicle Energy Network is launched in San Francisco
2028	All city-centre traffic in Shanghai is now electric
2029	Most homes in Western nations have at least one 3D printer, and many people now print their own products
2030	Computers are 1000 times as powerful and ten times cheaper than any available in 2012
2031	United States Air Force–staffed fighter jets are completely replaced by unmanned aerial vehicles
2032	Commercially farmed insects are used to provide protein in some microwave-ready meals
2033	Sixty-five per cent of the world's population have sequenced their own DNA

2034	Most machines are now operated via speech or brain–machine interfaces
2035	Eighty five per cent of homes contain three or more robots
2036	The first commercial mine opens on the Moon
2037	The world's fifth largest company is Syn-Bio, Inc.
2038	Every human-made physical object now has its own internet protocol (IP) address
2039	Google unveils the Space Mirror Project, which has an estimated cost of US$8 trillion
2040	People are able to record their whole lives via real-time video

4

Please Please Me:

a world of greed

With hindsight, the problem with forecasts made by some commentators during the volatile period of 2008–2018 was that they focused almost exclusively on potential problems and did not properly consider other, more positive, possibilities. In particular, economic forecasters, politicians, and even many futurists failed to grasp how developments in areas such as artificial intelligence, synthetic biology, quantum computing, robotics, geoengineering, and nanotechnology could combine with globalisation and population growth to usher in an era of unparalleled prosperity — an era where daily life for the vast majority of people got better year after year, at what felt like an ever-accelerating rate.

Perhaps the failure to see the second long boom coming was due to the usual problem of people projecting current trends forwards; or perhaps there was nefarious pleasure to be found in perilous prophecies of doom and gloom. We're told that conservatives are afraid of the future, while liberals are afraid of the past. Maybe this is true, but both failed to grasp the new zeitgeist until it was well underway.

Whatever the reasons, the state of euphoric optimism that started around 2019 and continues to the present day caught most people off-guard, especially those who assumed that many of the world's biggest problems were either insurmountable or could only be solved by accredited experts with access to vast sums of money.

Not everyone missed the possibility of such a shift, although you might have to go back more than 100 years, to the 1930s, to find someone who grasped what could potentially unfold economically. In the middle of the first Great Depression (GD1, as we renamed it, following GD2 of 2012–2017), the economist John Maynard Keynes wrote an essay called 'Economic Possibilities for Our Grandchildren'. He suggested that the harsh economic conditions of the time were not signals that capitalism and the Industrial Revolution were at an end, but rather that undreamed of levels of productivity would soon be unleashed, and that this would transform average living standards and material prosperity across many parts of the globe. He still got a few things wrong — most notably, that people would work fewer hours, not more — but he correctly predicted that one of the central problems of society 100 years hence (in 2030) would be dealing with the fact that the vast majority of humankind would no longer need to struggle to survive.

This, it seems to us, is exactly what has been happening for awhile now. The key concern of our times is how to deal with the fact that most people have ended up with more or less what they said they always wanted. This is obviously not quite the same as people getting what they really need, but suffice to say that the new mass affluence doesn't seem to worry most people. The fact is that the vast majority of the world's nine billion people (give or take) are now far better off materially than their parents or grandparents, many of whom are still walking around *tut-tutting* about the materialistic greed that consumes the rest of society.

Enough of 'We' — More About 'Me'

We are, by and large, better educated, better fed, and more informed nowadays, thanks in part to central government's investment in new skills and infrastructure, and the fact that almost everyone in the world is now online, with access to the latest information and knowledge — much of it crowd-sourced, or 'home-brewed', to the annoyance of the various corporations and bureaucrats running the more traditional media and political institutions.

Not that 'we' is a word you'll hear much in conversation these days — it's almost exclusively 'me'. (Or, more precisely, 'Money, money, money; me, me, me.') Most people today seem to be happy skimming along atop a sea of ruthless self-interest and hedonism. And most populist right-wing politicians (by definition largely opportunistic and status-obsessed) have bent over backwards to retain this world, in which status and financial success are unapologetic drivers, rather than challenge or change the system towards something more equitable, where concern for others and the health of our planet are taken into account.

We both know that everyone is supposed to be deliriously happy and lost in a labyrinth of consumerist existence, but in 2040 are we the only ones who worry that there might be something rotten — even in the happy-hippy state of Denmark, where we hear that the last of the communal gardens has now been bought by tanned, white-teethed, surgically enhanced celebrities? One of these rich new residents is watering her lawn with organic Welsh spring water, delivered by solar-powered tanker. Most say that's fine if you can afford it, but personally we think it's a frivolous indulgence, even if she is grazing a few Welsh spider sheep to satisfy the demand for local meat and super-strong silk for luxury fabrics. Never mind that 70 per cent of the planet is now water-stressed; if her lawn is looking good, why worry?

You think we're kidding about this? We're not — and neither are we kidding about a novelty-obsessed (and rather infantile) friend who recently set up a memory-hosting business in New York and, instead of carpeting the reception, laid biodynamic turf and brought in an organic lamb to 'cut' it. Neither the company nor the lawn lasted very long, but the exuberant libertarian view that he could do whatever he liked as long as he could pay for it still lingers in our minds, even without someone hosting our memories.

We guess that this is the view of politicians too, most of whom seem to believe that unfettered markets are the best mechanism to drive growth and that individuals (we'd use the word 'adults', but that's not always strictly correct) should look after themselves on virtually all matters, ranging from health, education, and pensions to physical security, no matter how stupid or short-term their thinking. User-decides and user-pays, they still call it, although quite how this works when a user has no money is a bit of a riddle. You'd think that many of the individuals who have been left behind by our 'get rich or die trying' culture would focus a bit more on the potential 'dying' bit, but no — people seem to have an incredible capacity to delude themselves that extraordinary financial success and instant global celebrity are still around the corner, even when they are temporarily sleeping in a tent without a pension. This attitude has even trickled down to pre-teens, 90 per cent of whom crave some kind of celebrity, according to a study in Google News. Maybe they are right; after all, recent experience would seem to suggest that once you're considered famous by 15 people, you can sell anything from jewellery to dog food.

It's like the whole world is now run by Walt Disney, and Hannah Montana has been put in charge of aesthetics. Again, if you think we're exaggerating, we'd draw your attention to the 250,000 Global Currency Unit (GCU) coat we saw in T&M

Stores last week. It was bright pink, the colour of denial, and covered in 18-carat-gold-plated buttons shaped like small bunny rabbits. It was aimed at eight-year-old girls, but there was a matching adult version, too. We assume that the big fluffy collars are so you can shield your eyes from people on the street asking for top-ups for their digital wallets.

While we're on the subject of dubious expenditure, it was also reported last week that one of the fastest-growing cosmetic surgery treatments in China is tongue surgery for kids. Why? To improve their accents, especially when they attend interviews for premium lifestyle schools — most notably Eton on the Hill (or the Shangri-La Hotel of educational establishments, as our old friend Douglas once called it). That's in addition to the facial surgery and body adjustment that is now more or less a standard feature in everyone's wardrobe of physical perfection.

Where are we going with this? The point is that when people of our generation were growing up, there was at least a modicum of self-restraint, modesty, and humility. These words have now been pasted into ancient history, replaced by our culture of me, which largely consists of self-gratification, self-entitlement, self-absorption, and personal indulgence. But we guess that's a by-product of a highly competitive, highly dynamic, and highly fluid global economy, where the spoils largely go to the fastest and the smartest.

It's All about the Cha-Ching

Apart from the explosion in obesity (now dealt with in some areas, but still a considerable problem in others), the result of this 'me' culture is physical and emotional separation from others, with the exception of those individuals — or institutions — that are temporarily seen as useful economically. A good, if somewhat tangential, example of this is something we spotted in Thailand recently. Apparently the government has been desperate to attract ultra-high-net-worth foreigners as residents, so they've come up with the idea of a VIT (Very Important Thai) Max Card. This nifty little card has a couple of chips in it, along with solar panels and wireless connectivity. As well as being a payment device and physically opening the doors of various black-card establishments (including premium police stations and hospitals), it allows foreigners to warn shops, restaurants, and clubs of their imminent arrival. Of course, it's backfired slightly because some people (we won't mention any nationalities, but let's say that vodka is frequently involved) are using it to be rude and inflict miseries on what they regard as 'the little people' — and that's not anything to do with their height.

What else is new, as everyone seems obsessed with saying these days? Well, the world's largely run financially by the Chinese, with a little help from the Russians, the Indians, and the Brazilians, much as Jim O'Neill at Goldman Sachs predicted back in 2001 that it would be; and there is now a significant gap opening up between what is, with a handful of major exceptions, an ageing and slothful West and North and a youthful and energetic East and South. The Chinese, in particular, have ongoing problems with spiralling wages and a lack of workers and key resources, but the fact remains that China and India combined are 300 per cent larger in GDP terms than the United States, so they are doing well. We must admit that we've been rather impressed with how seriously these two Asian nations have invested in education and skills, especially research and development — and the technology products they are now churning out are simply amazing.

Apparently, back in 2001, non-OECD countries' share of global research and development was around 17 per cent; it's now 67 per cent. This trend obviously surprised quite a few Western companies in the early days, but most of them have now been bought out by the Chinese. There's a level of resentment, and occasionally blatant protectionism, around some of the Chinese mergers and acquisitions deals, but mostly we seem to welcome their money with open arms. As for China setting the global price for labour — most people are still reacting to this ten years on. How long it will last is anyone's guess. Personally, we think you have to view China's economic miracle (and those of some other key nations) against the backdrop of a range of social, demographic, and environmental challenges.

Africa is doing well too, especially if you ignore the residue of corruption and their somewhat lackadaisical management of natural resources. Absolute poverty is still a problem in much of this region, as it is in a few others, but across much of the sub-Saharan things are better than they have been for a very long time (although, ironically, obesity within the African middle class has become a concern). The continent, especially North Africa, caught a few napping Western nations off-guard in the early days, yet China bought up some African land — and hence their food, for awhile. The deals also tied up most of the labour-outsourcing market, which was a serious problem until the impacts of automation, especially robotics, kicked in.

Africa also eluded people in other ways, too, notably the European and Australasian travel industries, which missed the influx of African tourists — although this wasn't quite as bad as their negligence in adapting to other new markets, especially to Asian tourists with different shopping and dining tastes. By the way, two things that still make us laugh are the fact that Russian and Chinese tourists now come to London and Paris to look for British and French counterfeits of Russian and Chinese luxury brands, and the fact that African companies (largely controlled by the Chinese) are now outsourcing their call centres to Northern England. We also bask in the glorious irony of the reverse colonisation of Europe by Asians, Africans, and those from parts of Latin America — although the fact that so many migrants display so little loyalty to their new host nations does worry us a little in terms of long-term urban planning

Latin America continues to boom economically, with Brazilian biomass industries doing especially well, alongside those developing in Africa. But we shouldn't forget the economic impacts of the democracy dividend in the Middle East, or what a few of the Gulf States have achieved socially and culturally. The fact that they have built many of the world's best new art galleries, libraries, and museums is hardly surprising when you consider how much money some of these nations have, and how quickly certain individuals have amassed huge personal fortunes through technologies such as solar power. There are, of course, some shady solar cowboys out there in the desert — they are more or less everywhere these days, due to the low levels of regulation — but the sands of time will likely sort these things out.

The long-term vision of several of the sovereign wealth funds in some of these regions is another thing we should be learning from. Then again, it's fairly easy to lay back and think about the future when you still have relatively large reserves of oil and the price is GCU$250 per barrel. The rest of us in the West are still suffering slightly, despite the penetration of new forms of energy technology and the stream of energy-related innovations. Until the new generation of low-energy nuclear reactors and fusion power plants come online, the Gulf States will maintain the upper hand in terms of re-drawing the map of art and science. Thank goodness for nuclear, solar, coal, and gas, without which we really would be in trouble.

Nevertheless, we shouldn't get so obsessed with cultural projects in the Gulf States that we forget about the new wealth that's flowing into grand projects in South America, China, and India. And let's not forget, either, about the good old US of A.

The Empire Strikes Back

Those commentators in the early years of the millennium who penned prophecies writing off the US economy (and the Canadian economy, to a degree) have been eating humble American cherry pie for a couple of decades now, thanks largely to the nation's favourable demographics (high fertility rates, plus a high percentage of women active in senior positions within the workforce), immigration policies, and large tar sands and shale gas deposits. Indeed, the United States is, as far as we know, the only OECD nation that has managed to grow the size of its workforce over the past 30 years and, despite globalisation, remains one of the few places on the planet where very big ideas rub shoulders with very large amounts of seed capital. We don't want to dwell on the economic situation of individual nations for too long, but we think the global economic context is important to understand before we dig into some of the other forces affecting the world.

The N11 nations (another Jim O'Neill forecast) have all done terribly well, too — especially Turkey, which has recovered quickly from the devastating Istanbul earthquake a couple of years ago. The Indonesian economy, in particular, is growing at an amazing rate: we heard last month that within ten years the Indonesian GDP will be greater than that of Germany, Italy, Spain, and the United Kingdom combined.

The United Kingdom is doing surprisingly well — still the world's tenth largest economy, and now the second largest in Europe by a considerable margin. We're told that this is due to favourable immigration policies and high fertility rates. (God bless those unwed teenage mums!) The same conditions do not prevail in Korea and, especially, Japan, who are ageing ahead of almost every other nation. The main problem, we understand, is that the lack of younger people in the population has had a direct impact upon innovation rates, with much of the innovation that does exist coming from older people in larger, more traditional firms, rather than smaller or more diverse sources, especially small entrepreneurial firms led by young people. To be fair, unified Korea is actually doing rather well on a straight GDP measure, thanks largely to its focus on automation, but this disguises the lack of technological breakthroughs. The low levels of immigration don't help, either, and the zero-tax policy for under-25s doesn't seem to be having much of an effect.

What concerns us most with regard to Korea and Japan are the almost suicidal hours that businesspeople work, and the fact that we in the West seem to be following closely in their tracks. They say that most Koreans now enjoy what is known as the one-day weekend, because it apparently takes most Koreans 22 hours to wind down from the previous week's work; Koreans only really relax after 4.00 p.m. on a Saturday. But by about 4.00 p.m. on the Sunday, they start worrying about work and begin working from home to 'get ahead'. (Does this sound at all familiar?) You can see similar tendencies in the United States, Northern Europe, and even the United Kingdom — although thankfully Australians have preserved their more balanced outlook on work — but Korea in particular seems to take working to a whole new level, especially with the company hotels that encourage employees to stay in the office even later, or not go home at all. And that's for the lucky ones. Vast numbers of employees now either work for themselves, doing projects from dining rooms, spare bedrooms, and McBucks coffee shops, while others work part-time, with neither option providing much in the way of security, training, or benefits. Many companies complain about a lack of loyalty among full-time staff, but if you ask us, that is partly a result of the companies showing zero loyalty in the other direction — and they started it.

Some of these companies are quite dreadful. We have a friend who was Chief Ethics Officer for MyWay Pharmaceuticals, and was recently 'managed for value' (that is, he lost his job). He told us that he was 'forgotten before he was even gone'; it still rings in our ears. No doubt MyWay will soon complain that working with 20- and 30-year-olds is like herding cats and will try to hire him back full- or part-time next year, pretending that nothing ever happened. No wonder that loyalty is so conditional and short-term these days.

Because I'm Worth It

Someone asked us recently how today's world is different to that of 2012. We suppose the answer isn't so much to do with the rampant optimism, the sense of economic wellbeing, the accelerated nature of everyday life, the constant urban clatter, or even the pervasive displays of greed and materialism, but rather the way in which everything centres on the individual — it's all about a person's rights and expectations. For example, most people now regard cars, expensive holidays, large steaks, and the latest electronic gadgets as 'rights', whereas we never used to think like that.

This optimism and sense of entitlement isn't quite the same as happiness. In fact, we'd argue that a great many people aren't happy precisely because they spend so much of their time and money trying to be. You can see this with cuddle parties, where middle-aged professionals, many of whom have recently popped into a 90-second divorce kiosk, embrace strangers in an attempt to persuade themselves that it's all been worth it. Several of these are the very same people that appear in *Bling* magazine's World's Top 500 Most Successful People list, but one suspects that the great job, huge smarthouse, and flashy electric trike don't quite add up to eternal bliss — unless they can afford regular bottles of Eternal Bliss™ to go alongside the cashmere shampoo and 24-carat-gold-flecked dark chocolate, in which case maybe it does.

That's too negative. Okay, things were perhaps marginally better before the mass media invented annual top-everything lists — which now, of course, includes the *List of Top Lists* annual — but let's not forget that there are many positive sides to our regained affluence, and our newfound ability to personalise our lives and even our deaths. The most notable example of this is the way that healthcare and medicine are now targeted towards the genetic blueprint of every patient. Personalised genome sequencing (free since 2025), together with personalised remote monitoring, sophisticated data analysis, and sentiment analysis, mean that individuals are now fully aware of what they will, in all probability, get sick from in the future, and can target specific treatments and personalised pharmaceuticals to unique genetic building blocks and environmental factors, changing both where desirable or where advised to by their insurance company.

Individualised treatment isn't limited to medicine. We've now got user-generated and individualised pension plans (although very few people seem to bother until it's too late), personalised curricula in schools, personalised media, personalised diets, and personalised ready-meals. Add a little bit of augmented reality, and it's not that far-fetched to suggest that each individual experiences the world in a fundamentally different way, based upon their personal preferences. In 2012 this wasn't the case — although, looking back, there were some weak signals emerging with Microsoft (as it was then known) and Google tailoring search results to individuals, and early social-media sites personalising retail offers and webpages according to who was looking at them, when, where, and why. There was also Levi's early attempt at personalised jeans, although this didn't really take off until everyone had a virtual 3D twin to try them on before the order was sent to the in-store factory.

There are some downsides to all of this. Pandering to instant expression and opinion sometimes comes at the expense of group wisdom and experience, although shallow knowledge and deep social fragmentation are hardly anything new. They have been growing since at least 2005, which is ancient history — as far away from today as 1970 was back then. On reflection, a culture of immediacy, novelty, and individual entitlement was also significantly present back then, but concerns about financial instability, environmental change, and respect for the rule of law often negated this. With hindsight, you can see the early impacts of personalised genome sequencing, a user-pays mentality, and micro-blogging too, but at the time we didn't recognise how this would lead to an outbreak of unapologetic narcissism, where individuals would become increasingly unable to accommodate the opinions, preferences, or beliefs of others. Perhaps we should have listened more carefully to authors Sherry Turkle and Jaron Lanier, who warned about the fragmentation and tyranny created by instant communication and by ubiquitous global connectivity. In theory, the fact that people expect more transparency and individual control is a positive development, forcing politicians and corporations to become more accountable and truthful. But this isn't always the reality, and many have found ways to get around the controls that technology seeks to impose.

Another downside is that managing individual expectations has, for many individuals and institutions, become cumbersome, irritating, and frustrating, especially when misunderstandings are amplified due to the use of text messaging and avatar assistants, rather than direct-voice or face-to-face communication. Constantly responding to individuals who won't admit that anything is their fault — ever — also means that less time is spent on developing the very products and services that these people are usually complaining about.

In addition, radical transparency has meant that it has become even more difficult to plan far ahead, as shareholders and the media have become even more fixated on a company's pipeline of new products, rather than on longer-term research and development. Maybe they are right: after all, what's the point in developing radical new thinking if competitors continually find out about your plans before you've properly developed anything? At least the intellectual-property lawyers are kept busy. Not that the problems surrounding too much connectivity and data overload are confined to large corporations and governments — decision-making on an individual level is also being adversely affected, as are relationships, sleep patterns, people's sense of privacy, and the general ability to reflect and 'think before you leap'. Or perhaps the problem of accountability isn't so much about transparency, but connectivity. If people had to think more rigorously before they criticised something, there would be fewer time-consuming, distracting, and irrelevant diatribes, many of which must, by law, be dealt with.

We sometimes see something vaguely similar occurring with money, in the sense that people often act without thinking. When we had physical money, especially bank notes, purchasing was much more considered; it was as though the money itself had real value. But since we've moved to the global e-standard, spending has become much more impulsive, which is possibly why we have more debt, more bubbles, and more systemic shocks. Bizarrely, nobody seems to think that this is a problem.

Maybe they are right. Few people today even remember that the global social-media crash, the Chinese real-estate crash, and the US nanotechnology bubble all happened within a decade of each other, which surely says something about our collective ability to be sidelined by endless optimism and greed. You might even argue that governments' responses to pressure to liberalise bankruptcy laws and force banks to lend to people with bad credit ratings or a lack of proper income might see a repeat of GD2, but nobody wants to listen. As far as most people are concerned, none of this is a problem because any losses will quickly be offset by endlessly rising asset prices.

Our focus on narrow, short-term self-interest, self-absorption, and invincibility also extends across nations, and means that global problems such as climate change and mobile and wireless radiation have remained largely ignored. There are, of course, numerous examples of local arrangements aimed at offsetting the impacts of climate change, but to date nobody has achieved anything significant on a global scale. The 'To Hell With Climate Change' T-shirt we saw yesterday on the beach in Brighton says it all, really, although perhaps the slogan had a subtle ironic twist to it. We're too old to know (but we're glad to see that slogan T-shirts are still 'in', and especially like the ones where the slogan is generated automatically according to what's trending on a particular day).

Somehow, millions of people walking around the streets with the same T-shirt flies in the face of individual expression, but we suppose you could say much the same thing about mobile ringtones and playlists. And there is, after all, a world of difference between an aggregation of individual choices and the insistence on uniformity from on high.

The Global Economy Greenwash

Despite the apathy towards climate change, it is still a concern — although, usually, if it doesn't affect people directly and *right now*, they ignore it. We've had a few run-ins with very wild weather recently, especially monsoon-like rains, which caused so much flooding that a number of electricity substations were damaged — and, of course, we had last year's heatwave and droughts, too — but these events tend to be quickly forgotten once the damage is cleaned up. Most people take the view that this is simply part of a natural weather cycle and that the threats of global warming that we were all so concerned about 30 or 40 years ago were largely exaggerated. Mind you, soil erosion, dwindling biodiversity, and ocean acidification will, without a doubt, turn around and bite us on the bum sooner or later. In the meantime, we guess that the world will adapt to whatever comes our way.

We suppose that on one level the social passivity towards climate change is a negative; but on the other hand, many believe that natural disasters often happen to people who probably deserve it. After all, if you are stupid enough to live right next to a beach or to build a luxury smart shack in a river basin, you can hardly complain when you get washed out, can you? Anyway, shouldn't we be focusing on ways to harness all this excess water, wind, and sun to generate a bit of power? If a few thousand people have to be moved out of the way to do this, so be it.

A handful of individuals, largely those that were pressing for zero emissions by 2040, think that this attitude stinks, but others just call it common sense.

The good news is that the high price of oil (along with coal and gas, thanks to the ludicrous carbon price adjustments) has slightly dampened demand — but the better news is that we've got a lot more oil than we thought. Add to this shale gas and light tight oil, and the lamp of heavy industry will burn bright for awhile longer.

The other piece of positive news is that high fossil-fuel prices have resulted in serious investment in alternative energy technologies, together with technologies related to smart-infrastructure and -transport. Given that the global energy demand has increased by 80 per cent since 2010, and that 75 per cent of this rise has been met by fossil fuels, you can perhaps see why there is now so much emphasis on nuclear, offshore wind, and solar. None of these are cheap, but solar in particular looks promising, and is already supplying as much as 10 to 15 per cent of several countries' electricity needs. The other big innovation has been the development of the grid, which is now starting to resemble the early internet, with people sharing and selling local energy to one another. Oliver's wife, Susie, is right in her belief that necessity is the midwife of all new thinking, and this continues to be the case — although we suspect that society's continued addiction to old-school fossil fuels has at least a few more years to run yet. If we could only cure our addiction to moving things, including people, from one place to another physically, or constantly connecting virtually with battery-powered mobile devices, we would be in an even stronger position. Personally, we're optimistic that this is exactly what will happen, and dream that one day energy will be almost free — in which case, we can all go completely mad and leave the heating on while having all the windows open, and buy every fabulous new gizmo going …

Another thing to mention is that the green economy has become something of a white elephant. Or is that a red herring? Whatever the terminology, beyond clean tech, energy conservation, and materials reduction, the green economy is something of a non-starter, much like the supposedly terminal effects of climate change. We suspect that the only reason most of the rules and taxation relating to sustainability remain is because they are linked to revenue maximisation or to resource shortages.

There are, of course, various eco-luxe and eco-novelty products aimed at people with excessive guilt, but there's not many of these people left. Even the leftist groupings that championed climate change in the 2000s and 2010s have moved on, either to promote the politics of embedded water or to rail against bio-hacking, bio-criminology, and the burgeoning transhumanist movement instead. (Personally, we're all in favour of transhumanism. Life has been good, and we'd like much more of it. Ageing is such a drag, so why not develop techniques and technologies to slow down the ageing process, or eliminate it altogether?)

The one area in which sustainability has made an enormous impact is travel and transport. You can thank the oil price for this, but it's also got a lot to do with governments trying to make urban infrastructure more frictionless from a local and global economic standpoint. High-speed rail travel is still enjoying something of a renaissance, and good old coaches are back on the roads now that the hybrids have got their act sorted out. Even air travel is looking promising again, thanks to Boeing's hybrid-electric Big Bird. Obviously we've still got large numbers of privately owned cars on the roads, but the numbers are starting to dwindle a little, especially since road pricing, based upon real-time traffic flows, was introduced. Personally, we find the logic of a Ferrari 4WD automatic biodiesel RV a bit dubious, but they tell us it's their best-selling eco-luxe vehicle to date.

A few other green plays have been successful too, but as far as we can see this is only when they tap into saving consumers either time or money. For example, one of the smart things the two of us did back in 2036 was buy into an urban mining company that was digging up rubbish tips, looking for old gold in early mobile phones and other large mobile devices. This investment had nothing to do with saving the planet, though; Noor Bank put us onto it as a sure-fire profit-making venture. They've been right, too: the shares are up 400 per cent this year alone, on rumours that the company is going to mine rare minerals on the Moon from 2050. It would have been over 500 per cent if it wasn't for the full-cost accounting model they've started using. We've also made a bundle on the back of the latest tech and biotech booms, which has more than made up for the money we lost a few years ago in the first clean-tech and carbon-offset futures markets. So the future is looking greener.

A Cocoon Culture

Speaking of profits, our biggest has been from Rent-a-Pet. We've made a 2200 per cent gain since February 2028, largely off the back of senior singles wanting a furry friend for the weekend and young, Type-A singles wanting to rent a fur kid for the appearance of empathy and warmth on first and second dates. Just recently, someone opened a hotel for animals at London's Terminal 6. Wait for this … rooms from GCU$800 a night, with suites starting at GCU$2000. The room-service menu for cats features Greedy Cat bluefin tuna steaks; while the juicy Wagyou bone-on-the-bed option for dogs seems to be asking for trouble.

On the subject of indulgences, we have to admit an addiction here ourselves, especially to the new iWrist Lick. We're just suckers for lime green and brushed aluminium, especially when twinned with any direct brain-to-machine interface. Even so, it's not quite as cool as the new iRobot Washman developed by the celebrity designer Frankie Ive. We didn't think an ironing robot would work, but it's brilliant. It can even talk to and locate your lost cashmere socks. The only problem is that it doesn't seem to recognise instructions made with a Scottish accent.

Not that you really need a domestic robot these days. Most appliances are networked with other devices and work out for themselves when to switch on or order spare parts. Add to this the boom in outsourcing household services and the new phase-five nano-fabrics, and you hardly need any extra help. (Mind you, while many of these materials look good, they contain inferior Mexican quantum chips, so the inbuilt health-monitoring function isn't that good.) Regardless, we're not sure that we could let Cherdonnay go. Admittedly, she's not that great at ironing shirts, but she's been in Oliver's house for years, and gets on well with the gardening bot and the pool bot. Half the time practical applications are not that important, anyway.

Domestic robots are just great to look at, and the endless variety of programmable personality chips make hacking them tremendous fun. They're also good companions, although you'd have to admit they don't quite have the warmth or the humour of a real human worker. Even the Creature Comfort SafeSitter range of childcare bots leaves us a little cold — unless it's the shock-pink-and-titanium version with the predictive wants and Naughty Stick upgrade. Who could resist one of those?

We're glad we didn't buy any shares in Safe Technologies, though. The Safe Sitter range is a beautiful suite of predictive machinery, but it has fallen rather flat sales-wise — which makes sense, considering that 60 per cent of households contain only one person nowadays, and that only 8 per cent contain children (whereas it was 58 per cent 50 to 60 years ago, we're told). Most kids have already got a companion bot and most older people, particularly those in the 80 to 90 age range, prefer a real pet, partly because the voice implants are so much fun inside something that's biological and partly because none of the boring recycling legislation applies to animals. If your cat with a Zsa Zsa Gabor voice implant dies, you just dig a hole at the bottom of your garden, whereas companion bots have to be delivered to an approved robot recycling centre, where you need to deal with several screens of information requests.

As for other ways in which the world has changed since 2012, we suppose it depends a great deal on whom you are talking about. Regional differences are still significant, but in our experience the polarisation is greatest within countries, not between them. While most peoples' daily lives have improved immeasurably, globalisation and technology have wrought misery for those who cannot learn the skills that are required to adjust to our new masters. The two of us must admit that we have very little experience of these people, largely because they tend to inhabit the fringe areas, especially Area 21, and are largely prevented from accessing areas one to five, but a small minority of this minority do take it upon themselves to redistribute some of the individual gains that they believe have been acquired. You can't really object to this, we suppose, because they are simply doing what the rest of us are doing, in the sense of taking whatever they can until someone tells them not to. In other words, it's only wrong if you get caught.

Overall, crime rates are insignificant compared to what they were 30, 40, or even 50 years ago, but a small number of individuals and criminal gangs do still try to extract whatever they can, either from those who are weakest to resist or those with the most to take. This is all largely contained to Area 21, with illegals targeting other illegals or addicts robbing other addicts, but occasionally they do spend time trying to incite others to take up what they sometimes refer to as the anti-capitalist cause. This explains the large amounts of money spent on internal security in most countries, and why around 25 per cent of the world's population now live in gated communities, typically in the centre of megacities or attached to corporate campuses. This can lead to what we've heard being called a cocoon culture, with some being whisked around in private cars and premium-class railway carriages while others look on and think, 'Why not me?' The answer to this is probably that they didn't pay enough attention at school. Tough luck.

Anyway, on a Friday or Saturday night the drinking and drug-taking tend to occur, and it's not particularly safe to walk around most cities centres wearing much more than a pair of Kmart jeans and a non-organic T-shirt. It's not always that the undesirables are even around, but that sometimes otherwise sensible people do silly things, ranging from verbally abusing anyone who is not dressed almost identically to others to, in extreme cases, 'taxing' others at knifepoint for the latest impossible-to-get electronic devices. Then again, better to 'recycle' within the community, so to speak, than letting the government walk off with half of everything.

Is all this a permanent condition? We're not sure. Some people are starting to argue that homemade pharmaceuticals and gene-hacks (most recipes are easily available on the internet), together with back-street brain implants and cheap, full-immersion alternative-reality suits, mean that most of the serious trouble-makers will simply stay at home in the future. We'd like to think that society will continue to use technology to enhance or improve reality, but in the future it may be that we use it to escape from it. Communities are seeing this already, in the sense that younger generations would much prefer to deal with a machine than a human — although in our experience this preference usually changes when they grow older; they soon recognise that you can't speak to a machine about what it means to be human. Machines are also hopeless at understanding what can be, to some, illogical choices — such as the desire for *that* diamond-encrusted gold watch, rather than for a much cheaper model.

Me, Myself, and I

Some people we know are saying that increased competition for resources is forcing an arranged marriage between globalisation and localism, in the sense that the cost of physically moving people and goods around is becoming so high that manufacturing and consumption are re-localising, while virtual data, information, and services continue to globalise. This is tricky to explain, but the analogy that illustrates it best is a herd of cows munching on grass that's been laid on top of a server farm: the carbon credits attached to growing grass and having bio-engineered cows offset the methane coming out of the cows and the emissions created by the server farm — or, more specifically, by the people searching online for information about locally produced beef and milk.

This probably sounds very harmonious and balanced, which things are on one level, but most of the time we succeed in getting things totally out of balance until we suddenly realise that something is wrong and rush to compensate, often sowing the seeds for a crisis of equal magnitude in the other direction. As we explained earlier, most of the time our worldview tends to be narrow, focused on the short-term, and self-interested, which means that countries are frequently unable to deal with matters on a global level. Ironically, globalisation and global connectivity accelerate this, as they allow us to quickly create turbulence and volatility around problems. Much of the time, we seem to get away with things by the skin of our teeth, but occasionally we do get into very deep water. Our self-absorption and xenophobic tendencies are also fuelling outbreaks of isolationism and protectionism, especially around resources, which flies in the face of liberalism, deregulation, and lowered trade barriers.

This leads directly to the problem of the heightened regional tensions, blockages, and cyber-skirmishes that started way back in 2013 and continue to this day. The historical reason for this friction was largely that nations were attempting to secure vital supplies of energy, food, and water. The food-and-water problem has now been solved via a mixture of new technologies, pricing, and taxation, but energy generation and access to key raw materials continue to be far-reaching concerns. And don't forget that quite a bit of the antagonism is deep-rooted, often based on age-old nationalistic and tribal differences, many of them fuelled by globalisation and open internet access.

It might sound a bit of a stretch, but we do firmly believe that the collapse of the EU in 2014 was an early example of this resurgent tribalism, with nations keen to belong to something much smaller (and, we suppose, much more accountable domestically). Maybe that's why other Western-inspired and -engineered organisations, such as the United Nations and the

World Trade Organization, have either fallen apart or struggled to find relevance; or perhaps it's down to the fact that, in an age of instant connectivity and feedback, people really don't need analogue intermediaries. All we can say for sure is that when it comes to holidays, many people in the West prefer to stay at home or stay relatively close to what they are familiar with culturally. There are exceptions to this — especially the invitation-only silence resorts that have sprung up in countries such as Vietnam and Tibet — but generally, most of the faith-based and exploration tourism has a distinctly local flavour, and revolves around resorts that are sealed off from wider society. Yes, there are Russian tourists flocking to Stonehenge and Venice, but you won't generally come into contact with them (or they with you in St Petersburg) unless you are invited in — and why, exactly, would they do that?

In short, these days it's very much every person, and every nation, for themselves, within what are generally regarded as open markets and liberal legal frameworks (with a few notable exceptions). Despite this, there remains a longing to be part of a group and, we suspect, to engage physically with others. We're not talking about sex tourism here, but rather the desire to laugh and cry with others, whether it's watching a movie projected from a mobile phone onto a car-park wall or watching a local football match. You can do this sort of thing alone at home — and we increasingly do — but somehow a live experience, which is often expensive and inconvenient, still delivers something vital that the cheap and convenient digital version doesn't.

Perhaps this taps into something that isn't generally commented upon. On one level, we are all becoming united around concerns such as individual rights, economic freedoms, and the search for personal happiness and satisfaction. But simultaneously, we are becoming more intolerant of anything, or anyone, that deviates from this norm or benefits one individual or group over another. This would be especially true of the stateless digital nomads, seemingly unconcerned by anything other than the size of their own pay packets and the speed of their internet and mobile-phone access. But for some others, the fact that we are becoming distanced from reality or cocooned in personalised bubbles of information and friendship, unaware of the conditions facing others outside, will, we suspect, eventually become a problem.

We don't want to dwell too long on downsides because there's a great deal to be grateful for in 2040, but it's the social changes since 2012 that worry us the most. Clearly, a few billion extra middle-class individuals are a force for good, even if one result is soaring demand for everything from automobiles (up globally 300 per cent since 2015) and apartments to meat, fish, and potatoes. We've also got increasing mobility, and most individuals have far more options and choices available to them than at any previous point in history. Product personalisation, and collaborative production and consumption, are often good things; they took off following the introduction of fabricators back in 2030. Extreme poverty is still a problem, largely because of local corruption and the impact of climate change and oil prices on food costs, but, bubbles and price volatility aside, more of the world's people now enjoy the fruits of our global and highly competitive economy. Similarly, infant mortality has improved, alongside literacy and general health for the majority, while democracy, urbanisation, migration, and electrification have all spread across the globe. Around 90 per cent of the world, including China, now plays by traditional rules on intellectual property enforcement; and 85 per cent enjoy growth rates of between 7 and 10 per cent per year. Add to this the boom in technological philanthropy, and things haven't been this good since about the 1960s — which is about as far back as most machines can remember.

Will the internationalisation of markets, goods, and services ever stop? Presently, the thought seems inconceivable. But it has stopped, or at least paused for breath, twice: the first time in 1914, and the second time exactly 100 years later. Rising isolationism and protectionism might suggest that globalisation and free markets will eventually be restrained, especially given the volatility they have created, but it would be difficult for more than a handful of nations to walk away from them, given the economic interdependence not only between states, but also between customers and suppliers.

It's also highly unlikely that individuals will agree to any level of restraint in terms of access to global communications — a point well made by a 20-something woman that we spoke to awhile ago, who said: 'Most people today exist in one of two states — online or asleep.' Quite.

Nevertheless, there is restlessness in the midst of this digital utopia and material abundance. For example, income polarisation is becoming a very serious concern, with the gap between rich and poor at an all-time record. We read recently (*Fortune* magazine, 25 January 2040) that the average CEO in 1965 was paid 24 times as much as the average shop-floor worker; it's now 595 times as much, and it can be even higher for financial traders and speculators, as compared to product producers. Clearly, the economist Joseph Stiglitz is still correct in that even the most efficient markets can create socially undesirable outcomes — although we'd add an important footnote to this, which is that global media and mass communications mean that many of these undesirable outcomes are now much more visible too. We think the growing sense of grievance and resentment among many is also linked to this connectivity, transparency, and cultural complexity. The question is, will this eventually lead to rising tensions and instability, and if so, what should we do about it?

Another undesirable by-product of global competition and 24/7 markets is a certain ruthlessness and impatience when it comes to getting ahead. This is understandable, given that society is increasingly divided into winners and losers, and that those in positions of influence and power are largely immune to many of the problems facing others. The situation is not helped, either, by the fact that social affiliations are much looser than they used to be, so if you do drop out (or never even make it to the starting gate) the consequences can not only be swift, but also severe.

To some extent, various online interest-based communities can help to offset the anxieties of daily life; but for many, these communities, and even one-on-one online relationships, are wafer-thin. Most people now have between 300 and 600 'friends', but a recent survey suggested that when the gambling chips are down, some individuals only have two they can really talk to, and 50 per cent have none at all. Therefore, it is relatively easy to drop off people's radar, which partly explains the recent explosion in the number of diagnosed mental disorders.

On a milder but more pervasive level, you can see trouble brewing every morning. Most days there's a traffic jam or an accident. Fifty years ago people would generally have amused themselves quietly in the jam, and would likely have compared notes on damage politely in the event of a minor accident. These days everyone is in such a hurry, pumped-up and self-absorbed, that even the smallest blockage or bump kicks off a flood of verbal abuse, and sometimes physical violence. We think this is partly due to the competitive workplace culture (the mentality of 'if I'm late they may fire me'), and is partly a way for some of the world's losers to extract financial gain, especially when the prevalent attitude is that nothing can ever be their fault.

Occasionally, things go even further. Last month, we were both aimlessly looking out of a window when we saw someone fling themselves in front of a new Apple iBike. The whole thing was clearly a stunt — and, indeed, it soon transpired that the unfortunate fellow was targeting what looked like a wealthy commuter to extract some compensation for his lack of luck in the city. It's easier to get hit and exaggerate an injury than to pick the right stock in today's volatile markets; no wonder all iBikes now have 360-degree onboard cameras.

However, what's so interesting about iBike technology is not so much the cameras themselves, but how they are being used and why. The onboard cameras and human-motion detectors are almost Stone Age tools, as is the constant capture of data and its secure archiving in the cloud. The fact that the driver feels he or she needs all of this surely says something about our current notions of vulnerability and insecurity. As for the fellow who flung himself, the fact that he was prepared to suffer physical pain for those few seconds before his clothing released painkillers surely indicates an intense desire to be compensated for what we imagine to be his disappointment that the benefits of globalisation and technology had not flowed in his direction recently. It could also be due to the fact that he failed to pay attention at school or came from bad breeding stock and could not afford the upgrades, but that's none of our business.

We've Seen the Future and We're Alright

Enough doom and gloom; let's end this on a high and get back to some more of the good stuff. Not that long ago, bookshops (remember them?) were groaning under the growing weight of perilous prophecies about the end of the world. Forecasts of imminent catastrophe have a long history, but this batch started around 2000 with Y2K and went on to include rogue asteroids, Islamic wars, internet addiction, cyber crime, global warming, peak oil, mass starvation, binge drinking, peak population, and the coming alien hordes. Panic-buying sold lots of books, but every single one of these doomsday dystopias is now gathering dust or is at the bottom of a landfill.

Why? The reason is that we're smart. In the short term we can be incredibly stupid and lazy, but over the longer term we always seem to invent something to get us out of trouble, or we adapt our attitudes and behaviours to solve the problem — or we eventually find out that a supposed threat is actually not a threat at all. We've kicked the victim mentality by breaking free from religious oppression and from the idea that our parents know best. We know best, and we know that we know.

Back in 2012, most people thought that capitalism was doomed and that bankers should be locked up for their own sanity and safety. The global population had just hit seven billion, and in the West, people were starting to adjust to what they perceived would be a slow and rather painful slide towards the living standards of distant ancestors. They were wrong. Yes, the East remained largely buoyant and optimistic while the West suffered, but things soon started to turn around, due to the coming together of some very positive trends. Population growth turned out to be a blessing, because more eyeballs could fix more problems. Rising migration rates (a curse of globalisation, according to many at the time) also acted as an accelerant to innovation because people brought with them ideas — the freedom that comes with being from 'somewhere else' — as well as hard work and, with business migrants, hard cash. As for the emerging middle classes in Latin America, Africa, and Asia, they soon created massive new demand for many of the goods and services that were still manufactured in the West. Connectivity spread knowledge and collaboration, and science and technology bolted on a rocket booster to the whole combustible mixture and off we all blasted, to places that a few decades earlier would have been totally unimaginable.

Welcome to 2040: it's been a bumpy ride, but the new view is out of this world.

Please Please Me Timeline

2012	The average working parent spends between 19 and 81 minutes per day with their children
2013	There are more than 1.2 million US-dollar millionaires in China
2014	HTC announces a tie-up with Bugatti to create the BLiNG phone
2015	Major droughts lead to a doubling of food prices in some regions
2016	Australia's Sydney Harbour Bridge is sold to a Middle Eastern sovereign wealth fund
2017	Investment in smart infrastructure starts to push the world out of the latest recession
2018	Africa records the world's largest ever annual GDP increases
2019	Mortgage arrears fall to the lowest recorded figure in 20 years
2020	Convenience is ranked above quality and price in a global consumer survey
2021	Companies are banned from discriminating against potential employees on the basis of intelligence
2022	Red Bull is the drink of choice at most company meetings
2023	A-list celebrities generate more profit than FTSE 500 companies
2024	Legal action from disgruntled staff is the number-one cost for many businesses
2025	HSBC announces record profits of GCU$72 billion for the 2024–2025 financial year
2026	Southern England is hit by worst drought in living memory
2027	Mozambique's capital Maputo is described as 'Gold-rush City' on cover of *Fortune* magazine
2028	Eighty per cent of police and healthcare services in most countries are privatised

2029	FTSE 500 companies begin to offer scholarships to kindergarten children
2030	The World Health Organization reports than one in every four people in the world is obese
2031	All of the globe's top ten companies are energy, nanotech, or synthetic biology firms
2032	The average person sleeps just five and a half hours per night
2033	Walmart begins to sell Chinese- and Indian-made cars
2034	A survey reveals that 67 per cent of US adults are single, up from 9 per cent in 1950
2035	The amount of meat consumed by the average person in China rises to 125 kilograms per year
2036	'Ceviche of Amazonian Rainforest Catfish' wins the Dish of the Year Award in the New York Restaurant Awards
2037	Twenty-five per cent of novels are customised to add name of the reader to the story
2038	Floods wash out central Brisbane for the fourth time in 27 years
2039	Eighty-eight per cent of 11-year-olds in the United Kingdom have a smart television in their bedroom; 29 per cent have a fridge
2040	Seventy-five per cent of world's population lives in urban areas

5

Dear Prudence:

a world of temperance

In 1888, the third most popular book in the United States was Edward Bellamy's science-fiction novel *Looking Backward: 2000–1887*. The protagonist was a Bostonian who fell asleep in 1887 and woke up in the year 2000. The novel essentially foretold of a socialist utopia and, looking back from 2040, we can say that the author got a few things right. Take this passage, for example:

> It was the sincere belief of even the best of men at that epoch that the only stable elements in human nature, on which a social system could be safely founded, were its worst propensities. They had been taught and believed that greed and self-seeking were all that held mankind together, and that all human associations would fall to pieces if anything were done to blunt the edge of these motives or curb their operation. In a word, they believed — even those who longed to believe otherwise — the exact reverse of what to us seems self-evident; they believed, that is, that the antisocial qualities of men, and not their social qualities, were what furnished the cohesive

force of society ... It seems absurd to expect anyone to believe that convictions like these were ever seriously entertained by men ...

Not bad. It's taken quite awhile, and some rather dramatic weather, but we think that people have now finally moved away from the idea that civilisation should be seen through an economic lens alone, or that business and money are the only things that matter. We can't remember for sure, but we think John Ralston Saul spoke of this in his book *The Collapse of Globalism* many decades ago. Whoever it was, they were on the right track — although, as usual, it took a head-on collision with reality to actually change anything.

All of us had been fed-up for some time. Since the early part of the century, humanity had known that the climate would become a problem, but most people largely ignored it (including business and government at any meaningful level). We decided to cross our fingers and hope that anything bad would more or less be confined to people in faraway countries.

Equally, many people had grown tired of a homogenised and commercially driven world, flattened by unfeeling global forces, and we all longed for local differences. It's ironic that it was the slowness with which environmental and free-market failures built up that caught some people off-guard. After all, it wasn't as though we hadn't seen both building from a long way off.

It's also been a little ironic, given the sense of urgency that surrounds many of these things nowadays, that slowness is precisely the solution that society has collectively reached out for. We're a little surprised that, while the world is all in a bit of a mess — to put it mildly — somehow we haven't seen so many smiles on each other's face in a long while. We are all pessimistic deep down, but our faith in each other appears to be stronger than ever. Strange days indeed.

Take the view from Richard's sitting room. Who could have imagined that, 20 years ago, the grass in the average back garden would disappear? We're sure a few people might have argued that a lawn in suburbia was a vegetative perversion, with a mono-chromatic sheen achieved through human-made fertilisers and pesticides, and through the use of precious clean water. But who would have predicted that lawns would be dug up and replanted with various African and South American grasses, from which people would make everything from ethanol to floor coverings? So much for the grass always being greener — ours is now black. Black mondo grass, to be precise.

Slow is the New Fast

Everyone thinks the change is because of our new moral mission: our renewed belief in community cohesion and cooperation has created a sense of hope, which pokes out from beneath the surface of our dour utilitarianism. We suddenly seem to know where we are going — or, at least, we've woken up to what we all need to do. There is, for the first time in ages, a fixed point that we are moving towards. This doesn't mean that everything will work out alright — very far from it, in all probability — but just sensing the right direction and knowing that we are all in this together does seem to have changed the mood somewhat. There is another book, Ivan Illich's *Tools for Conviviality*, written 67 years ago, which tapped into this idea. Illich argued that over-reliance on technology would not solve anything, partly because, unless there was a dramatic change in society's values, we would simply put off any problems into the future. Furthermore, he believed that automation would only end up making people slaves to the machine. What he, like Bellamy, could see was that we would only become happy and solve the problems we faced if we acted together and cared for each other.

One of the reasons that we feel the pressure is off, in one way, is because people have managed to achieve balance on a number of levels. The law limiting work to 22 hours per week has balanced overwork against unemployment. Similarly, education is focused on broader outcomes: it is more community-driven, and has been redesigned to exercise the soul as well as the mind. People appear to have restrained our competitive instincts at work, too, and we are now collectively fixed on a handful of very well-defined enemies from what you might call 'the outside'. We are fighting the good fight, we guess you could say, with less confusion between means and ends, and more discussion about who we are and how we should live.

One thing we are especially pleased about is that Western societies have discovered that doing things a bit slower is not an attack on productivity or the economy. This is a relief, because we find that we have more time, both for thinking about what lies ahead and for engaging more meaningfully with other people. We can hear the birds and take the time to smell the freshly baked bread. The new emphasis on local manufacturing over remote services and financial speculation has also brought an attitude of can-do resilience.

As a result, we all get far more done nowadays — especially without the crutch of various digital devices and the endless torrent of largely useless information that was such a feature of life in the 2020s and 2030s. Life seems more focused now, which means that we can let more things go, which means that we have more time. One of the great lies of the early part of the 21st century was that globalisation and technology would set people free. In our experience, they ended up moving things in the opposite direction, and it was only a matter of time until we found an excuse to ration and restrain both.

This will sound a little strange, we're sure, but it's similar to being given some rather nasty news about your health — perhaps that you only have a few more years left to live. At first your reaction would probably be disbelief, followed by anger, but after a period of quiet contemplation you might become resigned to the fact and start to put your house in order. Eventually, a sense of resignation and calm would likely descend. Some people, we're sure, still carry an element of bitterness and resentment about being forced to live with less, but we think they're in the minority. Most people we know accept that doing what's good for society as a whole is also good for them individually, and they are using their time to do what's most important for themselves, or to help others who are in a more perilous pickle.

It could easily have gone in the other direction. We're told that when people feel insecure they often feel a need to belong to a group, and can see any difference or diversity as a threat. This happened in the very early days. Yet, thankfully, we all soon realised that the only way to deal with free-market and environmental failures was collective action. This might sound all very Eastern European circa the 1970s, but while the threats are real enough — and despondency is most certainly in the air — there is a feeling that if all members of society act together and do the right thing, we will make a difference, if only to hold back a few worst-case scenarios.

The two of us share the view is that society is undoubtedly in a tricky situation, and we fear that the community may never return to anything approaching 'business as usual', but our instincts tell us that much of the cynicism that's around is unwarranted. We think — we hope — that eventually our society will invent our way out of this mess, or at least buy ourselves another century or two by living more within our means and becoming more resilient and self-sufficient.

Try to be as positive as possible, we tell younger people. There are tough times ahead, but remember that you are among the more fortunate, thanks largely to an accident of geography;

and, regardless of that, you are young and still have a lot going for you. You certainly have a great deal to be thankful for. Things could be much worse, believe us.

No Through Traffic

The localisation of manufacturing and consumption, originally triggered by energy prices and cemented by draconian emissions legislation, has brought a certain purpose to peoples' lives. The acceptance that there are now certain things you can't have — and, if you insist on pursuing them, you'll invite trouble in the form on punitive taxation or social abrogation — has also lightened the load. People and products just don't move around as much as they used to.

At first everyone thought that 'people miles' was a ridiculous idea, but limiting the number of miles that each individual is allowed to travel per year is actually a great idea. Five thousand miles for all combined forms of motorised transport (private plus public) isn't that bad. Walking and cycling are obviously excluded, and you can always pay to upgrade your mileage allowance if you do want to travel more than that. You can even fly, if you really want to — although as far as we can see, this method of transportation is on life support, much like the rest of the luxury goods and services industry. It is kept aloft by a few remaining members of what we recently heard being described as a mixture of minor-dictator sheikh and Eurasiatrash.

We guess that this attitude of 'don't tell me what I can do' will persist for awhile yet. There are still a few individuals, and even a few newly resource-rich countries, that are ignoring the looming environmental collapse, and are clinging on to the old-fashioned belief that someone will eventually hit a reset button and life will return to normal. As for everyone else, we think they've just accepted that the world has gone back to its original form: small and local, with a high degree of transparency. Weird that you can compare life in 2040 with life before 1750, but that's just the way that the dice have landed.

It's possible that all this is indeed a temporary state. But even if, against the odds, nature did somehow reset itself and humanity solved all of the resource problems and free-market failures, we suspect that most people on the planet have now moved on. Our motivation in the early days was purely physical self-preservation, but there has since been an important psychological shift. We can now see what matters more clearly and cannot imagine any way to retreat from that. Yes, there are certain things we can no longer do, certain things we can no longer have. Materially, most people are far worse off; but as compensation, life has become fairer, less competitive, and less combative. Why would the majority want to change that?

Let us give you an example. Most people weren't aware of it at the time, but between about 1960 and 2038, the acquisition of what the author and academic Fred Hirsch used to called 'positional goods' ('stuff' to you and me) was all-encompassing. Securing the latest must-have product, going to the hottest restaurant, or being the first to have an AIPhone was felt to signify, or confer, some kind of superior status.

It started innocently enough. We needed certain things — food, shelter, and so on — but once these basic requirements were met, we subconsciously moved on to acquiring goods that said things about who we were as individuals — and the answer in almost all cases was 'better than everyone else'. Well, that's a bit unfair, but the answer was certainly, almost universally, 'different to everyone else'. Some products did indeed offer additional benefits or features, but more often than not people didn't use them. It was more about what the acquisition and ownership of these products (and occasionally services) implied about you, rather than what you could do with them.

This wasn't a problem for a long time. Difference created a

certain originality of mind, which, combined with curiosity and imagination, led to a flowering of discovery and invention. For centuries this had occurred within a framework of shared values and moral certainty. But by the early 1980s, individualism and consumerism had joined forces with free-market capitalism and deregulation. The result of this was a certain focus on the self. Individuals were seen as being responsible for creating their own wealth, and wealth was seen as all-important. Obviously, this system, where the earning of money was almost the only thing that mattered, didn't benefit everyone: the millions of children who died from a lack of fresh water or basic sanitation every year might be one example. But, flawed as it was, this system was generally thought to be better than the long list of not especially inspiring or practical alternatives.

The system worked for awhile, but when GDP growth, salary maximisation, and material comfort became the only goals, things started to go awry, especially when global connectivity meant that the daily impacts of climate change could not be hidden or so easily ignored. The flooding of farmland, major landslides in urban areas, the disappearance of crop-pollinating insects, and GM crop contamination were not seen as problems when it was happening elsewhere in the world. Even tens of billions of dollars worth of property damage and the displacement of hundreds of millions of people due to what the media started to call 'weather events' failed to make much of an impact.

But when increasingly frequent and severe storms, for example, started to happen 'over here', the mood changed — although it was not until local food supplies were disrupted that people really woke up and realised that many of the resources that were previously seen as abundant and secure were nothing of the sort. The now infamous sign in a local shop window, 'No Bananas Kept on Premises Overnight', says it all. The irreversible globalisation of the mind meant that what happened anywhere now had impacts everywhere else. The flapping of a dying butterfly's wings in a field in Guangdong, China, had an impact on the price of rice, which could shift the mood in Chiyoda City, Toyko, or in Lagos, Nigeria.

This didn't happen for awhile. Until around 2020, what we now see was inevitable was still not widely recognised; but even so, the forces of change were building, and well-established trends were starting to bend. Yet being aware of a possible change of direction and doing something about it are very different things. For example, it had long been known that work had started to take precedence over family, and that the social costs of this were being borne by society as a whole. And a popular grievance back around 2012 was that bankers were able to individualise the profits when times were good (that is, when they got their big bets right), but when times were bad (read: they got it wrong), the costs associated with their bets were socialised, in the sense of being society's responsibility. There was panic and the odd witch-hunt for awhile, but when temporary and superficial calm returned to the financial markets, calls for more stringent regulation, and even the end of investment banking and capitalism, soon evaporated.

Much the same became true of nature. The thinking was to extract as much value in the shortest possible time and not to worry too much about longer-term environmental costs. If you needed more fresh water to service the expansion of an urban area, just build a dam — and if this caused a drought further downstream, no matter. In those days, that was your problem, not mine. If you needed more farmland, simply cut down more trees, and never mind about the thousands of species wiped out thereafter. We, like most people, know this now, but like most people we didn't do anything about it. It's just that it looked as though the party would go on forever, so almost everyone focused on our own backyards and on maximising material comfort.

The greenies were on to this. So were the anti-globalisation protesters, the anti-capitalism groups, and assorted global warming and environmental activists, but too often their solutions were not, at the time, seen as practical (too much mental in environmental, as Robbie, our hedge fund guy, said back then). Yet they were right. We just weren't ready to hear it at the time.

Things got even worse when digital technology gatecrashed the party. We guess this started around the late 1990s, exploding like a shaken beer barrel from around 2010 onwards. We know that we shouldn't forget the role of misguided politicians (arguing for the presence of weapons of mass destruction in Iraq, for instance), corrupt CEOs (such as the leaders of Enron, et al.), unrepentant religious leaders, and assorted 'experts' in destroying people's trust in the long-established institutions that had previously held things together, but while this ship of fools was the primary source of disillusionment at the beginning of the troubles, it was certain forms of technology that provided the critical oxygen to eventually burn the existing order to the ground.

The first real concern, which we still cannot believe nobody could see at the time, was that automation and, to some extent, virtualisation was only of benefit to countries with stagnant or falling populations. For countries with high levels of fertility or immigration (the United States, for instance), such technologies created massive unemployment, alienation, and social unrest.

The second problem — which, again, very few people took seriously in the early days — emerged when the ownership of, or access to, many forms of technology moved from being collective to individual. This is when the trouble really began. Up until that point there had been at least some semblance of shared decision-making; there was at least the pretence of tolerance, and individuals had to embrace the views and opinions of others, even if it was only taking into account the preferences of other family members. In 2040 it's difficult to get your head around this, we know, so allow us to put it into some historical perspective. Back in the 1970s, most households only had a single television with a handful of channels (three, in some cases, later expanded to a mind-boggling four). The television was fixed and was not generally moved, which meant that the family sat and watched it together. Moreover, the programs ended around midnight, with children's shows limited to a couple of hours after school. Hard to believe, isn't it?

It was much the same story with music — it was played on a turntable that could not easily be moved from one room to another, much less taken out of the home altogether. We had radio, too, which was available in more portable forms (transistors), but even then one could only listen to what everyone else was listening to. We had one fixed phone (and so fewer personal secrets), one car, and one family holiday. And we had public telephones, public parks, public libraries, public hospitals, public education, and public police (the latter sounds a little odd when you put it that way, but they were there to serve the public).

You're probably wondering where we're going with this, but stay with us. Our point here — and we'll skip a few years to speed things up — is that once Margaret Thatcher and Ronald Reagan showed up, they declared that society didn't exist and prepared the ground for an explosion of me-ism, a philosophy that didn't express too much care for the views or the needs of others. The social costs of Thatcherism were not to be found as part of accounting policy at the time. Similarly, Reaganism did not fully take into account income polarisation or environmental destruction.

Skip another decade or two and this focus on the self, be it on the individual or on economic self-interest, went into overdrive. We created a society long on rights and self-importance, but short on ethical concerns or responsibilities. Personal technology then amplified and accelerated this to a level previously unseen. We focused almost exclusively on what each individual wanted; individual desires were of the utmost importance. Everything became personalised and easily accessible. At a micro level, we no longer had to accommodate or tolerate the viewing or listening preferences of other people. More people had more money to spend on whatever they pleased, which included cars, so we became less reliant on public transport. We didn't need libraries, either, because we could afford our own books (downloadable in an instant). We had our own portable screens with our own information and entertainment. We didn't need public education, public healthcare, or even public security (during the period 2000–2020, private street security was all the rage — a must-have accessory to go along with the latest handbag and shoes). In short, fewer people needed to interact with other members of society, much less wanted their help. What this meant was that we could build personalised bubbles that not only filtered out opposing opinions and ideas, but also excluded any news about what was happening far from home. So resource wars could be fought, mudslides could engulf small cities, and crops could be washed out without many people even knowing, much less caring, that it was happening. Add a large dose of litigation culture (the mentality that 'I have been deliberately wronged or damaged and someone has to be made to pay') and, hey presto, we had a society where personal responsibility went out of the window, along with empathy, humility, and respect for experts or state institutions.

It all made perfect sense on one level, but we had completely forgotten about other people. Yes, it's convenient to download a book instantly or use a self-service grocery checkout, but what happens to the person who used to be behind the bookshop counter or operating the supermarket till? Humans were rendered passive and stony-faced by the cold and calculating logic of machines. As a result, family life was destroyed and loyalty disappeared, and trust evaporated, too. In its place was a culture that valued money, celebrity, status, and speed — a society almost entirely devoid of any real meaning or purpose, beyond personal pleasure and gain. The culture of Berlin nightlife during the 1920s and 1930s all over again, some people were starting to say.

Thank goodness that's all changed. Luckily, pleasure is no longer associated with purchasing, and consumption, greed, and envy have largely given way to equality, at least in terms of opportunity and desire. Divisions remain, but the pyramid has been upended, with the vast majority of the world's people now benefiting from human endeavour. It's not exactly Shangri-La, but it doesn't feel like the slippery slope to the end of the world and eternal damnation, either.

Even crime has become rare, although we cannot quite explain why. Maybe it's because there is less 'stuff' to steal; or maybe it's because there's less sense of injustice; or perhaps, again, it's due to the fact that people feel that everyone is in this together, more or less. It could even be that family has been rediscovered and embraced, or that the community spirit causes everyone to keep an eye open for local trouble. Whatever the reason, even the binge drinking and drug-taking that became almost universal displacement activities seem to have subsided recently. They're still taking place, we're sure, especially in the dark alleys and lonely bed-sits, but there are now fewer public displays of boredom or defiance. Again, maybe it's just because peoples' lives have more meaning now — there's a point to it all. You'd think that the opposite would have occurred, but so far there's very little indication that this is the case. Our collective standard of living, as economists would have traditionally measured it, has been falling for some time now, but every recent happiness measure has been moving in the opposite direction. We are worried — we've all got the collective jitters — but we seem to have discovered a sense of inner calm.

All Together Now

Do you remember 'reduce, recycle, reuse'? This was a tiresomely trite slogan for some people a decade or two ago, especially if you had school-age children, who would insist on switching the refrigerator and freezer off for Earth Hour.

We don't even know anyone these days who has got a freezer. They've gone, along with other unsustainable and unnecessary contraptions like electric toothbrushes, power mowers, battery-powered torches, leaf-blowers, children's toys with electrical components, personal media players, pleasure craft, and wireless telephones.

It's funny: we can remember so clearly the pronouncements of various journalists, futurologists, technologists, and other pseudo-professionals, who told us frequently that certain events would one day happen or that other events would not. From memory, by the year 2040 we'd no longer be reading newspapers (certainly not printed on paper), there'd be no physical libraries, cash would no longer be king, nation-states would have disappeared, obesity would have become a pandemic, and we'd no longer be smoking. (But hey, you need at least one vice when you're stressed out by the future, right?)

Okay, so we're still not exactly model citizens — it's hardly Athens under Pericles — but society as a whole has become more self-sufficient and, as a result, more resilient and rounded. We're dusting off our old do-it-yourself ways, and the push back from our addiction to technology and our obsession with work — especially the treadmill of needless and unsustainable innovation — has meant that we have let out a collective sigh of relief. Governments and businesses alike are much more responsible, and are focused on longer-terms goals than they used to be, too. Tax and regulation seems fairer, and the ethical, environmental, and social agenda seems more consistent, more balanced, and more inclusive. Global corporations spent years trying to avoid paying higher taxes, but when the international community developed a binding agreement on single international rates for individuals and corporations alike, they folded like a pack of cards. Obviously, not everyone is playing by the new rules, but in our experience those who don't generally don't last very long.

Organic farming, especially biodynamic agriculture, is back, and fair-trade values are the order of the day, too. This is partly thanks to the re-localisation of trade, but primarily because suppliers of products that do still come from far-flung places are legally obliged to publish every last detail about how, where, and when things are made, transported, and will eventually be disposed of or de-engineered. Dust-to-dust manufacturing, they call it. It sounds insane now, but once people would actually buy a product — often impulsively — and when it broke or became even slightly unfashionable, they'd throw it away and buy another. Now, obviously, the whole purchasing and manufacturing process is much more considered. Even power is more local and more sustainable, with local energy networks allowing communities to buy, sell, and share power without interference from others.

We hear that village wells are being used again, too.

We all endeavour to 'buy less and buy better', but when appliances do go wrong we try to fix them ourselves — or at least take them to one of the many repair shops that have sprung up across the country. There is a cachet these days attached to making things last as long as possible, the ultimate status symbol being to have something that's been around for years and has been repaired many times. The idea of helping others to build or fix things is also enjoying a renaissance, as could be expected.

Fixing and fair value aside, one of the most interesting things for the two of us — and it's something that we have been talking about for awhile now, much to the annoyance of some people we know — is the way in which a level of unplugging has led to a flourishing of intimacy and personal contact. Everyone still communicates remotely, of course, but we have also re-discovered the joy of physical contact, and even of slow media. Who, with Kindle or iPad in hand back in the 2010s, would have seen that coming? We suppose that the speed of change and the constant updating was starting to become too much for people. It's not universal by any means, although most individuals do aim for balance between real life and virtual reality, and between paper and electronic channels.

We relish this change. We know we're old-fashioned, but the pleasure of receiving handwritten notes that flop through the letterbox onto the carpet each morning is so much more satisfying than receiving emails and text messages. We're sure that part of this is pure nostalgia, but there is also something quite sensual about certain materials.

Similarly, we have noticed recently that many more people now seem to take pleasure in giving and receiving physical embraces. Again, you can put this down to some kind of romantic or nostalgic impulse, although we'd prefer to think of it in terms of basic human needs; we're all still human beneath the hubris, and perhaps deep down we are frightened, and need reassurance in the form of physical touch.

This will sound silly, but there were Huggable T-shirts back in the 2020s. The idea was that once someone had the shirt on, they'd text the sender, who'd press a button for the shirt to give a little squeeze. It was rubbish. It was incredibly smart on one level, but amazingly stupid on another. Similarly, the medical T-shirts that followed on from Huggable tees kept misdiagnosing complaints and giving rather stern, and incorrect, advice from the wearer's doctor for absolutely no reason. Technically, it worked because it encouraged people to engage in healthier practices, but it was to intimacy what budget white bread ordered over the internet was to an artisan organic loaf from a local bakery. Maybe it's just that people today like to know how things work, and feel distanced from things they don't understand.

Talking of local bakeries, we bumped into our friend Steve, from the co-op, last week, and he's opened a new store selling refillable cleaning products. It's a bit of a time warp, apparently, similar to shops back in the 1930s and 1940s, before car culture redesigned the retail landscape. Just goes to show that what comes around goes around. The big-box out-of-town retail sites are largely empty now, or have been dug up to grow food or house various community facilities. Seems incredible now, but Walmart used to have huge stores rather than small mom-and-pop shops on Main Street.

Keep It Local

It's strange: we know that we are all supposed to be dealing with our disappointments, but the more control we're given and the more transparency and ethical agendas are built into government, business, and public-sector services, the better we feel about the future. We both know that we've said this before, and for all we know the human species really is doomed, but it doesn't feel like that at this moment.

Okay, so adding carbon pricing to items has meant that almost everything has become more expensive, but the upside is we are eating less, walking more, and generally becoming less wasteful. Perhaps it's just our natural optimism (a hangover from surviving the Great Pandemic of 2025?), or maybe it's the new bond that been forged between producers and consumers. (We have vowed to stop using that word — our journalist mate Jane hates it; she says it's very 2020s and that we should be using the term 'customers'. But aren't we all supposed to be both producers and customers now anyway, what with the way that collaboration is encouraged at all levels?)

Sorry, we're drifting off into our own little world again, but it's an age thing, together with the fact that we can no longer get any Newtropic pills to enhance our memories. We each have to use a sprig of rosemary from the garden instead. That's something you find when you get older: the distant past starts to race towards you in high definition and surround sound, while the recent past and the present starts to disappear faster than an EU politician in 2014 at a full-transparency hearing.

Oh yes, we wanted to talk about why global warming and climate change seem so ethereal, and segue into localism (we picked up that dreadful phrase when we were working with the Global Business Network in San Francisco, on the FreeBay Project). The question we really wanted to discuss is why everyone didn't pay more attention to our changing climate. Maybe slowness was part of it, as we've already mentioned, but beyond this we're not sure what the answer is. We guess it was literally something in the air — something that the great majority of people couldn't quite pin down. It was a bit like pensions: we knew we'd need them, but didn't get around to organising them until it was too late. Had we paid more attention, we could now afford prescriptions for Newtropic!

Climate. The word sounded so ... elsewhere. It was big stuff that few people really understood at the time — or now, let's be honest — and, most importantly, it concerned a faraway future. A parallel might be us trying to persuade a teenager to stop smoking and eat more healthy food; 'as if' would be the response. Climate change sounded like something too vague or too distant to worry about. But when global climate got translated into local weather, the concept started to get up-close and personal, and everyone soon saw that it had the ability to bring real misery.

What was it Mark Twain said? 'Everybody talks about the weather, but nobody seems to do anything about it.' Our community tried, of course — all that hype about geoengineering in the early days, and all to no avail.

We guess humanity is not quite as smart as we thought. Perhaps this is some kind of natural justice, though, if you'll pardon the awful pun. We all got smug — we thought we understood everything, and subsequently we blew it. The rough justice here is that most of the people who fought not to change anything did okay for a long time; they were rich enough to adapt. It's a bit like the recession that started around 2007 and 2008: the people who caused most of the trouble by lending or borrowing too much ended up okay for awhile because inflation eventually degraded their debts and increased the value of their assets. But more frugal citizens saw their savings evaporate, and they had very few assets to compensate for this. Similarly, it's our poor cousins in some far-flung places that have really borne the brunt of whatever the weather has thrown at them. We're amazed that they are still talking to us, really.

As for people closer to home, there are clearly some that are still depressed about the situation we appear to be in. The idea of climate suicides seems far-fetched, even now, but we can remember something very similar happening to drought- and flood-inflicted farmers when we lived in Australia in the early part of the new century. In Japan, the latest spate of 'lonely deaths' has been partly attributed to the weather because flooding caused the rice harvest to fail, which in turn sent food and fuel prices rocketing, which then led to ... well, do you remember 'I Know an Old Lady Who Swallowed a Fly', the nursery rhyme that American folk musician Burl Ives once sung? Everything connects.

Personally, we take a more sanguine view of human lifespans and, especially, of the fallibility of individual species. The Earth isn't 'our Earth', and it is old enough and strong enough to look after itself. But even if the planet itself is in absolutely no danger, whether humanity will still be on it in large numbers in 100 years time is another matter. We don't believe that another species will take over; humans may have made some fairly critical mistakes, and life is going to be extremely difficult for a long time, but deep down we can't believe it's finished. It's more a case of adaptation than extinction — we all just need to adjust our expectations, that's all. Humans are actually quite a smart species when needed (adversity and necessity being the mother and father of invention, and all that). It may well be the end of life as we all know it, but the show certainly isn't over yet.

Anyway, think of all the positives. The economy is a mess, unemployment is sky-high, inflation is raging, and angst is in the ascendant but, despite all this, culture is booming and people seem to be laughing again. Logically, this shouldn't be possible. One could say it's because life has become a dark comedy, but somehow we don't believe that's it.

The existence of a single, well-defined external threat has made people much closer and much nicer. People like titanic struggles between what we perceive as good and evil; two poles somehow keep the word in balance. If you have three or more centres of gravity, with no clear sense of right and wrong or good and bad, things can get very complicated, and rather volatile and chaotic. Perhaps that's why American, Chinese, and Russian retrenchment seems to be making people happy. Maybe that's just nationalism rising again, but we don't think so.

We're prepared to admit to you that we may have got this all wrong, but our view is that it's a bit like when the Berlin Wall came down and communism collapsed. There was an initial phase of excitement, but in the West this soon died down because we worked out that things were no longer so clear-cut. We preferred things the way they used to be: in black and white.

As a species, we need something strong to push against, otherwise we get flabby physically and mentally. If the problems of climate and, to a lesser degree, the economy, were solved, we'd be lost. The globalisation experiment undoubtedly paid dividends in terms of incomes and material expectations for quite awhile, but it soon became apparent that it was failing people on a number of levels, and the silver lining that's emerged from the dark cloud of climate change is that the 'anything, anytime, anywhere' culture that followed in the wake of globalisation has been largely pushed back.

To our way of thinking, it is important that everyone has a sense of place. Individuals need to know where others are coming from, physically and metaphorically; otherwise, how is anyone to assess the authenticity or pedigree of another's nature? In a world where people believe that anything is possible — especially one where resources are infinite and anything can be acquired if you have the money — it possibly doesn't matter that people don't know or care where things are from. But in a world where resources are scarce, and where radical transparency and strong social, environmental, and ethical policies mean that you can be held responsible for acquiring something even if you honestly didn't know where it was made, we feel that it's important — vital, in fact — to be able to study and assess the provenance of things. Perhaps you'd call this authenticity. Whatever the phrase, it's to do with risk management: it's a way of ensuring that what little money one might have left is spent well, but it's also about treating people and nature properly. It's about making informed choices, but it also means connecting more directly with those who actually make the things that we use; and if these people are local, these connections can become quite significant. So, while regulation seems excessive at times, it's for our own good.

Together Again

While we're on the people thing, one trend that we did notice over the period 2000–2037 was that as the world became more globalised, people felt more disconnected. It's an idea that was first raised ages ago and that we remember professor Sherry Turkle writing about in 2011. Perhaps society has gone too far in the opposite direction, what with individual targets for personal community contact, but the legislation does seem to be working. Personally, there are quite a few locals that we'd rather not see, especially prickly Penny, but we're more than happy to share our experiences with younger people.

It wasn't just a lack of physical contact with people that started to cause problems, though. Previously, the more that products and services became globalised, digitalised, and virtualised, the more sameness there was. We know you'll accuse us of Douglas Adams syndrome here — the thought that everything in existence when you're born is normal, anything that is invented while you're young is fantastic, but anything that gets invented afterwards is probably dangerous — but with digital content everything started to look and feel the same. There was no real sense of provenance, and no patina that came with age or use. Nobody saw this for years, until early digital media became quite old. Every copy of every digital book suddenly felt the same. So did every high street, every airport, every office, every factory, and every house. It was boring, cold, and soulless. It's a bit like how ubiquitous global connectivity led to an outbreak of isolation in the 2020s: when we could be friends with anyone, friendship no longer had much value or meaning; when communication was instant, saying hello meant little; when information was free, it no longer had any worth.

Our view is that we need to know where we are from as well as where we are going. We need to recognise that cultural identity and history matter deeply to people, and we need to appreciate that nothing of lasting value ever came from anything that was easy — which is perhaps why this current darkness has led to an outbreak of unexpected euphoria. The enemy is at the gate, but there's a strong feeling that we are all pushing in the same direction and helping each other along the path to possible (but somewhat unlikely) salvation. The task at hand is difficult, even impossible, but that's precisely why it has meaning.

If you don't believe us on this point, just think about how collaborative consumption has blossomed. We mentioned this earlier, but cars were once owned by individuals and represented the freedom to travel independently. Now they, along with bikes and apartments, are often shared, and knowing that you are helping others — and that they are helping you — is satisfying, even if things are not as convenient as they once were. People obviously had some problems with this concept in the early days, largely because many of the companies running share-a-like services were crooks, but it turned out alright in the end.

Social lending is much the same story. You probably don't see it, but to eyes as old as ours these developments have been really significant. It's like Picasso said: 'Every act of creation is first an act of destruction.' If it weren't for the weather and the economic turmoil that resulted, we'd probably still be going around in circles doing things the way we always used to, and killing ourselves, and most of the other species on our shared planet, in the process. As usual, it's taken a near-death experience to frighten the living daylights out of us and put us on the path to enlightenment. Only when you are facing death do you see your life for what it really is.

Some years ago, there was a hastily scribbled chalk message on the old Yorkstone at St Paul's Cathedral in London, which said: 'Sharing will save the planet.' At that time it seemed that the message, along with slogans like 'We need to talk about capitalism', was just amusing idealistic nonsense that would be washed away by the weather. Thirty years later, these messages are very relevant. The weather has etched them into our collective consciousness.

Incidentally, our Sydney friend Sandy was asked the other day about how the Enoughism movement began. He said that it flowed from a feeling that people had had enough deceit and, more importantly, that they had enough stuff.

As far as we can recall, there wasn't an obvious tipping point, but a series of unfortunate events that just combined — as they usually do. Between 2010 and 2018 there was increasing annoyance about income polarisation, especially the bonus and share-option culture. There was also outrage over politicians' double standards, sparked by the ongoing expenses scandals and the habit that 'retiring' public servants had of profitably migrating into the very industries they had previously been regulating. Our friend Wayde, who used to work with Sydney Sandy, also mentioned that it could track back to a book published a long time ago by John Naish — around 2009, we think, well before the attack on the internet or the economic and demographic implosions of China and Russia. The book tapped into a desire for greater simplicity, springing from too much choice and complexity. We guess the movement then just expanded organically (or more accurately, perhaps, contracted bio-dynamically) from there. It also plugged into the European slow movement and a burgeoning global desire for fairness and equality. Perhaps there is only so much that people — or the planet — can take. A degree of environmental disaster or ethical ineptitude is fine, but when most of the globe starts an accelerated race to the moral low ground, a few people notice, and then some more, and then more after that.

We'll give you a silly example. For years nobody thought much about water. It was something that simply came out of a tap (or didn't, for a billion or so poor souls) and was taken for granted by most governments, corporations, countries, and households alike. It was only when terrorists poisoned a large part of London's water supply, and future, theoretically safe, supplies were handed over to entirely commercial concerns (Coca-Cola was a bad choice, in our opinion) that people started to wake up and question whether something as essential as supplying water should be a private, commercial initiative. A few older commentators pointed out that public ownership of water utilities was nothing new, and that all utilities and infrastructure providers should be re-nationalised, but it took rocketing prices, along with collapsing infrastructure and 'pay per sip', to actually change anything. On reflection, the water wars — both political and physical — were important, but it was more the fact that everything that was once free or very cheap became hugely expensive, and then an outright rip-off, that made people really mad.

To be fair (how often do we hear this phrase nowadays?), the idea of simplification and, especially, of responsible sharing isn't exactly new. Putting Bellamy back on the bookshelf, you could perhaps trace the philosophy back to the hippie movement of the 1960s and the birth of the environmental movement in the early 1970s. We'd argue also that it has origins in, or at least connections to, Buddhism and various forms of Indian spiritualism. As to whether it's in any way a Marxist movement, we'd say no: there is undoubtedly a side to Bellamy that taps into the ideas of Marx, notably the nationalisation of private property, but we'd prefer to highlight his connections with the philosophy of the early Rochdale pioneers.

Actually, when you come to think about it, what is going on now does have remarkable echoes of what was happening in Northern England in the late 1800s. For example, most people assume that the policy of workers who do the most socially useful jobs receiving the largest number of community credits is a recent invention. It's not; this idea was around more than 150 years ago. Similarly, we can remember taxation targeting individual excess way back in 2013, while maximum ratios between best- and worst-paid workers existed in various cooperatives as far back as the 1920s.

There's probably a lesson here for everyone, which, more often that not, is that society moves in giant circles. We think we're being clever, inventing all kinds of whiz-bang ideas, but most ideas aren't new, and very few actually work. One benefit that is slowly emerging from our current situation is perhaps that we now have more time to carefully consider what's worked in the past and what hasn't, and apply these lessons for the benefit of all mankind and the other beautiful things that we are, for the time being, sharing our planet with.

It's a shame that it's taken what appears to some to be the end of the world to create such a common-sense revolution, but life's just like that sometimes.

Dear Prudence Timeline

2012	Governments impose profit caps on major banks and limit bonus payments
2013	The European economy fails to recover after Greece exits the eurozone
2014	The slow-living movement gains momentum; public water fountains are reintroduced in many Western nations
2015	A new prime minister is elected in the United Kingdom, following the second MPs expenses scandal
2016	Global sales of fair-trade products hit an all-time high
2017	Washing machine and tumble drier sales are down by 75 per cent on 2012 figures

2018	Ratings.com, which allows users to assess the environmental impact of services, becomes popular
2019	*Ethical Investor* magazine reports 50 per cent year-on-year growth in ethical savings
2020	The US government announces full transparency targets for all companies
2021	Hackers break into millions of mortgage accounts and change payments
2022	The United States adopts a flat annual income tax charge of 1 per cent of total wealth
2023	The European Union legislation limits the working week to 22 hours
2024	A new local tax on the use of non-renewable energy sources is introduced in many Western societies
2025	A report finds that more people know the names of their neighbours than 30 years ago
2026	Sixty per cent of children walk or cycle to school (up from 9 per cent in 2007)
2027	Coastal erosion means that buildings within 1.6 kilometres of the coast become uninsurable
2028	The sale of imported bottled water is banned globally
2029	Global demand for flood engineers outstrips supply by 600 to one
2030	All consumer products feature ethical ratings, plus carbon, oil, and water labels
2031	Major crop failures due to cold weather and flooding
2032	*Survivalism for Dummies* is the most requested book in local libraries
2033	Report reveals that the number of disqualifications for company directors has doubled over last ten years

2034 Church attendance rises to record levels and leads to a church-building boom

2035 Drought in Africa kills an estimated 100 million

2036 The US government introduces a limit on the amount of screen time each individual is allowed per day (adults are allowed four hours per day, and children two hours)

2037 Eco-activists target supermarkets selling imported foodstuffs

2038 A survey reveals that 90 per cent of people want taxes that will hurt the rich

2039 Membership of cooperatives is up 900 per cent, compared to 20 years earlier

2040 *The Social Planet* newspaper launches the Top 500 Good Deeds list

6

Helter Skelter:

a world of fear

We didn't know it at the time, but 2016 was just a dress rehearsal for a much larger event that finally happened on 8 February 2038. It had been decades in the making, which meant the forces that had slowly built up beneath our feet exploded with tremendous energy on that particular Monday morning. Two years on and we're still reeling; two years on and life feels like the opening sequence from that old classic *Children of Men*.

Some said that they had seen the whole thing coming, but nobody we know was prepared for the speed with which things started to fall apart. Western society had been given a taste of the shape of things to come on a number of previous occasions, but everyone had worked diligently to convince themselves that things would always get better — that our community was smart enough to engineer a series of lasting solutions. The famed, and occasionally framed, 'Keep Calm and Carry a Teabag' posters sold well between 2012 and 2022, but they were soon edged out by 'Keep Calm and Save' and, in 2038, by the less hopeful American version: 'Place Your Faith in Bottled Water, Canned Beans, and Lots of Ammunition.'

Less than two weeks after the first tremor, a trapdoor opened beneath our collective feet, and we plunged into a strange and shadowy world. Most people's first reaction was disorientation, followed by disbelief: it just couldn't be happening, surely. This was the sort of thing that happened in novels, or to groups of people in the more hot-tempered parts of Africa, Latin America, or the Middle East. Could the same thing really occur in the leafy suburbs of countries such as Australia, the United Kingdom, the United States, and Canada? Digging up lawns to grow food or seeing rubbish rotting slowly beside hastily built fences were not things that most people were used to seeing — at least, outside of Jo'burg during the food riots of 2017.

Then we all did what we always do: we got used to it. Little by little we adjusted to the harshness of the conditions, and made the best of our new, shadowy world. We didn't spend much time worrying about the future. Even now, we rarely worry about what might happen next because we're all too busy dealing with what is happening right now.

1970s Revival

It's a shame that there aren't more people around from the darker days of the 1970s, because they could possibly provide wise and much-needed counsel. The 1970s was a long time ago and our memories of it are fading fast, but the energy crisis was followed by inflation, unemployment, and debt; and then more inflation and more unemployment. The situation today is remarkably similar.

We guess the differences between then and now would be the role of technology and the fact that everything happens so much faster. The alienation and endless, formless drifting seems to be similar, too. However, we don't remember the gathering force of nationalism based on fear playing such a part back then. Maybe we've just subconsciously edited that part out.

The few remaining centenarian souls that lived through the period 1939–1945 are perhaps the only people still alive who might have seen anything like the situation we face today — especially the speed with which open minds can be closed and iron curtains can be drawn across previously porous borders. They would also perhaps recognise the way in which feelings of deep insecurity transform into the need to belong to a close-knit group, and the way in which difference and diversity can soon be regarded as bitter enemies. Some of them would certainly be familiar with the fact that terror can show up wearing polished shoes and a smart uniform, and that with the right trigger or provocation all hell can be unleashed in a matter of minutes.

On the other hand, even if the people who had witnessed such events before had been given a voice, would humanity have listened? Back then we were all still too fond of our own voices, too distracted by our own greed, and too reassured by our recent and somewhat privileged history to believe that anything truly bad could ever happen to us. Surely we were too smart to be caught out by a kind of evolutionary backwash, we all thought. We were moving too rapidly down the scientific superhighway to do a screeching handbrake turn and rush off rapidly in the opposite direction. But it appears that we can and we are.

Both of us imagine that the 1 per cent found it the most difficult to adjust. Their shrink-wrapped, hermetically sealed lives had for so long allowed them to distance themselves, physically and mentally, from what had been happening to others. It was interesting, as bystanders, to observe how the wealthy's blind disbelief and denial soon coalesced into individual anger, collective bargaining, and then solitary depression. Almost everyone else, by then, had become somewhat accustomed to a degree of insecurity and hardship, largely as a hangover from the events that happened between 2012 and 2018. We had accepted our fate and simply did the best we could in the circumstances. What else was there to do?

The idea that current generations would always live more comfortably than previous generations has been abandoned for now. The future, as we used to see it, has been cancelled, and confined to the recycling bin of history.

The Good Old Bad Old Days

This is not to say that the new global landscape is without an upside. Economic turmoil and political ferment have created a chaotic vacuum that Western society is struggling to control; but the worse things get, the happier some people appear to feel. We can't explain this, except to say that perhaps it is a response to the fact that individuals are, strangely, more in control of parts of their own lives. There is also a seemingly contradictory idea that people have now come to understand: once things reach a certain level of complexity and interdependence, control is, effectively, lost. We all realise that some things cannot be controlled and that we are each, ultimately, at the mercy of random events. Many of us find this a liberating thought, especially when politicians launch new initiatives with tiresomely trite slogans, and endlessly call new elections and leadership contests, all to no avail. Occupy yourselves with this nonsense if you like, but don't try to occupy our minds with such irrelevances and distractions.

Anther reason that the politicians are on a road to nowhere is, of course, the fact that nobody knows how long this situation — what is increasingly being referred to as the Great Reversal — will last. The biggest concern is that, while economic matters are the number-one concern in the short term, it is economists and, to a lesser degree, assorted scientists and other so-called experts who have largely created this dramatic and disturbing mess in the first place; so how can society engineer itself out of this current economic quandary? Furthermore, governments and our new economic masters still view progress through an economic prism: they continue to measure all developments solely with figures, and to ignore the things that matter most to people. No wonder everyone is so cynical and disenchanted.

The governments' habit of continually renaming economic problems doesn't help their cause, either. Who do they think they are kidding? We both remember laughing over the fact that printing money in the 2010s was termed 'quantitative easing'. Now unemployment has been renamed 'temporary work dislocation', and inflation has become 'rapid asset revaluation' in most of our fellow Western nations.

Climate change is a contributory factor too, but this has been more or less sidelined by what are felt to be more urgent, and more threatening, matters much closer to home. That's tough for those most directly impacted upon by recent weather events, but it's really down to them to do whatever they feel is necessary. We each have enough serious problems of our own.

The politicians are still hanging on in most countries, but, as we've said, the longer they do the more they are seen as weak and ineffectual. They keep imposing new, and increasing bizarre, indirect taxes and profit grabs in a desperate attempt to claw back lost revenues and pay back loans, but such taxes are widely ignored and frequently circumnavigated. The widespread use of digital payments has made it easier for governments to get their hands on what they regard as their share from the squeezed middle, but the boom in bartering at the bottom end of society, and tax evasion and 'lifestyle migration' at the top, has meant that much more economic activity is now hidden from view.

Most people seem hell-bent on strict protectionism and harsh regulation. These measures, alongside oppressive immigration restrictions, are seen as a way of limiting the damage. These individuals could yet be proven right, and it's certainly true that a degree of resilience comes from localisation. But, in our view, the troubles go well beyond whether GDP is an effective measure of progress; they go to our relationships with our new economic paymasters. If automation had been limited to jobs that were dangerous or dirty, we might have preserved some semblance of humanity. But removing almost all unskilled workers from the Western workforce over a period of 20 or so years was bound to cause trouble in the end. And the end came soon enough, when our fiscally orientated owners failed to grasp that while cutting grass or filling up shopping bags by hand could be boring or monotonous, these jobs provided more than a low wage to people. They also provided human interaction and, above all, some level of purpose, and even dignity. Remove these jobs from human hands and human hands will seek other distractions, especially if they are smart and have access to what we think we can euphemistically call 'interesting materials'.

The wholesale loss of manual and unskilled work to the machines is certainly a factor that explains the general level of alienation and discontent. So, too, does the fact that profits flowing from newly automated and virtualised jobs were moved abroad. Without local profits or high-earning individuals to tax, governments under-invested in critical public services. They also failed to lower their levels of debt, which got them into even more serious trouble.

We give the current crop of politicians in this country about a month, anyway, and they'll be gone, especially when the summer riot season kicks off again. People have no patience for spin and ridiculous political chatter anymore.

Personally, we rather look forward to the summer. Unexpected forms of chaos and disorder can add a certain frisson to what would otherwise be dull days. Not that any of 'them' have experienced the riots firsthand; most aren't even in the country any longer. As soon as the extended downturn and mass unemployment reappeared, they, like the rest of the offshore aristocracy, were nowhere to be seen — except for their daily cameos on the big screens, which nobody watches anyway.

The riots began a few years ago. People's simmering resentment had been contained for awhile, even as public services were withdrawn or allowed to decay. The rotting rubbish got on peoples' nerves, as did the blackouts and the three-day working weeks that were intended to reduce energy consumption — but even among all this hardship, humour and fun could be found. Brushing teeth by candlelight was a novel experience for many, and even the compulsory switching off of the internet at 10.30 every night had its bright side (more time for reading and other nocturnal pursuits), as did being told to share a bath with near neighbours to conserve water. For a moment, we seemed to be up to our necks in this together.

But when the strikes started to close hospitals and schools, and cemetery workers refused to bury bodies (talk about having your work pile up!), anger reached boiling point. Global governments might still have sorted things out, especially when the temporary opening of the docks created a brief period of calm, but when tensions between Russia and Georgia sent oil and gas prices spiralling into the stratosphere, there was little chance of business — or anything else — returning to anything approaching normal for a very long time.

At the time, we all expected this to be the end. But it turned out to be merely the beginning of the end. Most people, quite reasonably, assumed that things couldn't possibly get any worse, but this belief was merely a failure of imagination. Things could, and soon did, get far worse.

The tipping point was not the fact that our leaders couldn't keep the lights on or the schools open. It wasn't even the price of food and water (all globally priced some time ago), or the fact that the value of everyone's savings had evaporated. This had all built up slowly, and people saw it coming. Rather, it was the collapse of Chinese cooperation around climate change and the knee-jerk reactions that followed — especially the linking of

Chinese non-cooperation with the forced imposition of Asian-style management techniques on Western companies — that really blew the lid off cordial relations, both inside and outside this country. All forms of global governance and understanding evaporated, and institutions and individuals alike began acquiring whatever they felt they needed by any means necessary, resigning from any universal moral or ethical framework. The ethos shifted from individualism, tempered, to a degree, by tolerance, to something much nastier: an extreme form of me-ism, underlined by the idea that it was foreign nations who had created our misery in the West. The Western world had seen this before, of course, especially the way in which the German acquisition of Greek debt way back in 2014 had triggered nationalist protests and revolt, but somehow such sentiments were not thought to be present in our country until then.

Society might still have recovered from this situation, but we were all clearly angry and needed someone — or something — to blame, so after we'd finished trashing various bits of foreign-made self-service machinery, we promptly rounded on anyone who looked different or appeared to be threatening our jobs, comfort, or security. It started, as it often does, with a rag-tag bundle of reasonably innocent placards, badges, and T-shirts triumphantly proclaiming sentiments such as, 'You flew here, I grew here.' Anyone who looked vaguely Asian was assumed to be Chinese, and was singled out for verbal or physical abuse. We're told that something similar happened in the United States and Europe in the 1940s.

And that's when things went far beyond bad, to totally crazy. Certain people should have stepped forwards to calm the situation, but by this time our leaders had cocooned themselves in their carbon-neutral cement palaces. They probably assumed that they would be safe, but these gated and video-monitored communities only provided physical protection. Mentally, many of them found that they couldn't cope with a world, their world, that had been set adrift — a society of anchorless institutions and rudderless young people. They refused to engage with the reality of the situation. We hear that some fled the country, but most, we're told, are still around, avoiding the limelight and, in many instances, never going out at all. The dangers they feared at the time were undoubtedly exaggerated, although it's reasonable to suggest that had some of them ventured anywhere public they would have received, at the very least, a verbal battering. Many of the unemployed and underemployed had long ago disappeared into a mixture of online fantasy worlds, cigarettes, and alcohol, and presented no threat to civil society. (We haven't used that phrase for awhile!) But enough angry young men and women still remained physically present to conjure up some serious trouble, as we eventually discovered.

We know that this is starting to sound repetitive, but even at this late point society might have recovered its collective sanity. If jobs had been maintained or recreated domestically, or if the Chinese had loosened their grip on some of the more iconic Western investments, or if they had pulled back from the rollout of their automated systems, things might have paused long enough for a plan to emerge. Most of all, if individuals had been given something of substance to believe in or look forward to, we might have clawed back from the brink. But this wasn't to be.

In other words, several things conspired to produce the catastrophic result. With reflection, it wasn't so much the unemployment, inflation, the lack of credit, the crazy weather, the price of bread, or the growing hold of machines that caused the problem, but the combination of all of these things, in conjunction with some psychological fragility that had been building for some time.

It wasn't even what happened on that Monday morning that changed the world with a mighty wallop, but sheer bad luck.

Why, for example, was the second meeting held in four simultaneous locations, and why did they choose places with such iconic significance? They must have known that these buildings could have been targets, but they probably assumed that they knew how to prevent certain elements or objects from entering. Unfortunately, the security people were looking for something that couldn't be seen — something that had never been used in anger before.

Only the Paranoid Will Survive

8.2.38 was clearly a significant event. It was disturbing, without a doubt. We had never experienced an event quite like it before, and the world (even in its newly non-cooperative and jittery state) was soon divided into a before and an after.

What happened next was the weird bit. A series of feelings, nothing more, quickly surfaced throughout large sections of the world's population, and before we knew it these feelings had a physical manifestation. This was unique. We'd witnessed a few occasions where people suddenly snap, but we'd never observed it occurring with large groups of people. The two of us tend not to believe the media anymore, but we think it's true that more or less the same thing happened at the same time in Melbourne, Moscow, Mumbai, and most other cities around the world.

The only comparable event we can think of was the parrot-fever pandemic in December 1929 when, without warning, America was suddenly gripped by a collective fear of parrots. This was due to a real disease, called psittacosis, but the panic that resulted was out of all proportion. One US admiral even ordered sailors to toss their pet parrots overboard, while *The New York Times* ran a story that read 'Parrot Fever Kills Two in This Country'.

Much the same thing happened on 8.2.38. Yes, quite a few people were killed, but the ongoing threat was blown out of all proportion. Even stranger was that, while the initial reaction was panic followed by self-imposed isolation, this was quickly followed by a kind of revelatory, 'a-ha' moment. It was as though the sleep was rubbed from our collective eyes and we all suddenly realised what large pockets of the planet had known all along, which was that the certainties of life in the so-called developed regions (including the self-congratulatory smugness of 'civil society') were a chimera. Things like savings, jobs, houses, a sense of personal safety and, above all, the attitude that 'I'm special' and 'certain things can't possibly happen to me' could be swept away in seconds. And they could be made to vanish with objects or events as simple as a handful of test tubes, the swing of a baseball bat, a newspaper headline, or the smell of petrol-soaked rags being pushed through a letterbox.

We suppose it's everyone's own fault, really. Had we paid more attention to the needs of others, or saved more (anything!) for the proverbial rainy day, we might have been more prepared. But the very nature of assumptions is that we don't know we're making them. In between the all-night parties, the make-up, and the money, few people were awake enough to be looking for events that might puncture the bubble. Admittedly, a handful of speculators were on the lookout for disruptive events, if only to anticipate future stock market, currency, and commodity movements, but they were all looking in the wrong place and for the wrong things. As we've said before and we'll say again, it wasn't one event but several, which then triggered some feelings, which then triggered more events.

The problem was that, once social movements achieve a certain amount of momentum, they are almost impossible to stop or turn around. You almost need them to run out of energy by themselves. People had always assumed that any future social or economic trouble would be localised and short-lived. This, after all, was how things had usually happened before: trouble occurred in one spot, and eventually faded away; problems emerged, but so too did solutions. There was time to think. The sources of future disquiet could be found on a list of the usual suspects and our nation could, to a large degree, be prepared for it. It's the 21st century, so nobody expected the Spanish Inquisition.

Neither did anyone anticipate that a combination of seemingly trivial things could expose a systemic sore — a boil that had been festering, out of sight, for more than two generations. Perhaps in 2038 we should have listened more carefully to Cormac McCarthy, rather than watching the multimedia version of *The Road* on our WristPads: 'If trouble comes when you least expect it then maybe the thing to do is to always expect it.'

So what's to be done now that big trouble has finally arrived on so many fronts? To be brutally honest, we have no idea, and even less advice. It's clearly every man, woman, and child for themselves these days (the part about women and children into the lifeboats first has clearly been forgotten). At least everyone in the Western world finally has something in common: mutual distrust and disillusionment. The only things people know for sure is that almost anything is possible and that you can only trust family. And many aren't even sure about family sometimes.

The best thing we can really suggest to any individual is not to rely on anyone for anything; do the best you can with whatever you've got and try not to focus too much on the mundane aspects of life. If you still have a job, make sure that you keep it. If you've lost your job, do whatever it takes to get another — or get money, or work credits, any way you can. Stick whatever valuables you still have in a shoebox under your bed and, if necessary, protect it and your immediate family with whatever comes to hand. Above all, do not answer the door at night unless you know who's on the other side and what they want. At least, that appears to be the government's latest rather flaccid response to the current predicament.

We still use the word 'government' with the obligatory sense of betrayal and bitterness, not that's there's much of the government in this country left to loathe. Personally, we cannot help but feel that this is all turning into a kind of sequel to the 1930s, but with lots more weather and heaps of debt. Others say that, while the unravelling of global markets, protectionist and isolationist impulses, a sense of grim survivalism, a culture of blame, anti-immigration rhetoric, narrow national self-interest, and xenophobia have all paid us visits before, this time it's different. This time it's not just our bodies that will have to weather a global storm, but our minds, too, and it's feared that people's minds are no longer resilient enough to cope, having grown feeble on a diet of convenience foods and flickering mobile devices. This is the weak spot that nobody saw.

Our mutual friend Henry will accuse us of being glib here, but at least the local garden centres are doing well. Admittedly, the outdoor-living and garden-style sections have gone, as have most of the ornamental plants, but the fear, uncertainty, and doubt section is doing a roaring trade, and growing your own food and digging for sanity and salvation are certainty all the rage — even if nobody has the vaguest idea what a victory might look like, or even who we are all supposed to be fighting. The Chinese are an easy target, but most of them are in China. And how exactly can any of us fight the weather? Or the rogue scientists in faraway lands, or invisible software algorithms and viral mutations? Maybe we should march against 'combinations of things', or proudly hold homemade placards saying, 'Individuals are against things they don't really understand.' (In fact, the two of us spotted an even more vague version of this message recently: 'People are against this kind of thing.') Personally, we both think that the best solution is to collect some blood and use an index finger to scrawl Howard Beale's line from the old movie *Network*: 'I'm as mad as hell, and I'm not going to take this anymore!'

A return to normal? We don't even know what this means these days. Is that even remotely possible? Deep inside, we suspect that everyone knows it might not be. It's too difficult to think about — and, even if it were possible to go back, surely all we'd be doing would be saving up trouble to start the whole sorry cycle over again. Best just to deal with things as they are now.

Maybe that's really our advice. Accept your disappointment. Let the fear, betrayal, and bitterness go. Acknowledge that everything material is gone, or soon could be, and make the best of what is a very bad situation. Breathe slowly and be aware of each breath.

If you don't trust the police to protect what you've built up, don't worry. Either protect it the best you can or, better still, exhale deeply and let it disappear. Most of it is only stuff, anyway. You were probably too busy previously to even remember that you had most of it. It's gone, or it's going — get over it.

We hope that this doesn't apply to people too, but it's probably safer to assume it could.

Get Your Revenge First

This is going to sound negative, but we want to point out that if you trust someone in the current circumstances, there's a strong chance that you'll eventually be disappointed. You could even get yourself killed. Blind trust in strangers and in things no-one understands partly got us all into this mess, so why would you expect such an attitude to get us out of it?

We're not just talking about the supposed wisdom of people on the bus here; listening to experts of any kind is a really bad idea. Learn to live with the disappointment that there's nowhere to go. Accept that there is no value in being nostalgic about a future that will never happen. Just live in the now and react.

On a rare positive note, don't forget that there are small pleasures to be gained in melancholy moments, much as there is unanticipated delight to be found in the misfortunes of others — especially the previous masters of the universe, who are now forced to queue for bread alongside everyone else, or grow potatoes on what were previously well-mannered and well-manicured lawns. Who knew that equality could roll out quite so fast or taste so sweet? Who knew that spending less time worrying about things you don't have or were unlikely to get in the future could represent a kind of freedom?

As for political freedom, forget it. You can't eat freedom, and you can't drink it or warm your hands with it, either. What you can do, though, is hope for the best. What else is there to do?

Do either of us have any regrets? We have a few. We feel sorry for a few people. Now that everyone spends so much time worrying about crises close to home, our society has almost no interest in the problems of people further away. The charity sector, small before this mess, has imploded, except for a small number of organisations with a domestic focus that continue to provide aid, mainly to urban areas.

Although perhaps this doesn't matter. One thing we can say about people living out in the middle of nowhere is that they are among the few who have been able to survive without the foibles and vanities of what used to be called a sophisticated urban lifestyle. If we had a way of getting to the outback, the woods, or the mountains, we'd imagine those people could teach us a thing or two about survival. For the rest of us, who live in cities — which we'd guess is now approaching 80 per cent of the world's population of almost nine billion — adjusting to a world where things have suddenly collapsed back into hyper-local economies based upon physical exchange has been difficult. No reliable electricity or foamy coffee, no civilisation.

Some people joke that it's like Soviet Russia before the wall came down, but at least there you knew that things wouldn't work. Here we sometimes still assume that they will, and then get taken aback (or is that forward?) by a world where you cannot bet on a 12-volt socket being able to deliver a reliable supply of electricity to charge up your phone (and no phone means no money and no work).

Equally, while the internet remains — between 9.00 a.m. and 10.30 p.m., anyway — you're playing Russian roulette if you rely on any information contained therein or attempt to post personal information. And don't even think of trying to buy anything online. At best it won't show up and at worst you'll lose your shirt, followed by your credit history, reputation score, and the contents of anything that might have mistakenly been left in a credit-union passbook account. (But then again, you'll likely forfeit all of these things eventually anyway, either to the government, to inflation, or to a criminal gang, so, in a sense, it's not that big a deal.)

We guess that's one of the central problems of life nowadays: it's totally impossible to plan ahead. Some might argue that nothing has really changed; even before the dramatic volatility commenced, people rarely thought much about their future. We saw this a few weeks ago, with some sorry fools pushing each other over in a shop trying to buy Valentine's Day cards on 13 February. You'd think that by now people would have realised that 14 February occurs on the same day every year and might organise things a little bit in advance, but no. Anyway, anyone that's really sensible makes their own cards these days. Maybe this is another example of residual behaviour, or what our friend Nick, at IBM University, calls the comfort of familiarity.

And maybe not thinking ahead is a good thing. Life is just what happens to people in between the to-do lists and the other plans we make. You can prepare all you like, but it will almost certainly be a wasted effort. None of us can change the past, and the future that we were promised will never come — it's receding like the tail-lights of a stolen car containing all of our worldly goods disappearing into the distance. We are all locked into the present, and the best thing we can do is look after our immediate needs. Live for now, accept your mortality, and make the best of life while you still have it.

Some people have accused us both of being needlessly morbid, but we're just being realistic. Society has gone too far down a very steep path and there is no longer any realistic way back — or not one that we can see, anyway. We could be wrong. Maybe it's our age. Maybe younger people have more to look forward to, but for us it's more or less over, and the best thing to do is manage the decline. This isn't advice for everyone, but we're saying that most of those close to us should allocate time for the things that they still feel are important. And not live a lie. Above all, people should be themselves.

The lights are about to get cut off again, but we will get back to this voice-recording tomorrow.

The 25 Horsemen of the Apocalypse

We were talking about our current plight last night and it struck us both once again that it was not just the combination of events that really got humanity in the end, but the human fallout from these events. In one sense, this reminds us of the black and pale green — and somewhat limp — copy of Alvin Toffler's book *Future Shock*, which is lying on Richard's bedside table. (It must be almost 70 years old now. He bought it for 50 pence from a shop called Junk and Disorderly around 2005, as far as he can remember. The paper pages of the book, the colour of brown paper bags, are falling out, and it smells slightly of dust or autumn leaves or something he can't quite place, not having been around old books for so long.) Toffler's point was that too much radical change over a short period of time is disorientating to both individuals and society. We were both struck that this hits the rusty old nail right on the bruised head.

Things have been happening too fast for a very long period, so it was really only a matter of time before the mental pressure that had built up found a slight crack and exploded through it. The first impacts were found in our own heads, but physical reactions soon resulted, which then fed back into our heads, creating a vicious circle of physical and psychological damage from which very few of us seem immune. To begin with, we thought this was just the two of us — old-person syndrome striking again. But we noticed similar effects with much younger people, too. We think this explains how young and old alike tipped from being anxious and somewhat jittery into a state of full-blown anger, with a desire for physical destruction.

Again, some signs had been around, but no-one saw them for what they were at the time. One of our friends set up computer destruction sessions in the city. He ended up making quite a bit of money for awhile. The idea was that office workers would show up around 6.00 every evening and he'd have what looked like a normal office, full of every imaginable bit of technology — old desktop computers, which most people hadn't seen for ages; tablet computers; smartphones; self-service ticket dispensers and checkout terminals; flat and foldable screens; 3D printers; telepresence terminals; wearable health monitors; computerised clothing; night-time solar panels, and so on. Every person was given a claw hammer and could smash anything they liked. The funny thing was, even back then the most popular things to destroy were communications devices and robots, especially anything made in China. Rage against the machine? Certainly. Racism against robots? Possibly.

Another of the problems that we all failed to take seriously was where individualism might take us. The initial idea was obviously a good one: everyone was different, but everyone was equal and important. We both suppose there was, and still is, the view that, morally, every person has some kind of intrinsic worth and should be left alone to pursue their own interests. What started happening, though, with reflection, is that this was taken to extremes. The idea that the individual should resist all external forces or interference soon created a culture of entitlement, and a society (we use that word loosely) of self-centred, egotistical, narcissist individuals that were all for individual human rights, but totally against any kind of responsibilities.

Again, the warning signs were around for decades, but we chose not to see them. We remember reading a couple of newspaper articles in England, back in 2012. One was about corporations discriminating against people by overlooking applicants without good qualifications. Apparently that was elitism, implying that one individual might have greater worth than another. The other article concerned the opposite end of the social spectrum: someone who had just earned a multimillion-pound bonus despite losing his firm billions.

Everything from schooling and parenting styles to legal frameworks obviously contributed to this sorry state of affairs too, but technology was the real culprit; technology could have pushed us in the other direction. There is no reason why the connectivity that flourished after about 2005 could not have led to a blossoming of collective wisdom. We all could have used the internet to better understand what was happening in and to the world. It could, indeed, have created creativity and generosity. But it didn't. It just brought out the worst in everyone. It promoted hate, anger, and falsehood. Most of all, it allowed us to collectively escape from reality and bury our heads in personalised spheres of 'facts' and 'friendship', where anyone or anything that disagreed with our narrow worldviews was excluded. After awhile no-one even realised this was happening; we thought that our personalised news *was* the news. We also, foolishly, started to disregard the opinions and ideas of people who were clearly much smarter than we were. And when we started to distrust and then loathe institutions that had grown up over hundreds of years, things really started to unravel because there was no longer any arbiter. Eventually the state just became one of many service providers.

Where's the Off Switch?

Previously, when things turned nasty, we would have fallen back on eternal truths or sacred institutions to keep us sane and to stop greed, envy, fear, and hate from spilling over. Failing that, we might have put our faith in religion or our political leaders, but our newly nomadic nature, along with our general transience and the fragmented quality of our relationships, meant that we had absolutely nothing to fall back upon. This is partly why we are now metaphorically sitting naked, either freezing to death or cooking under the blistering sun, while trying to focus on the opportunistic scavengers circling overhead.

We still can't quite work out exactly how this was allowed to happen. You can articulate it in something resembling logical speech (debatable in this case, we know; our neighbour George says we both have hidden shallows), but the disorder outside the kitchen window doesn't line up. A person can factor in the resource wars, skyrocketing oil prices, rising sea levels, water shortages, crop failures, and even the odd urban pandemic caused by the lack of antibiotic resistance. (Add a rogue asteroid and you'd have a full set.) But somehow they still don't expect any, let alone all, of these events to have an impact on their comfortable existence in London, Melbourne, Jakarta, Dhaka, or New York.

As for anyone living in Shanghai, we imagine that they wonder what on Earth has just happened. We mean, what did they do to the rest of the world to justify present attitudes and behaviours? They even bailed most of us out financially. But we all got caught out. Everything connects, as they say. How else can we explain an earthquake in Istanbul bringing down a Chinese bank, or a volcano in Yellowstone destroying the Russian wheat harvest, which led to the invasion of Georgia? Go figure, as our friend Wendy McKinsey used to say.

In truth, there's not much more we can say, largely because we have no idea what's going on or what's going to happen next. This is partly because so many of the traditional news and information sources have shut down, and much of what remains is old or untrustworthy. Take the economy as an example: last we heard, we'd had a second successive year with almost zero growth. What are interest rates running at? In a sense, who cares — more their problem than ours — but we assume they're at around 16 per cent. We can just remember when they hit 14 per cent in October 1990, but we doubt that few others can. As for inflation, let's just say that the Weimar Republic is back in a variety of digital disguises. If 2040 had a soundtrack, it would be Leonard Cohen meets Neil Young, with orchestration by Wagner.

Unemployment? We have next to no idea about that either, although someone last week told us that two billion are out of work globally, with another three billion mostly underemployed. That leaves about three-and-a-half or four billion (but who's really counting?) with something, or someone, to look forward to every Monday morning.

The environment? You tell us! It's all over the place: one moment we're dealing with floods, and the next we're battling a drought; we're growing peaches and nectarines on the South Downs one week and rice in fields surrounding the outer-west of Sydney the next. And don't even mention the winds. We'd reluctantly admit now that scientist James ('Gaia') Lovelock was correct about a few things, but we still maintain that all of this havoc has been caused by solar activity and has nothing to do with driving the 4WD down to the supermarket to pick up a few scrawny organic chicken thighs.

You know what hurts the most? We think it's the false sense of hope we were given a couple of decades back. We feel let down, but most of all we feel bitter because we listened to other people who said they knew what they were doing. If we'd followed our instincts, we'd have packed up the house, bought one of our builder-friend Martin Upton's smartshax, and headed towards the woods. We would have grabbed a bit of land with a stream on it and built a life. Nobody would have known about us. We'd have sown some seeds for the year ahead and gone off-grid; we'd have become self-sufficient and would have left anyone living in a town or the city to their own devices — literally. We'd have declared war upon anyone and anything that tried to stop us. Trusting others is partly what got us into this mess; we believed what others told us and stopped questioning.

It's just what US Unabomber Ted Kaczynski said would happen — the system narrowed our freedoms, and the social stresses that built up eventually blew up. We blame automation. Everyone was so delighted with their digital devices in the early days, including us; we were all drawn to them like a baby to a set of shiny keys. They took our minds off weighty matters and gave us a false sense of togetherness. But it was a lie. Our connected-ness was a sham, and our devices only served to increase our isolation. And then the powerful corporations started to suck in information about all of us under the guise of loyalty and personalisation. They grew to know more about us than we knew about ourselves.

Do we sound angry? We're livid. They stole our lives and sold it back to us in small, time-efficient pieces.

And then the machines really arrived. Nobody noticed at first. Some of them even proved quite useful. But they were all surrogates, and soon they started to steal our jobs. Much of the work that remained had no meaning. It was belittling. Our leaders didn't care: the numbers looked good; what could go wrong? They were making more and more money, and with global connectivity came greater influence and control. Cynically, they gave us 50 types of organic bread and 500 television channels. This was supposed to keep us quiet, as were the endless pharmaceutical breakthroughs, the ubiquitous screens, and the infinite digital distractions. Bread and circuses.

Crazy Ted saw this. So did our writer friend J.G. He said that society's taste for pornography was nature alerting us to a threat of widespread extinction. He was right.

Sorry, we're getting distanced and disillusioned again. On reflection, we do think that part of the problem has indeed been technology, but society's ridiculous adherence to human rights hasn't helped. We know this sounds xenophobic, but had society spent more time looking after our own and keeping others out, everything might have been more harmonious. We should have made things more local earlier on. No wonder we've kicked most of the foreign workers out now. Good riddance — go back to where you came from and explain to your shareholders what happened to their money.

Seeds of Hope

This morning we've been down to the market and exchanged some writing paper and pencils for coffee. We hate to think how old it is, but we're going to make a brew, just for ourselves. We've then got Emily and Jake from up the road coming over and we're all going to dig over the back garden to make room for some more potatoes, edging the whole thing with some flower seeds from a tin in the attic. We found some bits of old carpet, and these will be useful when laid out, to keep the weeds down. Sure, hardly anyone is growing flowers anymore, but we just feel like it. Maybe it's a sign. Maybe it's a Richmond Spring (most people are too young to understand that reference, but please indulge us). Let's start today on a positive note for a change.

One of the good things to have come out of this whole sorry state of affairs is that everyone looks after themselves a bit more. People obviously don't trust anyone from too far away, but on our own streets and in our own buildings there's a comforting sense of togetherness — us against them. We wouldn't for a moment leave the back door open or make eye contact with a stranger, but there is a pulling-together within a radius of about 200 metres, both in terms of local security and in sharing anything we don't want or bartering surplus goods.

It's ridiculous, in a sense, but even the local savings bank has become a bastion of good sense. We hear that, back in the 1950s, people used to ask their bank manager about all kinds of things, such as whether or not to marry a local girl or whether to stick a little something away for the future. And hey presto, our local credit union is thriving again. Gone are almost all of the global online exchange sites and peer-to-peer lending portals, and in their place are solid, bricks-and-mortar establishments offering advice on everything from healthcare options to short-term savings plans. Most people still prefer to keep any spare earnings under the bed or buried in the garden, but for those that don't trust a shoebox or 30 centimetres of dirt, they are not a wholly stupid alternative.

Even the local library is doing well. These were supposed to have died a death of a thousand cuts decades ago, but somehow our one clung on and is now dishing out everything from advice on how to get a job to instruction on erecting small wind turbines and solar panels. We hear that a few of them are even lending physical books again, although ours is mainly a venue for free community events, especially how-to sessions. The one we went to last week was called 'How to Stop Your Clothes from Turning Grey in a Communal Wash'. We have one complaint: personally, we thought that hosting the launch of the local branch of One Nation Conservatives was a bit insensitive, especially given the proximity of you-know-what, but we think that someone knew someone who could pull in a few favours. Anyway, it is one of the few local places with reliable electricity and bandwidth, so it was a natural choice.

While we're still in a rare upbeat mood, let us tell you about something we discovered alongside the old seed packets in the attic. It was a stack of Digital Versatile Discs. We'd guess they were from around 2008, or maybe 2010 or 2012. Finding something to play the DVDs on proved to be a problem, but Johnny Two Shoes (the dance-mad Italian from the food-swap shop) said he'd got an old iMac running OS X version 10.4.11 and this might work. Sure enough, it did. And guess what was on the discs? One contained some old family movies — two brothers passed out on the sofa listening to something on a pair of wired headphones, a boy named Matt fishing off the old pier. But the real delight was a series of discs containing some television episodes from, we'd guess, the 1990s. Fifty-year-old TV! It was fantastic. One disc was an entire series of *Teenage Mutant Ninja Turtles*. Another was *South Park*, and we even found *Flight of the Conchords*, which must have been later — the late 2000s, perhaps. It's a shame that we couldn't find the 1970s television series *Survivors* — that would have been rather pertinent — but that show predated even home video-recorders. All we need now is a jar of lemon sherberts and packet of Refreshers, and we could do the time warp. Who knew that nostalgia would be so big in the future?

Maybe that's a way of earning some work credits. We hear that sales of cigarettes and chocolate are booming, alongside teh use of home-brewed versions of Prozac, Diazepam, and Wellbutrin, so perhaps someone could cook up some Dip Dabs in their basement. We'll certainly take a small supply.

We've got to go: the power is about to get turned off again. But we'll be back talking again soon — we hope.

Challenge to the Moral Order

Us again. Let us tell you what happened yesterday. We know things are bad, but we somehow assumed that some semblance of right and wrong remained. We have no problem with people breaking into stores, especially the foreign-owned ones. We even understand people robbing each other if one person has more of something than the other. Setting fire to empty buildings might even be justified on one level (as a visual display, perhaps — flickering light to watch when the television is shut off again). But why do people think that killing someone is a leisure activity?

It happened again in the park last night. There was a 13-year-old girl walking home, and two 18-year old girls stabbed her for no reason. They even filmed it. When the police caught the assailants, they coldly explained that they did it because there wasn't much else to do. That was someone's daughter.

We're not sure how much more of this we can take. It's the not knowing that gets you in the end.

We can deal with the fact that we are largely on our own. We can look after ourselves in terms of food and money, even at our age. We don't expect anything from anyone, and they don't expect anything from us. That's fine. It works on many levels. But what is deeply unsettling is the fact that everyone has to continually have eyes in the backs of their heads. If it was merely a matter of being robbed, we could avoid that by not drawing attention to ourselves and not carrying anything of value. But if there's people out there who thinks that killing a person would be a laugh — an alternative to watching a movie — what can we do? Not go out, we suppose. Well, that's the seeds of hope dead before they've even had a chance to germinate.

You know, we were thinking yesterday about how, historically, views of the future were often polarised between utopia and dystopia, with younger sci-fi writers generally being optimists, while older sci-fi writers tended to descend into misery and darkness. Why were so few people back then writing stories that were closer to our current situation? That's surely because what most people expected back then was either a future that was a recognisable place or one that was science on steroids: either a bit like 2016, but with more batteries; or with flying cars, roast dinner in a pill, and jetpacks. You know what we mean, right? Maybe the expected future doesn't sell books or movie tickets.

Or maybe what's happened over the last 50 years is a kind of sci-fi fantasy. We didn't notice most of it because it crept up on us slowly — at least until 2019; then, even as the pace increased, it became so normal that we failed to notice it. To add further to the confusion, we still can't figure out whether most of what has happened since we were born has been genuinely important; we're not entirely sure whether it's progress or just rapid movement. Do we still crave the same things and fear the same things? Have the real basics changed?

We suspect that deep inside we all still long for and are driven by the same things. We know that family composition has changed (more single-person households, more couples without kids, more blended families, and more extended financial families). We've got richer, and then poorer; we became more connected, and then more isolated; we were optimistic about the future, and then didn't believe in it any longer. In this sense, 2040 is much the same as 2012. But throughout this, some old rules largely applied: you needed a motive to kill someone, you craved love and respect, if you stole something there was a good chance you'd be punished, and if you had money you could buy things. Not to mention that people liked to interact with other people, the weather could bring us misery *and* joy, people feared death, the young respected their elders, and you didn't get something for nothing. Disappointment was tempered by moments of satisfaction. People had faith in liberal democracy and free markets. You could walk home without ending up dead for no apparent reason.

Anyway, we showed them, right? Reminds us of that line by George Orwell. We don't remember it exactly, but it was something like: 'If you want to imagine the future, think of a boot stamping on a human face ... forever.' That's still a bit far off, but it's not that far-fetched in some ways. We figure that there are two possible outcomes. One is that things spiral into even more chaos: things will soon start to resemble *28 Weeks Later*, at which point the lights get switched off permanently, the food runs out, and it's a just a matter of time until human evolution starts to reverse. The alternative is that we somehow pull ourselves together. However, we suspect that the only way to do this would be to unleash the most extraordinary force. And even if we succeeded, Mother Nature is still on the run, and we doubt whether she can be persuaded to come home.

So that's all we have to say, really. The voice-recorder's battery is fading fast and we can't imagine that we'll find another. Look after yourself.

Helter Skelter Timeline

2012	There is a boom in exotic derivative securities
2013	The Asian tsunami wipes out much of Papua New Guinea
2014	Hedge funds target European banks, leading to the collapse of the European Central Bank
2015	A heatwave across the United States and Europe kills an estimated 600,000 people
2016	FTSE 100 drops 30 per cent of value in a single day
2017	US consumer confidence reaches an all-time low
2018	US schoolteachers reveal that they haven't been paid in three months
2019	A virus disables most internet and mobile payment systems across the Western world for a week

2020	Flooding destroys half of the world's wheat crops
2021	The United States pulls out of the World Trade Organization, citing national security imperatives
2022	US inflation hits 11 per cent and is high in other Western nations, although the UK government disputes its own figures
2023	A three-day working week is announced across the European Union
2024	Official statistics show a massive rise in marriage rates
2025	China leaves the United Nations after announcing that the organisation has a 'Western bias'
2026	*Practical Self-sufficiency* becomes the highest-selling book in history
2027	The average American is found to be 20 kilograms lighter than in 2012
2028	Russia stops supplying gas to Europe, in retaliation for NATO action
2029	A survey reveals that one in four adults worldwide takes anti-anxiety medication
2030	Sales of vegetable seeds are up 1500 per cent on 2020 figures
2031	The global airline industry, and so the travel industry, collapses
2032	A largely demilitarised Europe is unable to prevent Russia from annexing Georgia
2033	Ammunition sales in the United States are up by 800 per cent from 2032
2034	There is a massive increase in the demand for allotment gardens
2035	The G4S Fear Index reaches a record high
2036	Pirates block the Strait of Hormuz with mines, which sends the price of oil to US$600 per barrel
2037	A survey reveals that 85 per cent of adults have no savings
2038	Students launch simultaneous bio-attacks on the Climate Summit
2039	Inflation hits 16 per cent, with a forecast of 19 per cent by year-end
2040	Escapist drama and musicals enjoy unexpected revivals

Signs of change:
early warning indicators

The timelines at the end of the previous four chapters suggest a possible journey from today to each future. In order to confirm or deny one future against another, we need to identify the events that might signal that a particular scenario is beginning to unfold. Early warning indicators alert us to significant changes of direction — that is, to when the trends start to bend. Here are possible indicators for each scenario.

Imagine: a world of intelligence

» The value of new-media and technology companies far outstrips the value of those that manufacture physical goods.

» There is a decline in new-car sales in favour of leasing and partial ownership, and user-pays systems.

» The cost of solar power continues to fall, while efficiency continues to rise.

» Online shopping accounts for over 90 per cent of shoe sales.

» Smartphones exceed sales of PCs, laptops, and simple mobile phones combined. Battery life extends ten times over 2012 performance. Landline telephones become the exception, rather than the rule.

» More than 70 per cent of grocery purchases are made using mobile devices.

» More than 20 per cent of parents select genetic characteristics for their children.

» More than 60 per cent of children have a personalised avatar.

Please Please Me: a world of greed

» The richest 5 per cent of Americans control 75 per cent of America's net worth.

» The public sector, as a percentage of GDP, falls below 30 per cent.

» The number of children in private education in Australia rises above 55 per cent.

» The most popular degree courses are linked in some way to banking, commercial law, media, or business studies.

» There is a cosmetic surgery boom among teens.

» Charitable donations show a regular year-on-year decline. Tax avoidance services rise 10 per cent year-on-year.

» The average walking speed in major cities is up by 10 per cent, compared to 2012.

» Ferrari announces that China is now its largest market, followed by India.

» Morbid obesity affects more than 20 per cent of India's population.

Dear Prudence: a world of temperance

» There is an interest in social democratic–style legislation in health, education, privacy, and human rights. Left-ish and centre-left political parties gain ground.

» Community and town-hall meetings increase significantly.

» The impacts of climate change become increasingly volatile.

» Congestion charges in cities become ubiquitous, and as a result there is booming investment in public transport systems.

» NGOs, ethical activism, and philanthropy grows. Taxation is increasingly used to increase opportunity and outcomes for everyone.

» The demand for many goods and services falls due to cultural shifts relating to consumerism.

» Air travel and the physical movement of people and goods declines.

» There are falls in hospital admissions related to stress and anxiety, along with working days lost due to mental health.

Helter Skelter: a world of fear

- Voter turnout in the United States presidential election falls below 40 per cent.

- Far-right political groups grow in number, and attract significant numbers of voters throughout much of Europe.

- Trade tariffs, import taxes, and other economic protection measures are reintroduced. There is a reduction in multilateral trade agreements and an increase in bilateral trade agreements.

- There is a rise in the number of gated communities and home security products, and an increase in the ratio of guns per capita.

- A general decline in health is led by an increase in smoking, drinking, and drug-taking. Sales of prescription drugs such as Valium skyrocket.

- There is growth of private banking and local lending, and in boxes of cash under the mattress.

- An increase in petty theft and cyber crime is recorded.

- Use of the internet for information and purchasing declines.

Part II

Planning Scenarios

'The play's the thing / Wherein I'll catch the conscience of the king.'
William Shakespeare, Hamlet

7

Futurevision:

the role of foresight

Our four stories about the future are not simply flights of the imagination, filled with random occurrences. We built them by using a methodology, which we call 'the Scenario-planning QUEST'. We have developed it with our colleagues, in particular Richard Bawden and Melanie Williams, over the last 20 years. Yet as with all good theory, in the final product the methodology is hidden from sight — just like the best waiters in a restaurant are invisible.

In this part, we'd like to invite you in on our secrets: take you on a journey to discover how we go about building scenarios, in the hope that the stories in Part I will take on deeper meaning. We also hope that, in learning our scenario-planning methodology, you'll be encouraged to build your own stories about the future for yourselves, your organisation, your nation, or, as in our case, large parts of the world.

Taming the Crystal Ball

Before we show you how to create scenarios, let's explore the very thorny issues relating to perception — the ways in which we all see the world, and how they influence our attempts at making sense of the future. No individual or organisation represents the world, however self-centric they may be. In conversation about the role of the United States in global affairs, for example, we once noted the paradox that for most Americans the USA *is* the world, but for the rest of us, the world is not the USA. But at the same time, no nation, group, or individual is an island. As Shakespeare put it eloquently, we are '*this little world, / This precious stone set in the silver sea.*'

So how do we each engage with the silver sea in which we find ourselves? To the general public, futurists will always be heralded as heroes; people look to them as savvy know-alls who can predict what will happen. Individuals want to know the answers to questions, such as: Will the iPad kill off Kindle? How long are my children likely to live? What do you think about China as a world power in 2050? Will women ever rule the world? Is there really going to be a merger of humankind and machines — the creation of radical, non-evolutionary hybrid robotic creatures that cry when their robotic dog dies of old age?

If we ask ourselves 'is the future uncertain?', the answer is the only predictable thing: yes, every time we respond. Nevertheless, there is a limit to what we humans can imagine. In a delightful book called *The History of the Future: images of the 21st century,* Christophe Canto and Odile Faliu look back on what past thinkers from 1850 to 1950 have predicted about the future. Retrospectively, there is one feature that unites all of these thinkers, and that is how old-fashioned their future thinking was. It seems that we cannot 'think the unthinkable', despite admonitions to do so.

But while there will always be wildcards that dramatically change the shape of things to come, the most illuminating observation from our work is not the enormous gap between what is foreseeable and what is not, but rather the gap between people's expectations and what they could foresee. Foresight is really more akin to four-sight: it involves anticipating a range of futures and rehearsing them, by whatever means available, to take the surprise out of what might happen.

This ability to expand our peripheral vision, to look for events that may influence the future, is heightened when we imagine alternative future worlds. The process of scenario planning is about thinking; specifically, it is about engaging in deep conversation with others about what humanity is doing now and where this may lead us. When done well, the process is not rigid or mechanical; it is creative and changeable. And it is ongoing, for as we build a set of future worlds, so new influences emerge that will impact upon those worlds in new ways.

Avoiding the Inside-out Approach

A critical aspect of looking at the future involves us all stepping outside of familiar territory and, indeed, of our comfort zones. We must strive to avoid a natural tendency to look at the world from the inside out, as this will often lead us to generate futures based on implicit assumptions. It doesn't allow individuals or organisations to open themselves up to the profound uncertainty about the way things might turn out.

There have been some really bad management ideas over the years that have been based on the inside-out approach — none worse, perhaps, than the notion that businesses should 'stick to the knitting', or stay with what they know. Imagine that it's 1910 and we are running the London Hansom Cab Company. Colleagues suggest that the transport base should be diversified to include those new-fangled motorised carriages, but we decide to 'stick to the knitting'. Unfortunately, although our horse-drawn cab service kept going until the 1920s, cheap cars and the expansion of reliable mass-transport systems led to a rapid decline in usage. We went out of business, knitting needles and all, in

1932, with the last London licence for a horse-drawn cab being issued in 1947. The world changes — get used to it. Get ready for it. Or, as Charles Darwin is alleged to have said: 'It is not the strongest of the species that survives, nor the most intelligent that survives. It is the one that is most adaptable to change.'

There is an interesting sense of circularity to the inside-out approach to seeing the world. With the rise of psychology, psychiatry, and the cult of the self (incomprehensible to citizens much before the 16th century) came a growing inability to see the world from perspectives other than our own. The bias of our vantage point — as residents of this country, participants in this community, employees of that organisation, and so on — was magnified by the relevance we imposed upon it. That combination is the catalyst for the assumption we all make, as mentioned at the beginning of this section: that only what we know is relevant. But nobody owns the truth, however passionately each of us might feel about our own values.

Examples of this insularity abound. In matters of art appreciation people may be heard to assert, 'I know what I like!' But such is the fear of getting it wrong that what they really mean is, 'I like what I know.' Or there was the Guinness beer poster from the 1970s: 'I've never tried it because I don't like it.' And it's as true with ideas as it is with art and beer. We naturally prefer the ideas that we have grown up with, and we tend to reject those ideas that are new and unfamiliar, often labelling them as impossible, impractical, or silly.

Scenario planning invites us to set out on a journey, one that emphasises the importance of exploring the outside world and using as many tools as we can to enrich our sense of the possible futures we may need to confront. These tools include the usual literature reviews, deep-desk research, and brainstorming sessions with colleagues. But they might also include reading unusual books, seeking out people with unique and sometimes unpopular ideas, or going to places where very few have been before. The process is about learning by walking and talking, so ferocious curiosity and a technicolour sense of adventure are critical. It is also about following our feelings and noticing what isn't being said, because emotional issues are often the real drivers of change: while the discovery of physical phenomena is important, so too is the idea of getting to the unsaid stuff. It's therefore worth exploring things, such as emerging attitudes or behavioural trends, that people have noticed but cannot explain.

It has not always been fashionable to focus on the power of the mind to help us to get somewhere new. Businesses often undervalue the importance of reflecting and thinking, in favour of planning and acting. In our philosophy, you need all four: reflecting and thinking are essential precursors to planning and acting, which, in turn, stimulate more reflecting and thinking. One needs to first think about what kind of thinking one requires, and then set about thinking over what kinds of tools, environments, and people are best suited to this. We build all of these activities into all of our methodologies.

The term 'thought leaders' is often used in this context, but while such experts can be extremely useful, they can often encourage the perceived wisdom. That is precisely what we are trying to escape. Importantly, the scenario planning we advocate is not linear (as, for example, Otto Scharmer's Theory U) or prescriptive, but one in which we spin the activities like a drum major's baton, as our foresight team marches to the future with the band playing an inspiring song — and hopefully marching to the beat of at least one different drummer. In developing the scenarios for 2040, for example, we read contemporary literature in and around the topic, talked to social experts, thought about the meanings of contemporary films, and tapped into the global chatter that is the internet. This is a truly diverse collection of activities, but the consequences were revelatory.

The four alternative futures we wrote about emerged from our mass of data, prompted by the conversations we had and encountered, and by our sense of strategic purpose.

The Nature of Perceiving

When 18th-century Anglo-Irish philosopher George Berkeley said 'to be is to be perceived', he unwittingly identified the foundation of foresight studies. Reality exists in the mind. When we each think about the future, we unconsciously interpret masses of data to make mind-maps, which we can construct into scenarios that seem plausible and rigorous, and tell us a possible story about the way in which the world might unfold. These pictures do not represent a future external reality. What they do represent is the impact of our socialisation and cognitive development, and the biases that we have come to hold in the way that we interpret what is going on around us. Not only do we filter what we see, but we also fashion how we see it.

The anthropologist Claude Levi-Strauss discovered that the ancient people he was studying had many more words for 'grass' than existed in our lexicon. Digging deeper, he found that the major differentiator between these words was a suffix indicating how far from the village the grass was located. A complex taxonomy was thus being used to reflect the interests of the people involved. So much for the concept of primitive minds. Similarly, in our so-called sophisticated English-speaking societies, we continually confuse the notion of 'English' with the idea of 'language'. They are not synonymous. English is an example of a language, and each language carries with it a different way of expressing reality. There is a separate and important point to be made here about how understanding can be influenced not only language, but also by the medium with which the message is transmitted, but suffice to say that we do not have enough time or space to explore that now.

Basically, the way in which we see the world is not only an ontological matter of the nature of existence. It is also, as we've already hinted, a neurological question of how our brains work, and the way that neurological pathways — and possibly human nature — might develop as a result of influences such as information and communications technology. Much has happened and is happening on this topic, and it's important to take a look at the latest developments. Yet the key point here is that coming to grips with the multiplicity of ways in which people see the world (their worldviews) is a critical precursor to thinking about the future and what may happen. We'd go so far as to say that true leadership — in organisations, governments, sports teams, and so on — is as dependent upon a person's ability to embrace and consider diverging worldviews as much is it is about having a clear vision and being able to communicate that vision.

The actions that follow from such 'worldview-inclusivity' do not need to pay lip-service to all opinions. We would have hardly expected Winston Churchill to define his leadership by accommodating Nazi values into his battle plans. But to make effective battle plans a person does need to understand the worldviews of their opponents. After all, had Adolf Hitler studied scenario planning and asked the question 'what if …', he might not have invaded Russia, and World War II would have been his.

What Aren't We Seeing?

The way we see the world is both exclusive and inclusive, in that we all naturally edit out things that are not relevant to us. Take, for example, the new car test. Every now and then we hear of a person who branches out and buys a make of car they've never driven before. Imagine that you've driven Toyota after Toyota and now, as a welcome to middle age, you purchase the BMW 3 Series Convertible of which you've always dreamed. Out of the showroom and onto the road when, suddenly, you see convertible BMWs all over the place. The Toyotas you've become used to seeing have disappeared as you re-calibrate your perceptual response to the world outside.

There are legions of practical examples that show how we bring an innate bias to the way that we evaluate what is going on around us. American Football fans were once asked to identify the fouls committed in a game, and fans of the New York Jets overestimated the fouls committed by their opposing team, the Green Bay Packers, and underestimated fouls committed by their own side. Seeing is believing, but what you see is not necessarily the truth. Similarly, we regularly underestimate the degree of risk in tasks we are familiar with (driving a car or climbing a ladder, for instance) while overestimating — and, in many cases, becoming quite hysterical about — other risks, such as the dangers that come with boarding an aeroplane or jumping out of one wearing a parachute.

Pierre Wack, the early pioneer of scenario planning at Royal Dutch Shell, emphasised what he called 'the gentle art of re-perception' as the process by which we open up ourselves to new ways of seeing the world. There are many methods by which we can access new and different worldviews, and the most successful of these involve critical conversations with people whose experience and outlook are quite different from our own. These 'remarkable people', as Wack observed, are not necessarily experts in the field under review. In our scenario-planning work, we like to involve creatives from the arts, the entertainment world, and academia, as well as the scientists, engineers, and business types who are trailblazing within their specialist fields.

What Can Others See?

We all understand the concerns driving our organisations, which mean that we are all well on our way to creating scenarios.

Yet there are questions, opportunities, and threats that people around us can see, but to which we are blind or in denial.

You may remember a novel or a film called *Smilla's Sense of Snow*, in which the eponymous heroine's experience of snow in Scandinavia meant that she could see forensically how a murder had been committed in a way that no-one else could. It is with climate change and globalisation as it is with snow: it all depends on your point of view and your experience of the world.

Even obesity — and, with it, the risk of diabetes — falls into this trap. If you fell asleep in the 1970s and woke up this morning, it would be obvious that society is in trouble. But because our waistlines expanded over many years, and because society 'reframes' what it is to be fat, few of us notice. In America, there are now 'outsized' (XXL) coffins, while in Britain, ambulances have been redesigned to accommodate 'plus-sized' people — and even then we hardly notice, much less think about, the risks and, perhaps, 'growth opportunities' associated with obesity.

Of course, the distinction between the internal and external worlds is fuzzy. But the point is that point of view is all-important. An employee of one organisation will see the external world quite differently from those at other organisations engaged in the same types of enquiry. Similarly, an employee who has recently joined a company is likely to have a perspective on the organisation that is wholly different to someone that has spent their entire working life within it. Thus, tapping into the thinking of people that have just joined an organisation as well as those that are about to leave (due to time served, rather than misconduct) can reap dividends.

How Did We Get Here?

In his novel *Free Fall*, William Golding asks a very interesting question: when did the person I know I was become the person I am today? We might look back on our lives and, despite the power of our memory, still be perplexed as to how the people we assumed we were became the 'us' of today. If we dwell on this for a moment, we can untangle some of the factors that contribute to this sense of bewilderment, not least of which is the whole learning cycle in which we are engaged. We need to live life in order to learn how to live it, and in learning how to live it we are changed — sometimes in small ways, but on other occasions, momentously.

Futurists love this approach. We like to ask how the world we have lived through for the last 20 or 30 years became the world as we know it today. We wonder, what are the key events and influences that have shaped the world we now live in, and what has influenced the influences? Why, for example, did eight-track cassettes, which were all the rage in the early 1970s, disappear without a bleep; did the much-vaunted laser disc follow a similar path? What happened to Creole cookery, which blitzed the restaurant scene in the 1980s, to be swept away without so much as a gumbo or jambalaya left on the menu of fashionable restaurants today?

Looking backwards before going forward makes sense, especially if we can isolate the ideas and events that create change and assess whether or not they may continue to have an impact in the future. This process can take place with a simple discussion, but in our experience it is often better to treat it more formally: to map a series of events on a timeline, showing key inventions and/or 'extinction events'. You can guarantee an enormous degree of argument if this is done as a collaborative exercise, but that's precisely what should happen.

Some of the milestones we can unearth in this activity will be pretty obvious to everyone. If we were interested in the future of globalisation, for example, most of us would pick out the creation of the United Nations, the European Commission, the Association of South-East Asian Nations, and the North American Free Trade Agreement as critical stepping stones to the free-trade agreements and the activities of the World Trade Organization today. We would also spot the role of the internet in dissolving boundaries and creating global networks. But there are other features of this movement that will look very different if you are looking at the world from Beijing, Delhi, or Brasilia. These are the capitals of nations whose histories stretch back, and for whom globalisation is offering a fast track from a pre-industrial society to a postmodern one in a matter of decades, rather than centuries. The pace with which this is happening is astonishing. For instance, 25 or so years ago in China, private cars were banned. Now China is the largest market for cars on the planet.

The pace of change, and surprises it brings, make trend-based forecasting highly unreliable. We need multiple points of view from diverse sources to anticipate all of the possibilities.

Why People See Some Things and Not Others

Futurists are also concerned with what we can see that others don't, and why or how these differences in perception arise. The key driver here is the idea of interpretation. Every one of us has developed sophisticated ways of seeing that filter our experience of the world and lead us to certain conclusions.

This isn't rocket science, but it is close to brain surgery in the sense that our brains have evolved to deceive us. They are lazy, and they like things they've seen before. This is because our brains have already built the pathways and filing systems to transport and store information, and it is efficient to process only information that is 'familiar' or 'uncontestable'. Information that is too novel, original, or unclear needs new pathways and filing cabinets to be built, so we tend to resist seeing such things. However, the good news is that brain plasticity is not tied to youth and, if we try, we can reroute information and build new transport networks and filing cupboards any time we wish.

More worrying, in a sense, is the fact that no two people ever experience reality in the same way, thus creating more than one reality. Put another way, our minds are the personalisation of our brains, shaped by our individual experience, and no two minds are ever the same. No wonder that in some situations it can be so difficult for people to agree about what is happening and what should be done. For example, we were running a community workshop in the Australian town of Chinchilla in the late 2000s. It is located in the Surat Basin, north-west of Brisbane. The task was to moderate and mediate the process on behalf of the community, which was hell-bent on engaging with the mining boom that had placed Australia in the vanguard of global economies. An enthusiastic mining engineer got proceedings going by admonishing the community to take heed of the facts about the mining boom. He went on to lay out the facts that supported his pro-mining worldview as if they were the only bits of information on which to base policies for the future. An elderly farmer with a true love for prime agricultural land then expressed a contradictory worldview, which explained why mining development should be restricted from going anywhere it pleased, presenting his own set of facts to support his position.

Another story on the same point comes from the inspirational educationalist Sir Ken Robinson. A child was doing a painting in class when the teacher said, 'You'll have to do that again because clouds are not green.'

'But they are green in my picture,' the kid replied.

It is a highly subjective journey we are on, such that, as our colleague Richard Neville writes in his book *Footprints of the Future*, 'nobody owns the truth'. All we own are our worldviews.

The problem of subjective realities is compounded further by what is usually a rather narrow field of interest. When we worked with an Australian bank back in 2005, looking forward to the world in 2012, it rapidly became apparent that people inside the bank knew a lot about banking, especially in the Australia/New

Zealand region and in other areas that were culturally and commercially familiar (primarily the United States and the United Kingdom). But when it came to different regions, the knowledge was regrettably thin. Knowledge of mobile-phone banking in Africa, customer service in Japan, the role of the media in South Korea, and the housing system in Germany were all weak, perhaps much as you'd expect. You may ask why a banker in Sydney might need to know about mobile-phone use in Seoul. Our answer to this would be that they wouldn't — not if all they were concerned with was the next financial quarter or 36-month start plan. But some things spread and connect, and if one were concerned with the next 12 to 18 years, rather than the next 12 to 18 months, these things could become very important indeed.

In addition, the most important knowledge within an organisation is often unstructured or even unknown. Old ideas, good ones, gather dust in corporate attics because newer ideas have become more fashionable. Embodied knowledge — various routines, tasks, and aims that are understood without conscious thought — can become buried beneath the detritus of daily office life. It can be a challenge to reveal such ideas and understandings, but just looking and listening until it hurts can often pay dividends. One example that springs to mind is working for a FTSE 100 company many years ago, where we found out that one of the company's products was not allowed on the boardroom floor. Why? Because, while it lost money, it had greater recognition externally than the company itself. Once we knew this, certain other options began to reveal themselves.

Another method of getting at what really matters to different individuals or groups is a wonderful trick used by the management writer Charles Handy and his portrait-photographer wife, Elizabeth. Liz asks sitters to bring along five objects and a flower that represent what's important to them. These are discussed and photographed. It can be revealing, but what is particularly fascinating is when couples or even leadership teams are asked to do this, since the responses can be quite different, and potentially highly divergent.

We each have particular memories, hold certain values, and see certain things that others do not, and the same holds true for them. If we respect and value others' worldviews, we will be able to make the most of our collective knowledge to understand how we got here and where we might be going.

The Scenario-planning QUEST

Now, let us outline the basic methodology that we use when building scenarios for our clients across the world. As we mentioned at the beginning of this chapter, we've followed this process to create the scenarios in Part I.

To recap: scenario planning is a critical-thinking, experiential learning process that embraces the uncertainty of the future by asking us to imagine different ones. We are not trying to predict exactly what we believe tomorrow will be like, nor what we would prefer it to look like. Our aim is not to get the future exactly right, but to avoid getting it completely wrong. We use the alternative futures we develop as contexts for working out what an organisation or group of individuals should be doing to prepare for them (we call these adaptive strategies), or even what they might do to create better futures (generative strategies).

Scenario planning is based on three core propositions. The first is that what actually happens in the future is often a consequence of unexpected permutations between seemingly disconnected or unrelated events. We are interested in the often surprising process of how things affect each other. As social beings, we understand this intuitively when we say '1+1 = 3'. Could we, for example, have predicted that the US sub-prime mortgage disaster of 2007–2008 would, when connected to growing national debt levels, have precipitated the global economic downturn of 2008–2009? Or that the reforms of glasnost and perestroika would lead to the formal dissolution of the Soviet Union on Christmas Day 1991?

The second is that at least some of these influences will come from diverse sources external to the organisational environment. Conventional strategists are really good at defining the interrelationships between familiar variables, such as the demographics of socio-economics, personal achievement, and resource allocation, but they struggle when we throw into the mix 'contextual' variables such as environmental degradation, attitudes to religion, and urban tribalism. In our experience, large organisations are well aware of this weakness, but frequently struggle to engage meaningfully with such externalities.

The third is that organisations benefit from having a disciplined way to explore those kinds of permutations and study their implications. Through scenario planning, companies can sustain a strategic conversation over time, one that renders uncertainty into a set of opportunities for action (for example, by highlighting new avenues for growth or uncovering new risks). The key point here is that scenario planning is valuable for its ability to promote strategic conversations that engender practical action, not for its ability to predict the future.

A useful way of thinking about all of this is to imagine the organisation as a system that is being deeply affected by a set of influences coming from the external environment in which it operates — and, indeed, in which it must flourish if it is to succeed. At the heart of the organisation is a scenario-learning subsystem that has been created to monitor the environment, to design strategies in response to it, and to change it.

Stages in the QUEST

To illustrate our basic process, which consists of four inter-dependent stages, we use the acronym QUEST (questions, environments, scenarios, and transformations). The next chapter will introduce you to each of the stages in detail, but here is a quick outline of what they involve.

Stage One: developing framing questions
Learning to identify and focus the concerns

In our scenario-planning work, we create scenarios for alternative futures contextually, in order to address a question about which we would like to know more, or to explore a problem that we feel we would like to solve or address to generate a better future. These concerns are typically our framing questions, or focusing topics, for the project. In short, they lead us to ask: what do we want to know?

This stage begins with us immersing ourselves in a topic of interest: gathering as many observations as possible, and recording and sharing perceptions through a series of interviews and questionnaires that value opinion, experience, and intuition. It involves engaging with the stakeholders to clarify key concerns. Our purpose is to explore and map the external environment, in order to gain rich data. By keeping an open mind and suspending disbelief and judgements as much as possible, we will be aiming to discover unexpected new information and to find a new spin on the things we already know. The combination of discovery and perspective is at the heart of what we sometimes call 'joining up the dots'. The results, which we often compile in an 'issues report', are used to develop the framing questions that, in turn, help to frame the scenario-building process.

Stage Two: examining environmental influences
Learning to clarify the influences of environmental change

Our questions will play out in a certain environment, so this stage involves identifying the influences that are likely to interact (in specific and sometimes unpredictable ways) to change today's natural, social, political, economic, or cultural environment. These influences are sometimes called 'driving forces', but we prefer the more neutral terminology of plain 'influences'.

In this step, we use the INSPECT acronym — examining the topics of ideas, nature, society, politics, economics, culture, and technology — to ensure that we consider the key influences comprehensively, and to help in organising our thoughts. We then prioritise the ideas we generate by highlighting those that, alone or in combination, are:

» most relevant to the framing questions
» most likely to have the greatest degree of impact
» most likely to have the highest degree of uncertainty.

Stage Three: building scenario worlds
Learning to build alternative futures

Armed with our framework and the influences that will create the future, we now build our scenario worlds. There are several ways of doing this. Practitioners usually adopt either the matrix (inductive) method for creating scenarios, or the messier emerging (deductive) technique, both of which we'll explain.

Whichever road is travelled, the destination is a set of alternative futures that are imaginative and compelling. Scenario-builders are invited to open a door on these new worlds, to step inside and suspend disbelief. Scenarios are not predicted future states; they are anticipated futures, imagined spaces in which you can experience what it would be like to live in them. The test for these worlds is not their believability, but the robustness of their internal logic. Therefore, we build them with timelines and stories, which together make them plausible.

Stage Four: creating transformational strategies
Learning to use scenarios for strategic development

Lastly, we use the scenario worlds as the context for creating strategies that are focused on achieving our purpose. We move from finding out to taking action — or, at least, to designing plans for taking action. We use critical-contingency analysis to test the robustness of each strategy, working out how much it will change or improve the concerns outlined in stage one. We ask ourselves what we need to put in place today in order to be ready for whichever version of the future comes into being.

It is the strategies — the decision outcomes, as we sometimes like to call them — that transform the situation, and the behaviour of participants, into the future. As we learn about strategy, another transformation will be evident: a change in the way we see the world; a stimulus to help us to re-perceive the present.

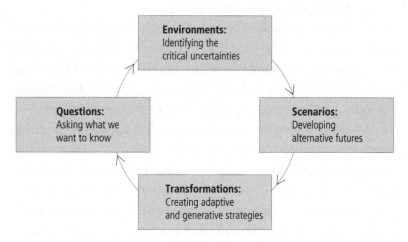

Figure 4. The four stages in the scenario-planning QUEST

8

The Scenario-planning QUEST:

introducing the four stages

Scenario planning, or the practice of building scenarios, is part of a strategic planning and development process. It involves learning to see the future in different ways, and using these futures as a context for doing different things today — in essence, it involves 'learning from the future'. And it changes the way in which each of us sees the world.

As we mentioned in Part I, scenario planning is not simply about predicting the future. It is a process that, through imagination and analysis, broadens the current approaches to strategy by looking at the complex future environments with which the organisation might have to engage and seek to flourish. It moves the strategic conversations away from the immediate future, to a more distant one, allowing participants to step back from examining individual influences and events, and concentrate instead on the bigger picture. Most importantly, it is a method that has strong theoretical and philosophical foundations. A key benefit for participants is being exposed to these theories and principles, and learning how to employ them critically.

Many consider scenarios to be more practical and more useful than most other processes of planning for the future, especially when a diverse group of people come together. But there are no shortcuts: it is a demanding and rigorous process that has sound intellectual foundations, with roots in cognitive science, in systems theory, and perhaps most importantly, in experiential learning.

The scenario-planning process consists of four major learning stages — questions, environments, scenarios, and transformations — which are neatly captured in the acronym QUEST. These stages takes us through four cognitive activities: divergence (observation), assimilation (making sense of what we've observed), convergence (planning), and accommodation (acting).

Stage One: developing framing questions

'Questions are never indiscreet. Answers sometimes are.' *Oscar Wilde*

We begin by focusing on our framing questions. Every inquiry needs a purpose; without one, it will flounder. Determining the purpose is of course a critical component of the scenario-planning process — it will reflect the scope of our search for knowledge, and for understanding, of the potential futures we might want to embrace. A puzzled student once asked the painter Frank Freeman how best to appreciate an abstract artwork. The reply was precise: 'First you must ask this question: what is this a painting of?' And so it is with scenarios; it is not enough to merely ask the question, 'What will the future be like?' That is too broad and open-ended. Imagine instead that you met someone who had travelled back in time from the future to the present day. If you were allowed to ask this person one question, what would it be? What about if this person suddenly arrived at your office while you were engaged in a difficult decision regarding long-term capital expenditure — what would you ask then?

Simply asking what the future will look like is not going to work. We need to ask specific questions, and the more narrowly we can orientate our interest, the clearer and more illuminating the answer. Getting the question right drives the scenario-thinking process.

But what are the problems that we need to know more about? Do they relate to our business, or to the country in which we live; to family life, or to the impact of global technology? In this stage, we will explain how we go about creating framing questions, and how far into the future we need to look in different situations. We will also explore the importance of listening carefully to people inside an organisation and of creating an issues report based on the problems that they see confronting them. This is how we end up with framing questions that really address the challenges that lie ahead.

Who Should We Listen To and What Should We Ask Them?

Conversation is the critical activity if we are to use foresight to tackle the uncertainties of the future. The most important voices to listen to as we start creating our framing questions will come from within the organisation undertaking the project, not from any consultant brought in from the outside — although it is often true that it takes someone from the outside to unleash such thinking. After all, it's the staff within an organisation who engage every day with the complexities of research and development, competition, market share, community engagement, career advancement, stakeholder management, takeovers, mergers, ethics, profitability, margins, brand relevance, and so on.

Listening to others is critical in order to refine the framing questions, too. As our colleague Richard Bawden discovered in a scenario-planning project, his client thought that their concern was how to be the biggest company in their field. But as the conversations deepened, they discovered this wasn't so at all; they wanted to be the most profitable. Size didn't matter, after all.

We have developed a simple questionnaire based on work done by the scenario-planning pioneer Kees van der Heijden and his colleagues at the Global Business Network and Royal Dutch Shell (and some other companies). It attempts to map out the concerns of the client organisation, whether this is a government, a business, a pressure group, a community, or even a nation. A typical questionnaire for initiating the conversation with stakeholders in any scenario project might look like this.

Questionnaire

1. The Big Picture
What things are happening now that have the potential to make a major difference over the timeframe of our project?

2. Wildcards
Have there been any events or developments over the course of your career that have come as a complete surprise to you?

3. Asking the Oracle
If the oracle at Delphi were alive today, what questions would you ask about the world at the future date for which we are building our scenarios?

4. Nightmares
What are the things about the future that keep you awake at night, and why?

5. Who's Sleeping in My Bed?

Innovative strategies sometimes call for strange bedfellows. What are the major unexpected alliances, partnerships, and conversations that could advance the future?

6. Missing Links

Most fields require a solid infrastructure of information technology, communication channels, incentives, revenue models, and other underlying support. Are there key pieces of infrastructure that seem to be missing in your organisation or industry?

7. But for the Grace of God ...

What major constraints, internal or external, are you experiencing? How do these limit what you can achieve?

8. It's Now or Never

What critical decisions have to be made soon? What forks in the road are coming up?

9. I Did It My Way

What core values would you like to see driving development into the future?

10. RIP

If you were looking back on your time, what lasting contribution would you hope to have made?

It is worth noting that these questions are always couched in the present tense. This is not accidental. The most important feature of foresight work is imagining that we are living in the future so that we can feel what it is like and experience the quality of life. As soon as we talk about the worlds as if they are not yet here, the experiential nature of the exercise is diluted, and the worlds just seem to be arbitrary predictions.

Compiling an Issues Report

This questionnaire activity is internal, conducted with the key staff in the organisation. We usually present it in the form of an interview, which can be done face-to-face or online. If conducted in person, these interviews are always one-to-one. We then usually gather the responses to the questionnaire in a dense summary document we call an issues report. We use this as a guide for asking the right questions when engaging with the future.

When the results are written up in a report, all responses are presented anonymously. Interviewees are aware of this when they answer the questionnaire. This is very important, to provide them with confidence to speak their minds without fear of repercussion. For example, if the CEO is a bullying, aggressive male and is impairing the function of the organisation, we need to elicit such information as part of the process.

In the report itself, we usually synthesise the responses by question and present the aggregated information as a narrative (rather than as an interminable list of bullet points). The ideas that come from this activity provide a strong anchor for scenario building and are used to create the framing question for the project. The issues report is also used during the environmental scanning activity in stage two, and in the workshops to build the scenarios in stage three.

Types of Framing Questions

The type of framing question depends, of course, on the purpose of the project. The framing question can be very specific, such as what sort of research and development prospects there are in information technology, whether the business should invest in a new factory, or whether it is justifiable to diversify from the core business to embrace new opportunities. It can also be broader, such as what sort of global prospects might be offered by genetically modified organisms or nanotechnology, what sort of new funding avenues could be available for not-for-profit organisations, or what the likely business climate for a nation or a regional economic community will look like in the future. It can be a bundle of these sorts of questions, too.

Here are some examples of questions that we have employed in our work over the past decade or so. Some of the dates are no longer especially futuristic, but that's because some of the questions were asked many years ago.

> » **For retail bankers.** By 2012, how will we have succeeded as a sustainable growth–driven financial services leader? What roles did organic growth, acquisitions, alliances, innovation, technology, intermediaries, staff, leadership, and the customer of the future play in this success?
> » **For teachers.** What sort of environments will the teaching profession be operating in by 2030? What will the profession have to do to be successful in those times?
> » **For insurers.** How might we be achieving health gains for individuals in 2020, and how might the growth of real-time data impact on behaviour?
> » **For the business community.** How do we identify alternative, plausible scenarios for the future of business in 2015? How do we explore strategies that maximise our ability to generate wealth and jobs, integrate us into global markets, and contribute to a rising standard of living for the community as a whole?
> » **For power generators.** What do we need to know about the future between now and 2020 to help us at the negotiation table for the takeover or the merger of our business?
> » **For printers.** What are the future customers' and consumers' demands and preferences likely to be? How do we create sustainable business models for that future?

» **For the book-publishing industry.** How will the book industry supply chain in Australia be affected by digital technologies, taking into account their impact on authors, publishers, printers, wholesalers, retailers, and consumers?

Here are some examples of questions that we might employ in the future.

» **For news media.** What will the newsroom of the future look like? How will publications source and publish content, and will journalistic standards be similar to today?

» **For retailers.** How will most goods be purchased in 2035? Should we be investing more in digital technology, or in expanding our bricks-and-mortar stores?

» **For charities.** How will not-for-profit organisations be funded in 2040? What role could digital technologies play in this?

» **For the mining industry.** What will the regulatory framework around mining activities be in 2030? What sort of challenges may the industry have to address between now and then?

» **For sporting organisations.** What will sport look like in 2030? How will changes in technology, wellbeing, demography, and societal attitudes towards leisure, drugs, regulation, and globalisation change the participation in sport, and its business models? What should we be doing today to prepare us for these futures?

Stage Two: examining the environmental influences

'The environment is everything that isn't me.' *Albert Einstein*

Foresight is about imagining what the future might be like in a range of different ways. We make these predictions, explicitly and implicitly, every day. Imagine, for example, that you are bored with your job and feel the need to move. You outline for yourself the opportunities that seem realistic, based on your experience and desires. You attend some interviews and eventually get offered a position at another company, which you need to decide if you will take. Everything about what you are doing is explicit, as you weigh up this with that.

But imagine another scenario: you are happy with what you are doing when your boss offers you the chance to transfer to another department. You turn it down without a moment's thought, having implicitly weighed up the pros and cons of the move. Both decision-paths involve foresight, but one is more 'foresightful' than the other.

We are now going to explore the environment around us by asking ourselves about the major influences that are shaping the world, and how foresight can help us to determine the direction in which they are moving.

Influences

Agents of change, or influences, are those things that shape the environment around us. A word about describing these agents for change as 'influences': in literature on foresight, the favoured description is 'drivers of change' or 'driving forces'. But we think this gives the wrong message: it anthropomorphises influences, as if they had a will and a direction in which they want to travel — a life of their own. The reality is that they are completely neutral as to their role in shaping the future. In the same way that cancer cells are not inherently evil or that nature couldn't care a toss about whether it is sustainable, these influences have no hidden agenda that turns us from being heroes to victims. They just 'are' and, importantly, they are dependent on the way we interpret the world and edit what's going on for relevance and meaning.

In this stage, we map out the influences so that we will be able create a table of those that seem to be the most important on the future stage, and their key characteristics. We can work out how they relate to the framing questions, how they might play out, and which appear to be critically uncertain. And at that point, we will be just about ready to build our scenarios.

Let us now undertake the environmental scan of the world around us, to see what's coming up that is relevant to our future.

Interviews, Presentations, and Literature Reviews

In this stage of the scenario-planning process, we conduct qualitative research in an attempt to unearth what people are saying and thinking.

We do this in several ways. For example, we often make audio or video recordings of peer interviews or of discussions with 'remarkable people', and distribute them to the foresight team before or during a group scenario-planning workshop. We've also brought people into a workshop to freewheel around the key questions. (Our 'people net' is wide and includes stakeholders, academics, government regulators, advisers, and sometimes even friends.) Asking staff to present work-in-progress at workshops and similarly interactive gatherings also works well because it can trigger new ideas and reveal the need for further research, which can have the potential to transform the way we see the world and lead us to different futures. The key point is that this stage is truly divergent, so we are not simply looking for people to tell us the solutions to problems.

Another valuable step can be using the internet and research libraries to put together a literature review. This will give an overview of the field of inquiry: who has been saying what, who the thought leaders on the topic are, what their prevailing theories and hypotheses are, and what questions they have been asking.

We often use all of these research findings to create a brief 'thought-starters report', which is made available to the group involved in the scenario-planning process. Typically, these reports are four to eight A4 pages long, and are designed to open peoples' minds to the changes that are occurring, or may soon occur, in the external environment. They can be text-based, visual representations, or a mixture of both, and can feature any commissioned research as well as links to previously published works on relevant topics.

There is an interesting link between the internally generated issues report and the externally derived thought-starters report. The issues report is based on the worldviews of the participants from within the organisation, worldviews that have a tendency to converge because of the power of the organisational culture, a shared vision of its future, and the work already undertaken by the participants to achieve that vision. The thought-starter material is the reverse. It focuses on the worldviews of people *outside* of the organisation, who have no skin in the scenario-building game. The collision between these two reports creates the kind of tension out of which creativity grows, and can facilitate for participants the magic moment of suddenly seeing things differently.

Interviews with 'Remarkable People'

As we mentioned, it can be very useful to bring together creative people and those from government and business, to explore the new external realities that may have surprising consequences for the business or organisation under review. Let us tell you why.

These 'remarkable people', to borrow the term adopted by Pierre Wack at Shell, taken from the work of George Gurdjieff, are those who stand out from the crowd due to their mental resourcefulness. They are not necessarily celebrities, but they can offer special insights into our framing questions. They may be science-fiction writers, painters, poets, scientists, musicians, historians, economists, or philosophers; they could be experts in almost any field, but they are also people who have distinctive worldviews. At one of our meetings, for example, an artist and a computer programmer got very excited about the link between the topology of Aboriginal painting and circuit diagrams, thus bringing together two radically different skills to focus on the future of the organisation on hand. You never know in advance when and where unusual insights like these might occur. After all, as Jorge Luis Borges wrote, 'a wood is a garden of forking paths'.

We often conduct interviews in a workshop setting or during a panel discussion. Interview questions will depend on the level of expertise that the 'remarkable person' has on the topic. Obviously, the more qualified in the area he or she is, the more specific we can be in our queries. When interviewing, we may ask questions like these:

» How do you see this situation?
» What experiences do you have that are relevant to our area of inquiry?
» Would you interpret the situation differently from us?
» Who are the important actors in the stories that might unfold, as you see them?
» What are the deeper pressures driving this situation?
» What is the conventional wisdom? How do you see things differently?
» Who else should we be talking to?

These directed questions often give rise to fascinating insights for those in the organisation, who have the opportunity to see their situation in a new light.

Brainstorming using (I)NSPECT

Having undertaken the preparatory research and generated a thought-starters report, we then ask the scenario team to build upon all this thinking they have heard with their own ideas. To facilitate this, we have developed a process, with Richard Bawden, that we call the (I)NSPECT method. We ask participants to cluster their brainstorming under seven headings.

[I]: interpretation

N: the natural environment

S: society

P: politics

E: economics

C: culture

T: technology

The 'I' is in brackets as we do not list data under it. It stands for the idea of interpretation, or the role of worldviews, which together shape everything we see and record.

This activity, which works well in a workshop environment, is the foundation of building scenarios. A similar process that is sometimes used in scenario planning is STEEP (examining the topics of society, technology, economics, environment, and politics) and we have also come across the use of STEEPEN (examining the topics of society, technology, economics, environment, politics, energy, and nature). Whichever variation you use, the results will be similar.

The influences we are researching are mental constructs, which are totally dependent on the 'I'. We defy anyone to point out to us, as you might a mountain or a bird or a river, things like health, welfare, happiness, or mobility. The influences are also not simple, but complex and interrelated — and abstract.

In a recent and interesting piece of work, Vodafone sponsored the creation of a collaborative think piece about the future, in which they reported on four 'certainties' that would govern the future to 2020. They were: the imbalance in population growth, key-resource constraints, accelerating Asian wealth creation, and universal data access. But each of these items was an abstraction, dependent on an arsenal of assumptions and a cacophony of causes, which together rendered the idea of certainty wrong at best, and irrelevant at worst. For example, the imbalance in population growth leaves people in certain regions prey to health pandemics, the effects of climate change, problems with food supplies, and geopolitical tension. Key resource constraints are circumscribed by energy technology, transport economics, global climates, and geopolitics. Accelerating Asian wealth creation is dependent on cyber security, the future of the US dollar, regional political stability, and the capacity of India and China to provide its burgeoning middle class with political power. Universal data access is dependent on net neutrality, cyber crime, upward social mobility, and global economic wealth, among other things. And all four 'certainties' are defined by methodologies relating to measurement systems and the integrity of the findings.

In short, nothing is inevitable. We may anticipate that some influences are more volatile and unpredictable (for example, climate change) than others (say, demographics). But because of the inherent complexity of the systems that create the environment, and the worldviews that ascribe relevance to this construct while ignoring other possibilities, all influences, taken on their own, are unpredictable as to how they will interact with any others. The idea that some influences may be more predictable than others is potentially misleading.

When we work with (I)NSPECT, we often, as a warming-up exercise, ask the foresight team to identify the influences that have created the world as it is today. How do we describe the present? It is helpful to go back at least the same number of years as the foresight team will be directed to move forwards — so, for example, on a scenario-planning project oriented towards what the world will be like in 2052, we might ask people to identify the influences from 1972 to 2012 that have made the world as it is today. We find that this exercise frees up people's ability to lock horns with the future.

To record the ideas that come up through the (I)NSPECT process, we use Post-it notes, butcher's paper, and whiteboards, but the data can also be captured electronically. Whatever you use, it is important that all materials are retained, and recorded in the form of a report or summary. These reports do not seek closure; their purpose is to record what happened as it happened. They are designed to give the scenario-building team a grasp of what is going on externally and how the influences they have identified may impact upon the future.

Stage three: building scenario worlds

'… one of my strengths is my storytelling.' *Quentin Tarantino*

By the end of the environmental-mapping process, we will have created a rich and diverse catalogue of influences. We usually record at least 100 influences, but in some cases we have identified and recorded over 500. As publishers know, you cannot edit material to make more copy; you can only edit down. So more is … more!

Now we will outline how we can go about evaluating this bundle of influences that are changing the world in which we live. We will also try to provide a clearer understanding of the different types of influences: the trends, critical uncertainties, and the wildcards, which all shape the future in a series of directions.

Wildcards, Critical Uncertainties, and Trends

The aim of our conversations about the future is to open up and broaden our thinking, to help us think 'outside the square' and to identify those influences that have a profound role in shaping the future. But not all influences are the same, and some are easier to locate than others. They can be divided into three groups by asking a simple question: how unpredictable is this influence?

The extremely unpredictable influences are the wildcards — events or phenomena that would emerge as discontinuities, and whose determinants are very difficult to identify. Usually these wildcards are one-off events. Examples include pandemics, tsunamis, world wars, dramatic scientific discoveries, and religious subversions.

Wildcards can be distinguished from critical uncertainties: influences that are highly unpredictable, but whose determinants are more open to enquiry. They are the stuff that scenarios are made from because they present themselves in different states depending on the confluence of factors. Take economic growth, for example: we know that it is a critical factor, but we also know it is very difficult to predict. We can imagine futures in which economic growth is steady-as-she-goes; as volatile as a cat on a hot tin-roof; or in deep, prolonged recession. Then again, we may get a repeat of the long boom (1992–2006), where every day seems to be a continuation of the one before.

The more predictable influences are the trends. Trends, by their nature, are not futuristic at all, as they are retrospective in character — we trace their significance back in time to a point when they emerged. Some 60 or so years ago a feisty literary critic from Cambridge University, F.R. Leavis, wrote an appraisal of the English novel called *The Great Tradition*. He discussed how the traditions in novel writing were never prospective. Jane Austen, George Eliot, Charles Dickens, and James Joyce did not really deliberately start anything, yet as critics we like to ascribe to their ground-breaking writing the shock of the new, as if they created the fashion for realism and modernism that followed. But the reality is that the tradition we identify when we do this is retrospective. We trace back from later times to the point of difference or divergence and assign a somewhat misleading sense of purpose to these beginnings. And so it is with all trends: we trace significant events back to a pivotal moment and then posthumously declare it a trend. The Beatles did not create the future that followed, but we can trace relevant social history since back to their first steps in Germany and Liverpool.

Trends are therefore the easiest influences to uncover because they are embedded in and point to the past. They can be observed easily, and we like to think that they will play out in the future in a reasonably predictable way. However, by now the idea of absolute predictability should be well and truly consigned to the forecaster's rubbish bin. Whether you are a chartist following stock market activities or a climatologist grappling with climate change, or even a demographer counting the number of new babies, none of the data you assemble to analyse what's been happening can be used as cast-iron, predictable indicators of the future. As we like to say, the future is not at the end of a trend line; trends bend.

One element that affects all of these influences is the uneven pace of change. Although the last two decades have borne witness to a mind-blowing acceleration in the pace of change in some areas (for example, in information and communications technologies), in others the pace of change is highly volatile (for example, global free trade, the rise and fall of Hollywood, the use of bicycles, or the number of beer brands). It can even seem non-existent: democratic political institutions like the US presidency seem stuck in an antedeluvian past (although by saying this we will, naturally, inevitably invite some kind of rapid shift). Such complexities bedevil futurists of all colours. In every field of enquiry, we struggle to get right our judgements about the importance and uncertainty of the variables we are considering, including the frailty of the human condition and the bias that we bring to analysing influences in the first place, which forever dogs us in our pursuit of strategic nirvana.

Generally, the pace of change has four possible phases. At one end of the continuum, there is no change. We then move through incremental change to a state of disruptive change to, at the other extreme, a state of cataclysmic change. These four phases often line up with four states: business as usual, trends, critical uncertainties, and wildcards. Of course, not all influences are so amenable as to fit into this neat framework, but many of them do.

Focusing on Critical Uncertainties

As looking for potential wildcards would be close to pointless, given their unpredictable nature, and evaluating trends would be similarly silly, due to the fact that they may not continue into the future, foresight planning concentrates on analysing critical uncertainties. So, having categorised our influences, we can now narrow our focus to critical uncertainties.

Critical uncertainties are indeterminate for two reasons. The first is because we cannot easily establish a reliable behavioural outcome from them. Current critical uncertainties that fall into this category include climate change, exchange rates, attention spans, birth rates, social networking, cyber security, generational change, geopolitics, and food provision. The second is that no influence exists in isolation, and it is their systemic commingling with other influences that creates outcomes. Almost all sorts of technological change fall into this category: experience has told us that the invention of new technology itself is never a sufficient condition for change. We can see futures in which the iPad and Kindle co-exist, and others where either or both are assigned to the technology scrap-heap. But these possibilities are dependent on non-technological influences, such as timing and fashion, pricing and substitution, utility and generational change. Another way of expressing this is to say that technology itself can sometimes be neutral, but what it always does is accelerate and amplify existing feelings, needs, or trends.

In fact, critical uncertainties are usually 'neutral' at first — that is, they do not have a particular state that we can ascribe to them. So 'economic growth', 'climate change', 'mobile communications', and 'biotechnology' are influences, but at this stage in our process we have not yet thought about how they may play out, and whether they will have a positive or negative effect on the world in the future. Yet when we set about building scenarios, we give these chosen influences a value, placing them on a continuum. So they become 'poor economic growth', 'highly volatile climate change', 'universal mobile communications', 'radical biotechnology', and so on.

Narrowing the Influences

Our long list of influences has now been reduced to a clutch of influences — the critical uncertainties. Our first task is to go back to the framing question(s). We may wish to amend it or them as a result of our research, and it is crucial that any changes are recorded now.

The influences have been grouped or clustered according to the (I)NSPECT categories. We can now go through them to ditch any that do not seem relevant to the framing questions. Bear in mind that relevance is not based on proximity; an influence will often appear to be distantly related to the framing questions, but can in fact be intimately linked to it.

A tip to reduce the number of influences is to flick factors that are not measurable: that is, they cannot be placed on a continuum, as outlined above. If an influence has only one state, it will not change the future in a particular way. For example, if we were building scenarios for the future of happiness, oxygen is not a relevant influence — even though of course it is incredibly important, as without it there is no life. But there is no continuum for happiness with lots of oxygen at one end and no oxygen at the other. Yet if we substitute 'money' for 'oxygen', well, that is a different matter. Clearly, money is an influence with measurable values.

Armed with our revised list of influences, we now need to review them systematically. Are the factors we have brought to this stage events or patterns, and thus consequences? For example, in a project looking at the future of Africa, a workshop created a series of influences, including governance (autocratic versus democratic) and orientation (internal versus external). However, the two are linked: if democracy were to spread, surely the orientation would become more external? In short, you could use one, but not both. We can work through the remaining influences, merging and purging them to get a final list. Influences can be merged when they seem to have related effects, and they can be combined and better expressed in new wording, as in the example about Africa; influences can be purged when they are effectively duplicates.

Another question to ask is whether the influences will really have a deep structural role in shaping the future. One way to test for this is to ask what lies behind them. Is the birth rate, for example, a function of economic performance, community health, or job prospects? What's the real influence here? Similarly, when looking at Africa, the management or governance of natural resources might be a function of the type of government that exists (autocratic versus democratic again), but is there a deeper driver than even this?

This stage is all about digging deeper to make sure that we have enough diversity, richness, and depth in our thinking. The means are not as important as the outcomes; we open our minds and ask, 'Why?', 'Why?', 'Why?' to create the mental maps we need to build the scenarios. As we do this, we begin to see how the influences generate interrelated themes. For example, we may become aware that curiosity about new technology has a big impact on a business's performance in mobile communications, and that the ability to harness consumer attention is inextricably linked to device design — which in turn relies on the psychology of perception. This is the idea so exploited by Apple that their brand has become synonymous with the generic naming of the devices: just as all paperbacks used to be Penguins and all vacuum cleaners were Hoovers, so all MP3 players are iPods and all tablets iPads. We can now build a systemic view as to how these deep-seated influences (curiosity and psychology of perception) are reflected in the architecture and design of mobile and handheld devices, and how this can drive sales.

When we have our final list of influences, we are ready to begin the exciting process of building scenarios.

Creating Scenarios

There are, broadly, two ways to create scenarios. The deductive approach involves taking the clutch of influences and playing with them by selecting, say, five or six. Each is given a state: high this, low that, volatile the other. Then we can say 'This is a world in which …' and paint a broad picture of the emerging future. After that, we can take another set of influences (it's fine if the same influence is used more than once) and give them distinctive characteristics in the same way. We might end up with ten different scenarios as a result. These can be merged and purged to bring the number down to a more manageable three to five. We thus have a series of alternative futures that can be deemed 'as expected', 'better than expected', 'worse than expected', or 'weirder than expected'.

In the second, inductive, approach, we play with the critical uncertainties, pitching any two influences against each other in a matrix. We need to ensure that the chosen influences are as different from each other as possible. In a business-scenario context, we might oppose supply and demand influences; for political scenarios, voter and party drivers.

We have coined the term 'impaxes' as a way of identifying the influences that we are looking for when doing this. Impaxes are influences about which there is great uncertainty: it's unclear how they will perform when placed along a continuum. They have an impact along an uncertainty axis — thus the name 'impaxes'.

In teams, we and the participants review the influences and place them onto a matrix. This step is all art and no science. The aim is to identify a total of about a dozen or so impaxes to focus on further. If we were working with eight syndicate groups, we would ask each to select two or three and put them up to the plenary group. In a larger workshop setting, we may wish to implement a voting system whereby individuals allocate a total of 25 points among the influences they feel have most 'impax'. We usually limit the amount that can be given to any one driver to ten points, and allow people to give as little as one point to other choices.

Here are some examples of matrices that we developed as staging posts along the journey to a final set of scenarios.

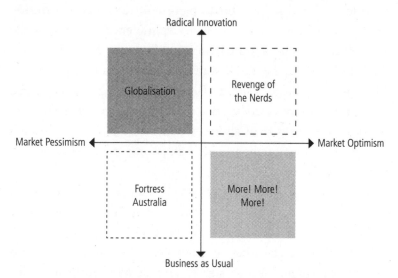

Figure 5. A scenario matrix for the financial services industry

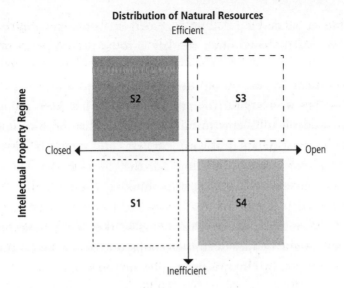

Figure 6. A scenario matrix for a tertiary faculty of design

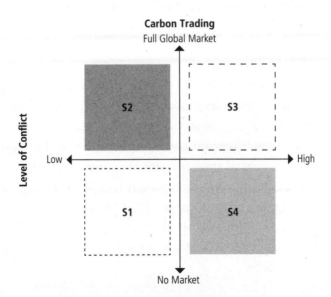

Figure 7. A scenario matrix for consulting engineers

Whether we develop deductive, emergent-based scenarios or inductive, matrix-based ones, the key is to be playful. Suspend disbelief; there is no right answer. Despite the frustration that can be present in developing the charts, trial and error — and time — does wonders for the creative process. Just keep going until it suddenly all seems to fall into place. This more or less mirrors how our brains deal with problems and solutions. First, we gather information relating to the problem at hand, educating ourselves. Then we stop thinking about it. This is often referred to as the incubation or fermentation stage, and patience is undoubtedly a virtue. Finally, there's illumination when an insight or idea seemingly pops out of nowhere. The trick, as with many things, is not to give up too soon.

Enriching the Scenarios

We don't live in a two-variable world, so we can't stop at matrices. We can only find out how plausible these worlds are when we go about the task of fleshing them out — moving from the skeletal matrix to full-blooded imagined futures full of history, sex, colour, and movement.

Once we have a scenario matrix that looks promising, we can set about enriching that matrix by loading other influences into each world in a non-deterministic way. We try to avoid deterministic outcomes: logic that would argue, for example, that in an economic scenario unemployment has to be high if inflation is high, and if unemployment is high then exchange rates would fall and interest rates would rise. We are imagining alternative futures, and the greater their difference from each other and from conventional ways of thinking, the more likely we are to prompt the moment when we begin to see the world differently from before.

Despite this plea for a non-deterministic approach, the scenarios do need to be robust and logical. They must be plausible and avoid fictional nonsense if they are to be effective. The test is not based on the probability of the world ever emerging, but on the internal logic that has been used to create the story. Creating timelines for each future world is one of the most successful ways to bring the stories to life and test their plausibility. How did this world emerge from today's reality? Can you map each key stage in the process? If you cannot imagine a plausible way of reaching the world, then it is very likely an implausible future. Scenarios are not fantasies — they need to link to the world we've got. But when they hold together and pass the tests for robustness, they are fantastically illustrative, as we shall see.

It is also helpful to name each of the scenarios and summarise them in short narratives, as we have done with our Worldview Scenarios, to help to bring them to life.

In a workshop setting, the techniques to find the right matrices may appear to be mechanistic and unimaginative. This is because in the longer-term scenario-development process, this step involves the scenario team researching over weeks, and sometimes months. The scenarios and the analysis techniques will develop from the logic of the analysis. In a workshop setting, the technique must be quick and reasonably simple to implement. But however we get there, we have created ingredients for our scenarios. The next step is to use them to develop strategies.

Stage Four: creating transformational strategies

'The future belongs to those who prepare for it today.' *Malcolm X*

The idea of futurism can come under fire because, as John Thackara, the founder of event-production company The Doors of Perception, notes, 'It's the present that matters, stupid, not that old paradigm, the future.' Well, the good news is that our whole methodology is about the present — the goal of scenario planning is 're-perceiving the present', in the words of Pierre

Wack. We interrogate the future as a means of freeing up our view of the world, our role in it, and what we might want to do about it.

This is perhaps the little-known secret about scenario planning. Most people who have heard of it but not done it think it is about the future. Ultimately, it is not. It concerns the future and draws on what we can imagine the world to be, but it is about using the future as an excuse to think long and hard about what we are doing now, and where we may profitably and purposefully go next. As Friedrich Nietzsche said, 'The future influences the present just as much as the past.'

The challenge is in making the journey from scenarios to strategy. It involves two steps. The first is to focus on the future worlds we have created and identify the sorts of things we would be doing in each of them, in response to the framing questions. This 'doing' is complex, in that we first have to discover the appropriate areas for action. If we are building scenarios for the future of our family, there are clearly domains in which we have the power to act — choosing schools, deciding where we live, adjusting employment, pursuing leisure pursuits, and so on. We are, of course, constrained by such things as our family income, house prices, our values, religious beliefs, job prospects, and available educational institutions, but we accept these as being part of family life.

Our options for action in these alternative futures are further complicated by the way in which we evaluate opportunities. Our responses usually fall into two categories. One is where we believe we have no power to change the environment, and need to put our heads down and be nimble and smart so as to optimise the outcomes for our group. Here, we are adapting to the new environment, making the best of it. The other type of response is very different: we no longer see ourselves as victims of the slings and arrows being thrown at us by a wicked world (unless philosophical determinists have their way), but as able to make generative, game-changing responses based on our ability to change the environment, rather than be cajoled by it. Our colleague Richard Neville summed this up perfectly when he said, 'The future can no longer be taken for granted; it needs to be rescued.' Vision, mission, and purpose all fit in here beautifully.

The second step, once we have mapped the sorts of things we might be doing in a future world, is to assess the strategic options that seem to be on offer. At one extreme, we will discover actions that are relevant in all of the scenarios, and at the other, those that seem to be appropriate in only one scenario — and, of course, everything in between.

Preferred Futures

At the beginning of this book, we mentioned the importance of worldviews and the notion of a preferred future. Let's now explore this idea a little futher. As we create scenarios for the future, it is obvious that some worlds seem better to us than others. A scenario set will often present two extreme scenarios — one utopian, maybe, and one dystopian — and two relatively benign scenarios, which seem to be based on current trends morphing incrementally from where we are today. But perhaps none of the scenarios present a future that we actually like: our preferred future.

Nor should they. Scenario building is not about our preferences, our hopes and fears about the future of our organisation. Yet, at the same time, it is natural for nearly all of us to want a vision for a better future. It therefore makes sense to call our collective view our preferred future not because we can will it into being, but because a clear vision of the world we want to live in is the best way to help us articulate a generative strategic response. It encourages us to ask: what can we do in this or that scenario to change the world, so that it moves closer to our preferred future?

Identifying Strategic Domains

A strategic domain is an area of influence within which we have the capacity to act strategically and make decisions. The strategic domains at the global level are different from those at the national level, those at a national level will be different from those at a regional level, and the regional domains may be different from the local, too. Even within the local domains there may be smaller relevant groups, such as families and/or households, and so on. This continuum, or move from the macro to the micro, is typical of all scenario inquiries. Our client and the framing questions usually determine the locus that we focus on.

It is best to choose the domains to focus on after the framing questions have been decided. Keeping the framing questions in mind, select an appropriate set of domains from a suggested list. For practical purposes, we might select the five to eight domains that seem most appropriate. As an example, here is a draft list of domains that came out of a project on the future of the teaching profession.

>> communications and public relations
>> curriculum
>> engagement with external groups
>> funding
>> infrastructure and resources
>> leadership
>> networking
>> organisation and structure
>> professional capabilities and competencies
>> recruitment and succession planning
>> teacher pre-service training

» technology
» teaching practice and pedagogy
» values and shared assumptions

In this example, we begin to see how the organisational focus will affect the selection of the domains and the activities that each domain covers. The focus for a school, a group of schools, a local council, a department of education, a teachers' union, and the teaching profession as a whole will be quite different from one another.

Developing Strategic Implications

The next step is to brainstorm the strategic implications for the domains in each of the scenario worlds. A strategic implication is a course of action that would lead to a desired outcome if the scenario it relates to came into existence. By 'desired outcome', we mean something that enables us to be successful in that future and to respond positively to the challenges that the framing question(s) asks us to tackle. The desired outcome is therefore linked to our vision for the future, even though the future in question may be highly undesirable. This link may be explicit, or it may be assumed.

It is important to undertake this activity with a mindset in the present, but to respond to the questions as if you were living in that world. Desired outcomes are not just adaptations to the future — they include strategic actions that seek to change the world through intervention. This assumes that the future is not a given, but can be modified by positive action. Strategy can involve:

» acting adaptively, by responding to factors outside of our control
» acting generatively, by attempting to shape things within our control.

Normally, at least five implications will emerge for each domain in each scenario, but there is no hard-and-fast rule. The freedom to deliberate is the key. Think the unthinkable; go beyond the obvious.

Moving from Implications to Options

A list of implications is not a call to action. We need to assess them in terms of their status. Are they, for example, relevant to all of the futures we have imagined, or perhaps only to one?

We like to rank the implications as 'high', 'medium', or 'low', according to their strategic importance. We can then sort them into three groups. Group one are the implications that are highly relevant in all of the scenarios. These are the strategies that we believe we might put in place whatever the future might bring. Group two are those implications that are highly relevant in two or three worlds, but not in all. Group three are those that are highly relevant in no more than one world. We've now created a typical strategic options table for the framing question. We often find that participants get enthused at this point because they can begin to see how they are 'learning from the future'.

The strategies in group one are things we have to do, as they feature in all the imagined futures, while those featuring in only one future, as in group three, are very specific to that future and will only be implemented if it comes about. The middle-ranking strategies in group two are relevant in most futures, and will more than likely become part of our action list. In this we practice the precautionary principle, which suggests that even if you can imagine a future in which the strategy is irrelevant, it would be foolish not to adopt it in view of its importance in the other futures we have imagined.

Blaise Pascal, the 17th-century French mathematician and philosopher, nailed the precautionary principle with his famous wager: as the existence of God cannot be proved through reason, there is more to lose by not believing than believing. His is the first example of scenario thinking. Using a matrix, as would any good mathematician, he created four worlds from the 'yes, God exists / no, God doesn't exist' and 'belief in God / disbelief in God' axes.

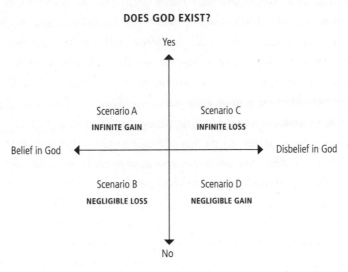

DOES GOD EXIST?

Yes

Scenario A — **INFINITE GAIN**

Scenario C — **INFINITE LOSS**

Belief in God ← → Disbelief in God

Scenario B — **NEGLIGIBLE LOSS**

Scenario D — **NEGLIGIBLE GAIN**

No

Figure 8. Pascal's matrix, which demonstrates that it is better to risk believing in God — even if you are later proved to be wrong — than disbelieving in Him.

We can see that if we believe in God, there is only one scenario in which espousing that belief is negative — that is in Scenario B, where my belief in God has no relevance. But the loss is of little consequence. Yet if I *don't* believe in God, I get hammered in Scenario C, miss out in Scenario B, and pick up very small bikkies in Scenario D. *In nomine Patris, et Filii, et Spiritūs Sancti ...*

Developing Environmental Awareness
We now jump forwards to a time when our scenario-building and strategy work has been completed, and strategic options are now

part of our planning cycle. All too often foresight-based strategy work is not integrated fully into our day-to-day activities, and the benefits of the work we have done are not felt. The first task, after we have decided upon the strategic options, is to develop ongoing environmental awareness in some shape or form.

This awareness has one major purpose: to allow us to be sensitive to changes in the environment, so that we can identify as early as possible the weak signals which will tell us that this future world, rather than that one, looks as if it is coming in to view. We need to be alert to events that tell us, in effect, which scenario might be emerging.

Of course, new worlds will not come into being in a linear way. Our allegiance to things temporal gives the illusion of a linear unfolding, but the present is always emerging through the interplay of hundreds and thousands of influences, which commingle to reveal new worlds. We suspect that 'future-casting' is like weather forecasting: it is hard to do, and yet we must do our best to read the indicators of climatic change. The earlier we can identify the signals and see their links to other events, the greater our ability to survive and thrive, and to build resilience in the face of what seems to be an increasingly turbulent environment.

There are two methods for performing the environmental sweep: scanning and monitoring.

The Difference Between Scanning and Monitoring

The basic difference between these two approaches is that scanning finds answers while looking for questions, while monitoring is based on working from questions while looking for answers.

Scanning takes a wide sweep, looking for events and trends that may signal new developments. These may be front-page news items or more subtle movements and trends. They are sometimes referred to as early warning indicators. Early warning indicators may be anomalies in polls and consumer surveys; changes in what we see on our supermarket shelves; or things that we come across in specialist magazines and journals, during innocuous conversations about football or on the train, amid the television ratings, on the book bestseller lists, or in any of myriad other sources. Monitoring reduces the range of the sweep to focus on specific events. It is a more quantitative approach than scanning, and can be linked directly to a particular scenario.

When we build scenarios, we create systematically designed snapshots of how the world might turn out, and these pictures can be confirmed or denied by monitoring relevant activities in the environment. A future built on the increasing volatility of climate change, or on escalating housing prices, will tell us where to look for early indications that the future is nigh. Scanning is less systematic than monitoring, but it is no less dependent on our understanding of the logic of the scenarios we have made and their reliance on the external environment. For example, science and technology may feature strongly in the futures we have designed, but the way in which breakthroughs will play out are largely unknown. We thus need to maintain a very broad sweep, to scan for unanticipated discoveries in this field (in particular areas such as climate change, biotechnology, robotics, ICT, and nanotechnology) in addition to monitoring the known concerns that have been revealed by the work we have already done.

Of course, these unknowns may catapult us into a completely new world not envisioned by our scenarios. Imagine if, as a result of a sudden scientific breakthrough, children born in 2015 need never die; or a world where nanotechnology actually enabled goods to be manufactured in single units close to where they were purchased. These would be game-changers. But all we can do is work with what we have to see the future.

Weak Signals and Deep Change

In the field of commerce, organisations that are first at identifying the possibilities being created by the influences for change — particularly those influences that appear to be more certain — have a unique competitive advantage. This was clear in the market advantages delivered to Royal Dutch Shell by the scenario work they undertook in the 1970s and 1980s. But how can we do this — how can we be ahead of the curve? Here is a checklist of some of the proven steps to take.

» Think of the preconditions needed for the scenario to unfold, and their likely precursors. See how far back you can go. The deeper your understanding, the greater your advantages.

» Identify small signs of change. Early indicators are not usually front-page news. Watch for unusual events in your peripheral vision, as they may gravitate to a more central role and require monitoring.

» Look to your customers' customers. If you are a car shipper, for example, the number of motor vehicle registrations might be a critical guide — or the number of people taking driving tests, or patterns of demand from consumers as to brand selection and added features.

» Look to your suppliers' suppliers. If you are a customs agent, for example, what is happening to immigration laws, and how does that affect the movement of domestic goods around the world?

» Keep an eye on the competition. Find out what your competitors are doing in terms of hiring, outsourcing, disinvesting, acquisitions, and so on. Identify new business entrants or unexpected competition. What were they doing previously? Where are they coming from, and why?

» Stay abreast of changes to your industry. What new patents have been lodged that are relevant to your business? What are the universities doing in terms of training and research that might help your company? How are new business models being achieved? Where is the new, low-cost competition?

» Be aware of the political climate. What kind of people are running for political office, and how is electoral voting behaviour changing? Track what is being legislated for. How does this reflect social change?

» Think about how social attitudes and values are changing, and how quickly the community is responding to innovation and adopting new ideas and products. Find out what is happening with innovation in technology — its pace, investment levels, demand (pull), and supply (push).

» Review what is happening with economic policy. Will this make it harder or easier for you to do business?

» Look to general trends. For example, the balance between globalisation and localisation — is it moving, and why?

Here are some examples of places to look for indicators.

In society

» fashion trends
» food purchases and prices
» job ads, especially what's rising or falling
» makes and colours of cars that people buy
» new subjects being offered in postgraduate degrees
» relevant signs, street art, and posters (for example, a poster reading 'Business as Usual is Dead')
» the most popular children's names
» things people complain about, or questions they ask
» what children want to be when they grow up

» what things people spend time or money on, and what they do with their free time
» what people worry about, and what makes them happy
» where people go on holiday, and why

In the economy
» expenditure on research and development
» head-office relocations for big business
» stock-exchange movements, and why they occur
» unemployment rates

In technology
» patent applications
» Google searches
» website hit rates
» YouTube views

In the media
» attendance rates at conferences or seminars on certain topics
» innovative publications, such as *Monocle*, *Wallpaper*, *Wired*, and *Fast Company*
» newspaper front pages
» science-fiction bestsellers (books, movies, and magazines)
» subscription rates for specialist publications
» the top ten television shows and books (especially the top ten business books)
» incidence of key words or phrases used by journalists, and rises and falls therein

In other nations
» literacy rates in developing economies
» migration rates, both formal and informal
» political rhetoric and debate

Everywhere
> » general anomalies: things that are rising or falling very fast, or things that seem odd and don't make sense

Implementing an early-warning-indicator program is quite simple, provided that it is not viewed simply as a service that the strategy team provides to the rest of the organisation. While we must have (preferably internal) resources to do this — particularly for monitoring — it's a good idea to get everyone involved. An interactive intranet site, with a facilitator, can work very well. It might include not only a scenario scanning and monitoring component, but also provide a full presentation of the scenario worlds for colleagues. Shapingtomorrow.com is a useful resource, as are springwise.com and nowandnext.com (full declaration: this last is one of Richard's websites). At a minimum, post the scenarios in summary form and, for each, list the strategic implications and early indicators. Then invite people to supplement the work done by the scenario team. Have meetings to review what's happening on a periodic but regular basis, and update the scenario information accordingly.

Kees van der Heijden, the great scenario thinker and champion, was asked by a client of ours, 'How should we use the scenarios we have created on an everyday basis?'

'Well,' he replied, 'let's start by reviewing your government's budget policy, announced last night, against your scenarios — where does it think we are heading?'

Use foresight work to inform current decision-making. The best scenario projects get integrated into existing strategy cycles and become a powerful tool for increasing our vision of the future.

Overview of the Scenario-planning QUEST

Stage 1: developing framing questions

1. Interview key staff and stakeholders

2. Record their concerns and collate an issues report

3. Develop the framing question(s)

Stage 2: examining the environmental influences

1. Conduct research (including literature reviews) and interviews (including with 'remarkable people'), and collate a thought-starters report

2. Create a timeline of key influences that have created the present environment

3. Brainstorm future environmental influences using (I)NSPECT

4. Make a list or map of influences that are impacting upon the external environment

Stage 3: building scenario worlds

1. Identify the critical uncertainties

2. Refine and confirm the framing question(s)

3. Narrow and refine the relevant critical uncertainties

4. Choose a scenario-building approach

   a. The inductive method: create as many as ten indicative scenarios, then merge and purge them to generate the most compelling three or four.

   b. The deductive method: map sets of critical uncertainties (impaxes) on to impax charts to identify the three or four most compelling critical uncertainties.

5. Enrich the first-cut scenarios and create timelines to test their plausibility; write the names and narratives for the final scenario sets

Stage 4: creating transformational strategies

1. Decide on a preferred future
2. Identify relevant strategic domains and implications
3. Map the implications to create a strategic options table
4. Divide the options into groups one, two, and three, and formulate a strategy action plan
5. Conduct ongoing scanning and monitoring
6. Periodically update the scenarios to keep them current

9

Developing Framing Questions:

the first stage

The previous chapter outlined our QUEST methodology. In the next four chapters, we are going to show how we employed this methodology to create the Worldview Scenarios of Part I. In this chapter, we'll focus on the first stage: developing framing questions.

Let's take a brief look at the ideas we have about human nature. Is the nature of human existence 'nasty, brutish and short', as Thomas Hobbes suggested in *Leviathan*, where the law of the jungle governs our lives? Or are we born free, as Jean-Jacques Rousseau argues, but are 'everywhere in chains'? Is human nature a constant, as so eloquently suggested by E.M. Forster in *Aspects of the Novel*; or is it open to transformational alteration (think biotechnology, genetics, and pharmaceuticals), as suggested by Joel Garreau?

The nature of human nature has intrigued writers and philosophers for the last 2500 years, from Socrates to John Ralston Saul, and from Shakespeare to William Gibson. We tend to bifurcate the debate into two camps. The first believes that there is nothing new under the sun: human nature is constant, and the humans of ancient classical civilisations are no different from those of the Americas in the 21st century. This school of thought holds that there really are no differences between the generations — generational difference is no more than cosmetic, as the rites of passage are unchanging. It focuses on the idea of the natural: that there is an innate process we go through as we grow up. This process sometimes becomes masked by external forces, but exists nevertheless.

The other group believes in the transformative potential of technology and related synthetic interventions in the evolutionary process. Consider the impact of the GRIN technologies (genetics, robotics, information, and nanotechnology). In *Radical Evolution*, Joel Garreau explains: 'These four advances are intermingling and feeding on one another, and they are collectively creating a curve of change unlike anything we humans have ever seen.' The change is not just quantitative: the difference is qualitative, and will take us to a new space in which human nature has actually changed. This school of thought holds that we should not necessarily think of the next 30 years or so in terms of the last 30 years; rather than less change or a similar level of change, it's quite possible that the level of change we collectively experience will be a minimum of five times, a probable ten times, and a possible 100 times the rate we have seen before. Yikes.

The current debate about climate change, for example, shows this dichotomy. The positivists adduce data to show how we are warming the planet, claiming that the human-made component in the build-up of carbon dioxide in the atmosphere is changing the climate critically, and that we need to intervene now in order to save ourselves from an early bath and possible extinction. The sceptics pour cold water over the arguments, arguing that climate change was ever thus and that we are not the critical change-agents in global weather patterns — and, most importantly, that we should not be increasing the cost of living by levelling carbon taxes or emission trading schemes on our economies. Combating weather is merely a matter of dams, dykes, and giant sunshades.

The debate about climate change is clearly not about science. The sceptics criticise science for being uncertain in its findings about climate — but uncertainty is fundamental to science and scientific thinking, too. Nowhere is this uncertainty more evident than in the concept of the singularity. There have been very different applications of the singularity: for example, in the work of physicist Stephen Hawking, or in that of futurist Ray Kurzweil. Let's look at one, which is concerned with the dilemma about what happened before the Big Bang. Everyone knows that every event has a precursor. But if that event is the beginning of the universe, how can that have a precursor and still be the beginning? Enter Mr Singularity. Even though we know there must have been prior events, we are going to assume that the Big Bang has no antecedents unless science eventually proves otherwise. Compare this with the Bibilical view of the creation of the world: 'In the beginning God created the heavens and the earth' (Genesis 1:1). This verse describes the transformation of invisible energy into all of the fundamental physical matter that would be formed into stars, planets, and everything else — including us. The purported existence of 'invisible energy' bears some similarities to the concept of Big Bang singularity. Science and religion collide by using assumptions to create some sense of certainty in a sea of uncertainty. And what is it that underpins each approach? To an extent, it is the worldviews of the authors, which support a set of beliefs from which they hope to create knowledge. Fantastically, all knowledge is based on belief. 'We don't see things as they are. We see things as we are,' a quote often attributed to the Talmud, is apt here.

The Challenges Facing Western Democracy

We decided that we would investigate the questions concerning us about the future for Western democracies in a global context. Then we completed the questionnaire. Please note that our responses to the questions were based on our opinions about the future. These opinions provided inputs for the creation of the scenarios, but they were not necessarily what emerged undiluted in the scenarios themselves. We should also point out, as we did in Chapter 2, that we have created what follows purely for the purpose of this book, and in normal circumstances we would work with a client to develop a custom-built set of questions that would obviously generate a very different set of answers.

1. The Big Picture

What things are happening right now that have the potential to make a major difference over the timeframe of our project? There are five areas that jump out at us when we look at what's happening right now.

» **Weather.** The impact of global warming and the melting of polar ice looks set to be a persistent concern, especially given the volatility of these changes. Actuaries worldwide are factoring climate risk into insurance premiums, whatever climate-change sceptics are saying about the science of change. The United States Environmental Protection Agency states, 'The last 10 five-year periods have been the 10 warmest five-year periods on record.' Some could argue that this statistic is of no great significance. But what is emerging is the consistency with which unprecedented statistics like this are being recorded in some parts of the world. Volatility is the name of the new game.

» **Finance.** The world's financial climate is suggesting a drought for economic growth outside of the Asian region.

Coupled with this is political risk, linked to country debt. The spectre of a final collapse of the euro, the marginalisation of the greenback, and the money-muscle of the Chinese yuan are fuelling deep uncertainties in the future of global finance at present.

» **Oil and other natural resources.** The rapid depletion of oil reserves and the environmental unfriendliness of coal have already been game-changers, but we all do seem to be in denial as to what happens next. Market-driven approaches to the adoption of alternative energies are not working, as they still seem less attractive businesses for new investment.

» **Religion.** Religions worldwide have responded inadequately to the task of improving the sustainability of the planet, and seem undaunted by any rational analysis of what we might need to do. Whether we focus on Catholic attitudes to birth control, Muslim attitudes to women, Protestant attitudes to same-sex marriage, or Buddhist attitudes to communitarianism, the values espoused often form obstacles to progress.

» **Technology.** It's hard to grasp that the iPod has just turned ten, that Facebook and YouTube are much younger, and that the iPhone and iPad are under six. The impact of technology — in particular, information and communications technology — is dramatically changing the face of interpersonal relationships, politics, and social activism, as well as the boundaries between reality and the virtual. Add to this what is happening in robotics, nanotechnology, genetics (especially the mapping of the human genome), and neurology, and the pathway to a radically different future is already in place.

2. Wildcards

Have there been any events or developments over the course of our careers that have come as a complete surprise to us?

Looking at the history of the world since 1970, in the context of future social attitudes to consumerism and globalisation, the most significant event may be the tearing down of the Berlin Wall in 1989 — some 28 years after East Germany built it. It is ironic that the wall was constructed as the liberal reformist John F. Kennedy came to power, at the beginning of the psychedelic 1960s, and dismantled at a time when the restrictive tenets of monetary economics were being introduced in the 'greed is good' 1980s by Ronald Reagan in the United States and Margaret Thatcher in the United Kingdom.

The end of the Cold War between the East and the West and the dismantling of the Soviet Union has had a dramatic effect on the way we see things and, in particular, on the way that we perceive Western capitalism. As Charles Hampden-Turner and Fons Trompenaars wrote at length in the book *The Seven Cultures of Capitalism*, what it revealed was that capitalism was not a monoculture in direct opposition to communism, but as variegated in its blooming in different countries as the exhibits at the Chelsea Flower Show. They contrast the individualistic capitalism of the United States with the communitarian capitalism of some other nations. For example, the American dream asserts that if I do what is good for me, it is good for society; while Japanese values suggest if I do what is good for society, it is good for me. It is small wonder that John F. Kennedy's exhortation in his 1961 inaugural address, 'Ask not what your country can do for you, ask what you can do for your country', did not find a ready-made market. He would have been more successful in Tokyo than in Washington!

The acceleration of the speed of technological change has been a big surprise — although, from a third millennium point of view, it has been locked in for some time. Look, for example, at this table of what has been happening technologically in the lifecycles of music-reproduction technology.

TECHNOLOGY	INTRODUCED	DECLINED/ RETIRED	LIFESPAN
The phonograph	1877	1920	43 years
The gramophone			
78 records	1910	1950	40 years
Vinyl records	1950	1985	35 years
Audio cassettes	1964	1995	31 years
8-track cassettes	1965	1975	10 years
CDs	1982	2005	23 years
MP3 players	1997	—	—

It's hard to grasp that a technology as old-fashioned as the 78 gramophone record lasted almost half a century, while the CD has fallen from its perch in almost half that time. A similar acceleration could be seen in regard to adoption rates for telephones in the United States. Back in the late 1800s and early 1900s, it took 50 years for half of American homes to acquire a fixed-line phone (it was originally seen as a business, rather than a domestic, device). It took just seven years with mobile phones. The adoption of Facebook is probably even faster (over 50 per cent of Harvard undergraduates had joined Facebook within four weeks of its launch in 2004). Use of Twitter has expanded at a similarly quick pace: according to Dick Costolo, CEO, speaking at an event in San Francisco we attended recently, it took four years for the company, founded in 2006, to reach a billion tweets. Nowadays a billion tweets are sent every four days.

In the world of welfare economics, the 'brave new worlds' heralded by the New Deal in the United States in the 1930s and the welfare state in the United Kingdom in the 1940s have long been abandoned as neocons, and monetary economists have become key influencers of policy. The abandonment of the concept of the public good is the surprise of the last 30 years. The provision of public services such as health, education, and transport may never be delivered successfully using free-market economics. The Australian economy, for example, provides incentives for private education, with over 30 per cent of children in full-time secondary private education. But just think of the opportunity to improve health, welfare, and superannuation (pensions) for families if the capital going into funding private schools was available for investment elsewhere.

Another surprise has been the shift in the world of employment, promoted by the changing attitude to jobs. The idea of lifetime employment has fast disappeared, but only very recently. As a somewhat jaded human resources manager said to us, the difference in attitudes to work between baby boomers (born between 1945 and 1964) and Generation X (born between 1965 and 1982) is marginal and has been incremental; but that between Gen X and Gen Y (born between 1983 and 1995) is huge. Gen Y and their successors are from another planet. They don't even always regard physical presence as a prerequisite for employment. (Maybe they are onto something?)

Our last surprise has been the dramatic fall in the real cost of air travel and the impact it has had on how we in the Western world see ourselves. The cut-price air ticket haltingly pioneered by the likes of Laker Airways, and more solidly in recent times by Ryanair, EasyJet, Southwest, Jetstar, Air Asia, and many more, has produced an interesting outcome: increasingly, we find that we all know more about countries other than our own because we spend more leisure time overseas than within our own nations. This is particularly true for Australians, who rarely travel interstate for pleasure and prefer to head to Asia, Europe, and the United States for holidays. But this could change very rapidly, due to regulation, taxation, or the oil price.

3. Asking the Oracle

If the oracle at Delphi were alive today, what questions would we ask about the world in 2040?

A common response to events after they have happened is to say, 'Silly me; I should have known that was going to happen.' We all kick ourselves for our lack of foresight, but nevertheless continue to be surprised by what happens, again and again. It's almost as if we wilfully fail to learn from our experiences. Most of us do usually, however, have some insight into the big questions that are full of uncertainty and seem to be so very important for us get our heads around in preparation for the future.

In developing a scenario-planning project, we ask individuals in the organisation to plump for one question they'd like answered. As a result, we can put together a hit list of the top questions that a group of participants most often asks. Among the many influences that are shaping values, which in turn shape society in Western democracies, we isolated six things about which we would dearly love to have prescience. Again, these are merely examples, and would be different in different situations. Sorting them by our (I)NSPECT categories:

> **Nature**: What is the prevailing global climate like in 2040?
> **Society**: How is global population and income distributed?
> **Politics**: How strong is democracy around the world?
> **Economics**: What is the dominant global currency?
> **Culture**: What does social media look like and who owns it?
> **Technology**: Has human nature been altered by technology and, if so, how?

4. Nightmares

What are the things about the future that keep us awake at night, and why?

Imagined futures are always linked to the present in some way — we can step into those future worlds and think about what might have happened for them to emerge like a phoenix from the ashes of the present day. These links lead to, in most cases, one of three types of futures. The first is utopian. This future is strongly preferred by many, and it is one in which their key concerns have been met. When building scenarios for the future of school teaching, the group we worked with designed a world called 'A Farewell to Arms', which evoked a society where social values had become strongly feminised and schools were a significant part of a broader collaborative social fabric.

Here is a tag cloud of the influences that were seen to create this optimistic future.

Tolerant
Optimistic
Community engagement
Socially cohesive
Family life valued
Green technology
Economy less important than family values
Gender balance
Innovation
Sustainability
Schools respected

Figure 9. A tag cloud of the utopian future for the teaching profession

Two of the other futures in the same project were built on incremental or organic linkages to the present day, where change was driven by current trends. 'Under the Volcano' focused on the impact of generational change, which was already visible in the conversations about Gen Y and the Millennials, while 'The Magic Mountain' picked up on the potential for schools to become even more privatised than they already are (particularly in Australia and the United Kingdom).

The third type of scenario is dystopian. The link to the present is discontinuous — an unexpected left-field event suddenly snaps us into a different, and gloomier, world. Events like 9/11, the Bali bombings, the splintering of an iceberg twice the size of Manhattan from Petermann Glacier, the Iraq War, and the sub-prime mortgage disaster were surprises that have had a significant impact upon the world we try to make sense of as we go about our daily business. Surprises become causes. These surprises foster fundamental changes in how we make and implement strategy in a world where we are at the mercy of the slings and arrows of outrageous fortune. Causes have effects. None are one-off events; rather, each represents visible and politically significant manifestations of turbulent systems in the geopolitical environment. Effects are linked systemically.

It is these dystopian influences that are the stuff of which nightmares are made.

The teachers also created a dystopian future around environmental degradation and economic collapse, which they called 'The Grapes of Wrath'. Interestingly, recent experience suggests that dystopian scenarios are on the increase — certainly in the sense that they are more readily created or accepted — but one suspects that this is merely another case of projecting forward recent experience, especially in the West.

So what are the influences at play in 2040 that hold us in fear? Here are our top six prescriptions for insomnia.

» **Nature.** We really do run out of oil and there are no cheap, environmentally friendly alternatives to fuel our lust for energy. Have a look at James Kunstler's *The Long Emergency*, which is about surviving the end of oil.

» **Society.** The great divide emerges in many shapes and colours, but the prevailing gloom is that in a world which is getting more affluent, albeit in an unsystematic way, the gap between rich and poor, top and bottom, gets wider and wider until something snaps.

» **Politics.** The pursuit of the public good is finally vanquished in favour of economic efficiency. The neocons rule supreme! And the handbasket is full of people on their way to hell.

» **Economics.** The until-now cyclical world recession becomes permanent due to the pressures of a global population of nine or ten billion people, many of whom demand upward social mobility, and some two billion of whom are squatters at the fringes of megacities. Slumdog millions, not millionaires.

» **Culture.** Relationships become the dominant basis for social action, as opposed to rule-governed behaviour. Think of William Golding's *Lord of the Flies:* in this new ending, Jack's anarchic tribe wins out over Ralph's rule-followers.

» **Technology.** The prospect offered by an orderly and independent internet is abandoned as cyber wars, brownouts, identity theft, trolling, and the politicisation of web neutrality take hold. Not *1984* but *2044*.

5. Who's Sleeping in My Bed?

Innovative strategies sometimes call for strange bedfellows. What are the major unexpected alliances, partnerships, and conversations that could advance the future?

We all make assumptions about what is possible based on things to which we have become accustomed. If we think about the world as a collection of nations (united or not), we assume that the geographical boundaries that frame a nation and define sovereignty and culture are fixed. But why should this be so? If global corporations can merge, as did AOL and Time Warner, Pfizer and Pharmacia, and the awkwardly named Belgian/US beer conglomerate, Anheuser-Busch InBev, why shouldn't countries merge voluntarily? Just imagine what the Netherlands and Australia (Hollandoz) or Brazil and Singapore (Brazinga) could do as new countries, combining assets in a new framework.

An equally powerful theme is the replacement of physical boundaries by virtual ones. Perhaps the joker in the pack of wildcards about the future is social media. The Western world has, as noted earlier, moved very recently from an internet of information to an internet of relationships — from Google to Facebook, from what to who. The realpolitik of virtually defined entities is not yet known, but we have a sneaking suspicion that we ain't seen nothing yet.

What we do know, however, is that the mechanistic reality of representative politics, with its political parties and electorates and candidates and branch stacking and polls, has been traduced by the viral power of social networks. Every day we see another example of the marginalisation of conventional politics. Whether it is the catchphrase of the Occupy Wall Street movement of 2011 ('We are the 99 per cent'); or the invitation from YouTube to 'broadcast yourself'; or the power of crowdsourcing with sites such as freelancer.com, with more members worldwide than there are soldiers in the Chinese army, the democratic king in parliament is dead — but how long will it take to bury him? And how will his demise, if it continues, change the distribution and exercise of political power?

6. Missing Links

Most fields require a solid infrastructure of communication channels, information technology, incentives, revenue models, and other underlying support. Are there key pieces of infrastructure that seem to be missing in our organisation or industry?

This question is, really, less worried about missing infrastructure than it is concerned with the lack of alignment between the pathways to power in Western democracies. It's also about the culture, which binds us together as social animals. In times of stress, we all look to our cultural values to provide the inner resources that we need to deal with adversity. Whether London in 1940 or New York in 2001, Japan in 2011 or Ireland in 1848, we frequently draw on these resources. But the question for the future is, will these resources be there?

There are clear signs that we need to be concerned. Could mental health problems, caused by rapid social change and a lack of physical community, be the biggest battleground of the 21st century? We'll no doubt find out sooner or later. Prime among other concerns is the changing face of the media. The role of the fourth estate as the independent commentator on news, politics, and society has been eroded by the muscle of its owners, who often prefer to use the media as a tool for influencing politics, rather than commenting on it, and as a channel for commercial sponsors to access new and existing markets. As the writer John Le Carre said about the media in the United States, when we look back on its role in the early part of the third millennium, we will be staggered at how poorly served we have been. It hasn't been telling us what is really going on. Small wonder there is an American website called What Really Happened (www.whatreallyhappened.com).

Another concern is our declining ability to stay focused on any topic. Teachers complain that young students behave much like bees, flitting from the equivalent of one bright flower to the next and never stopping to complete any task. The reduction of attention spans is not a new concept, but the increasing pace with which it is diminishing is. What will be the consequences?

Last but not least in the 'what's missing' segment is the question of wealth. In the last 25 years, the increases in average wealth have been astronomical. Take a look at this graph.

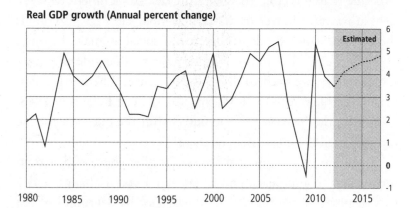

Real GDP growth (Annual percent change)

Figure 10. A world getting richer — but will the trend bend?

Source: International Monetary Fund

Yet while growth rates are up, inequality in the distribution of wealth has increased. The great divide is on us. And as the global population soars, the divide will certainly get wider because the urge to grow capital is inextricably linked to self-interest. In recent years, stock-market activity, particularly in the United States, has been focused on companies buying back their own shares. The driver for this activity is the manipulation of the share prices to increase the wealth of owner-managers. This concentrates ownership and provides very little social benefit, as the rich just get richer.

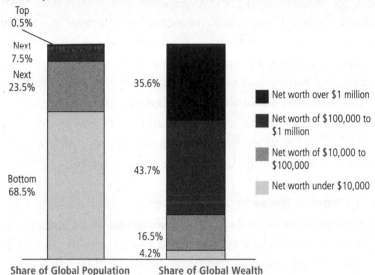

Figure 11. The demographics of wealth in 2010

7. But For the Grace of God ...

What major constraints, internal or external, are we experiencing? How do these limit what we can achieve? Responding to this question requires clarity about our point of view and our starting point. If we consider a topic like the future of international taxation, although we can identify laws and regulations that are global in reach and have universal application, it will largely depend on the jurisdiction in which we are based. When we think about the future of our world, the internal constraints will be different depending on where we live. These cover things like the efficacy of democracy in our country (the degree of transparency, accountability, or corruptibility), its communication networks and infrastructure (such as telecoms, transport, and logistics), social welfare (such as health, education, and community care), and the cost and standard of living (GDP, investment/saving, and inflation). External constraints will be driven by macro influences such as climate change, cyber security, global networks, geo-politics, religion, the world economy, the supply of natural resources, exchange rates, and political and national risk.

When considering the limits of humanity's capacity to change, we usually end up in Reality Street. We have passions, hopes, and fears about the future, but the great leveller is the turbulent nature of the influences and our increasing collective inability to respond to them appropriately and to mediate them, where necessary, in order to build the future we want.

8. It's Now or Never

What critical decisions have to be made soon? What forks in the road are coming? Many assume that foresight activities should be undertaken with urgency, during a short period of time, to prevent looming crises, but this isn't true. History is full of moments when a crisis appeared to be on us or was beckoning, but the future turned out somewhat different. The influential Meadows Report, *Limits to Growth*, sponsored by the Club of Rome in 1972, is a case in point. Its doomsday predictions were elegantly presented but, according to some critics, they were based on assumptions that proved to be false. Other commentators have applauded the report for identifying uncurbed economic growth as a major problem for our planet. Similarly, the climate-change sceptics and those denying the global impact of resource depletion have a view that may be out of alignment with some alternative futures.

These two topics — climate change and finite resources — head our list of critical concerns for which action seems to be needed, based on current knowledge. And we would add to them the impacts of technology on the human mind (read Alvin Toffler's 1970 classic, *Future Shock*, for an inkling of what we might mean); the issue of economic competitiveness in some countries; and the problem of global liquidity and debt, which is to an extent linked to competitiveness and looks as if it could tear the world apart unless China steps into the breech as the fixer. China, of course, has its own problems. But even if China were to save the day financially, how would the rest of the world react?

We are also concerned about the increasing levels of social and political disaffection in the United States, as reflected by the Occupy Wall Street movement of 2011, which looks to have the potential to cause a political and social implosion, leading it to retreat from its role as a superpower. Once again, China beckons.

9. I Did It My Way

What core values would we like to see driving development into the future? Our strongest wish is for a future that combines the virtues of fair play, respect for life, and collaboration and community with those of anticipation, excitement, self-realisation, and fun. We can imagine dour futures in which life is lived respectfully without enjoyment of the moment, and we can imagine risky futures that sacrifice sustainability for hedonistic pleasure and repress the equality of opportunity we feel is needed. Finding a balance between the needs and wants of institutions, especially large corporations, and the needs and wants of individuals and society — across the planet as a whole — is surely one of the biggest challenges that we and our children face.

10. RIP

If we were looking back on our time, what lasting contribution would we hope to have made? One of the enduring responses to this question has been the universality of people's need to 'make a difference'. Making a difference involves two ideas. Firstly, it recognises that each of us individually has the power to act, to do something. Secondly, it invokes the idea of change. If things stay the same, there is no difference in play.

Our feeling is very much that most people would like to do something to make life better, rather than worse, for others, or for a patch of the planet. But to do this requires time, and a degree of security that modern life sometimes makes elusive. Some individuals devote their entire lives to such deeds, but for many others the chance to sit quietly and reflect upon what they have achieved and to do things that are important, rather than just urgent, only seems to come when the final curtain is about to fall. It might sound overly theatrical, but one good trick to sort out what is really important, compared to more mundane matters, is to pretend that you or the institution for whom you work is facing an extinction event. The threat of death, it seems, creates a clarity of vision that is generally lacking in everyday life.

Addressing the Framing Questions

So where are we headed, in this turbulent world, and what alternative scenarios present themselves? What opportunities and risks would each trajectory represent, in terms of sustainable lifestyles that are socially, culturally, and ecologically desirable, and what can we do to influence the future as it unfolds? How, as Socrates might have said, do we want to live our lives, not only to do things better but also to do better things? These ideas are perhaps connected to another question that is asked very infrequently: what are we *for*, as individuals and as organisations? It is assumed that most commercial organisations exist merely to make money. But can that really be it? Is there not a greater or more satisfactory reason for existence?

After surveying some of the challenges that humanity might face, we decided on the framing question — or, as it turned out, two questions: *What opportunities and challenges might we face in 2040, in terms of lifestyles that are socially, culturally, and ecologically desirable? What can we do to influence the future as it might unfold to promote more resilient and successful ways of living?*

The future, here we come!

10

Examining the Environmental Influences:
the second stage

The framing questions have helped us to define why we are interrogating the future, and what we hope to find out. This process of interrogation will fuel insights for those in the organisation who take part in it.

We like to think of the organisation as a system that interacts with all sorts of other systems and is thus embedded in a larger universe. The context might be local, national, or global. It might be the organisational landscape, or something quite different. This stage looks at the environment outside of the organisation. What's going on 'out there' in the world that will change how we go about our business in the future? Who should we engage with to find out more about the all-important environmental setting in which we will have to make our way? What are the key influences that are going to bring about important changes?

How Did We Get to Where We Are Today?

Before we explore the key influences that might change the world in the future, let's look at how we got to where we are today by analysing what has been happening in the world since 1970, in an annotated timeline. This will help us to uncover broad patterns that may continue into the future, and to help us separate 'signals' from 'noise'.

So, let's ask: what things have helped to shape the world? What have been the major steps along the road from the 1970s to the present day? How has humanity sought to engage with life's challenges, and have we been successful?

1970s

» **Nature.** There were three key developments: early DNA testing was introduced, the environmental movement was born (Greenpeace was established in 1972, in Vancouver), and the first genetically modified organism was developed (also in 1972).

» **Society.** The growth of feminism saw a movement for equal pay for women, and identity politics came to the fore in the form of the gay and lesbian movement, and in the focus on multiculturalism. The contraceptive pill continued to open up new avenues for sexual freedom, while the countercultural movement blossomed through the growth of the drug culture and increases in alternative schooling. The global population reached four billion.

» **Politics.** The Vietnam War grew increasingly unpopular, and moratoriums were held across much of the Western world. Meanwhile, the first Vietnamese boat people, refugees from the war, began arriving on the shores of Western nations. Idi Amin seized power in 1971, the same year that Bangladesh was created, and his regime lasted until 1979, the same year that Margaret Thatcher was elected prime minister in the United Kingdom. In between, the Watergate scandal broke in 1972, with Nixon resigning the presidency in 1974; and the 1973 oil crisis led to high oil prices and rationing. A second oil crisis occurred in 1979, in the wake of the Iranian Revolution.

» **Economics.** Fuel costs rose and growth rates slowed in many nations, and inflation hit 13.3 per cent in the United Kingdom. There was a shift away from heavy industry in several Western nations, and Britain launched a 'Made in Britain' campaign to offset their lack of competitiveness. More women entered the workforce, as a result of feminism and better conditions for female workers, and the development of package holidays expanded tourism.

» **Culture.** In 1970, the Beatles broke up. The media's coverage of Vietnam expanded, and nations worldwide saw graphic images of what was happening on the ground. Nuclear families expanded, while postmodern ideas began to take hold following the 1968 protests in Paris. New York's World Trade Centre and the Sydney Opera House both opened in 1973. The first facelifts were also conducted in this decade, by cosmetic surgeons.

» **Technology.** Colour television became dominant; the silicon chip became ubiquitous; and pocket calculators, barcodes, floppy discs, and liquid crystal displays were invented. In 1976, Steve Jobs, Steve Wozniak, and Ronald Wayne founded Apple, to sell the Apple I personal computer. The first MRI machine was developed (in 1972) and the first test-tube baby was born (in 1978). Our lifestyles continued to improve as the microwave came onto the market and air-conditioning became widespread.

1980s

» **Nature.** Several natural and human-made disasters dominated the decade: the 1980 Mount St Helens eruption, the 1984 Bhopal chemical disaster, 1986 Chernobyl nuclear disaster, and the 1989 Exxon Valdez oil spill. The threat of global warming loomed, and the environmental movement gained strength. The Ethiopian famine of 1983–1984 claimed over one million lives, and in 1985, French foreign services sunk Greenpeace's *Rainbow Warrior*.

» **Society.** Activism continued as aid organisations were established, opposition mobilised against Apartheid in South Africa, and political correctness came to the fore. At the same time, there was a shift towards the primacy of the individual. AIDS was clinically observed in the United States in 1981, and the HIV/AIDS epidemic began. Crack cocaine and arcade video games entered society. Urbanisation increased apace and public surveillance rose, and the world population reached five billion. Mobility grew, while overseas travel increased.

» **Politics.** In the United States, Republican Ronald Reagan was elected president in 1981; in the United Kingdom, the Falklands War and the miners' strike of 1984–1985 dominated the headlines; in Poland, the Solidarity movement began; and in Afghanistan, Soviet war continued. The European Union expanded during the decade; in 1988, Mikhail Gorbachev became the USSR's head of state; and in 1989, the Berlin Wall fell and the Tiananmen Square protests ended with military suppression. Environmental politics entered the mainstream in many Western nations, and Green political parties were established.

» **Economics.** The 1980s was dominated by neoliberal economics and economic rationalism. The impact and influence of multinationals grew, outsourcing began to take hold, trans-Pacific trade rose, and there was widespread privatisation of publicly owned companies. There was also economic recession and high unemployment in many Western countries. In 1983, the Australian dollar was floated; in 1986, the Big Bang (the sudden deregulation of financial markets) occurred in London; and in 1987, stock markets around the world crashed. Credit cards and EFTPOS facilities became available to consumers.

» **Culture.** In 1980, CNN was established to provide 24-hour news services; in 1981, music-video channel MTV began broadcasting. LiveAid, a concert to raise funds for poverty and starvation in Africa, was held in 1986; around the same time, there was a rise in individualism and the philosophy that 'greed is good'. Hip-hop music gained popularity, as did acid house during the Second Summer of Love (1988–1989) in the United Kingdom.

» **Technology.** The Apple Macintosh was introduced, leading to a rise in home computing and word processing. Computer viruses also came into existence. Compact discs and CD-ROMs were launched, fax machines replaced Telex, and video cameras and camcorders became widespread. The Sony Walkman and mobile phones also gained penetration, allowing music and communication to become mobile.

1990s

» **Nature.** Concern over global warming grew, but society became desensitised to global disasters. Hurricane Andrew hit Florida in 1992, and there was local action against Shell in Nigeria.

» **Society.** There was a decrease in community spirit, and the growing need to accommodate refugees became a polarising problem. In 1990, the UK poll-tax riots affected England and Wales, and in 1992, the Los Angeles riots, sparked by the beating of Rodney King, resulted in 53 deaths and 2000 injuries. The number of home alarms grew, women worked large numbers of hours outside of the home, and there was concern over 'stranger danger' for children. There was growing recognition of gay and other non-nuclear families, and multi-literacies developed as new media emerged.

» **Politics.** This was a decade of conflict, which saw a rise in jingoism. In 1990–1991, several Western nations sent troops to fight in the first Gulf War, while 1994 saw the beginning of the Chechen wars and the Rwandan genocide, and in 1998–1999 the Kosovo war raged. The US 'war on drugs' also continued throughout the 1990s. The Soviet Union collapsed in 1991, with Boris Yeltsin elected the first president of the Russian federation. German reunification took place, Nelson Mandela was freed from jail, the Apartheid system collapsed, and an Earth Summit was held in Rio. The Maastricht Treaty was signed in 1992, and the Belfast agreement in 1998. That same year, Indian and Pakistani nuclear tests took place, and the Bill Clinton scandal came to light.

» **Economics.** In business, there was a desire for transparent accountability and performance reporting. The preoccupation with triple-bottom-line reporting began. Globalisation took off, and we saw the rise of the new economy. In 1995, the euro was officially adopted, and in 1997, the Asian financial crisis hit. Privatisation continued in most Western nations, and there was an increase in disposable consumerism.

» **Culture.** Email went viral, mobile-phone penetration increased, and people were able to communicate instantly, becoming more globally connected. The concept of the knowledge economy was born, there was hysteria over health and safety, several 24-hour news channels were launched, and in 1997 Princess Diana's death raised concerns over privacy and the role of the media. That same year saw the release of the first Harry Potter book. The approaching end of the millennium saw the rise of Y2K anxiety.

» **Technology.** Mosaic was credited with popularising the world wide web, which became a commercial reality. Amazon was launched in 1994, and Google in 1998. We also saw the rise of electronic gaming devices, laptop computers, digital cameras, DVDs, and answering machines. The human genome project was launched; Dolly the sheep, the first cloned mammal, was born in 1996; and there were significant advances in research on brain dynamics and how we learn.

2000s

» **Nature.** We saw the environmental impacts of economic growth as we became aware of water shortages and witnessed increasingly volatile natural-resources prices, including for oil. The Asian tsunami hit in 2004, Hurricane Katrina in 2005, and Australia recorded the beginning of its worst drought in 2003.

» **Society.** There was continuing social liberalisation and consumerism, and there were changes in the way that families operate, and in how we planned for and thought about the future. The internet became a place for relationships (MySpace, Facebook, and Twitter), and for publishing (YouTube, Flickr, and the rise of blogging). Napster came and went, but introduced the idea of file-sharing. Baby boomers began to retire, and the global population hit six billion.

» **Politics.** The 9/11 terrorist attacks on the World Trade Centre saw the beginning of the War on Terror, led by George W. Bush; further terrorist attacks occurred in 2002 (the Bali bombings) and 2005 (the London bombings). War began in Darfur in 2003, and the Beslan school hostage crisis occurred in 2004. The African Union set up its own parliament, former Warsaw Pact members were allowed to join NATO, Australians took part in the Walk for Reconciliation, and Londoners marched in support of rural communities.

» **Economics.** Most developed countries turned to the free-trade agreement regime. The sub-prime mortgage disaster in the United States triggered global financial collapse, followed by recession in many countries, and disarray in the PIIIGs (Portugal, Ireland, Italy, Iceland, Greece, and Spain). The European Union continued to expand, the euro became widely used, and the concept of the BRICs (Brazil, Russia, India, and China) and the N11 (Bangladesh, Egypt, Indonesia, Iran, Mexico, Nigeria, Pakistan, the Philippines, South Korea, Turkey, and Vietnam) took hold.

» **Culture.** There was a rise in reality television and celebrity culture, an interest in extreme sports, growth in interactive gaming through programs such as Second Life, and a heightened interest in blogging and bloggers. There was also a continued boom in nostalgia, and an interest in simplicity and slowness.

» **Technology.** There was an internet explosion, as global communication and connectivity reached new heights. Apple introduced the iPod, the iPhone, and the iPad; ebooks.com was launched; and camera phones and wireless internet networks became common. Most households had access to the internet. There was a rise in social media, such as Twitter and Facebook. Radio-frequency identification was introduced, and the human genome project was completed.

2010s

» **Nature.** The effects of climate change are becoming increasingly volatile as we worry about melting ice-caps, endemic resource depletion, continued destruction of rainforests, loss of biodiversity, groundwater contamination, aquifer reduction, and ocean warming and acidification. In 2010, BP caused the Deepwater Horizon oil spill, and in 2011 an earthquake and tsunami in Japan triggered a nuclear meltdown in and around Fukushima.

» **Society.** There is endemic volatility and uncertainty, and deepening income polarisation (dividing society into the 'haves' and 'have-nots'). There is also a growing incidence of mental-health problems; increasing automation and virtualisation; and growth of mobile internet, mobile-phone retail, and digital payments. Most Western societies are ageing, fertility rates are declining, and immigration levels are causing tensions in some countries. The world population has reached seven billion.

» **Politics.** The Arab Spring, the capture of bin Laden, WikiLeaks, and the Occupy Wall Street movement (and related protests and 'banker-bashing') all made global headlines. The European Union is in turmoil, and there are calls in many Western nations to back-source outsourced jobs. There has been a rightward shift and a rise in nationalism and jingoism, but there has also been a rise in localism, and a developing culture of 'hacktivism'. Pakistan and Afghanistan present instabilities.

» **Economics.** The long slump looks set to replace the long boom as the US dollar, the largest reserve currency, weakens; there are problems with solvency and competitiveness in parts of Europe; and many countries are having jobs-free recoveries. The prices of food, energy, and raw materials are rising, and some developed nations have seen a decline in real wages. There is a bifurcation between developed and emerging markets, as growing BRICs and N11 countries are leading to the emergence of a middle class. We are seeing multi-speed economies and the re-emergence of city-states.

» **Culture.** The last of Gen Y is reaching adulthood, the nuclear family is declining, we are shifting from paper to screens, attention spans are shortening, and culture is becoming increasingly visual. Social media and microblogging are becoming ubiquitous, and the number of virtual friendships is growing; email is losing ground, in favour of Facebook posts and tweets. There is declining trust in institutions and individuals, authenticity is becoming a questionable concept, and there is debate around privacy and what constitutes social connection.

» **Technology.** We have seen the rise of cloud computing, crowdsourcing, 'big data' and data analytics, smartphone apps, geo-tagging of information, and personal genome sequencing. There is continued growth in smartphones and tablets (over personal computers), for the mobile computing and retail purchasing they allow. The use of voice communications are declining, in favour of text. The open-innovation movement is gaining ground, and UAVs and robotics are in use.

Looking to the Future

The (I)NSPECT (ideas, nature, society, politics, economics, culture, and technology) approach recognises that we operate within a complex environment. While we can influence some elements in the environment, we control very few. As we have seen in Chapter 8, the way in which we might expect these influences to play out varies from the relatively predictable ('organic' population growth and ageing) to the critically uncertain (economic growth, informal migration, stability of the internet, and the impact of disintermediation), to the complete surprise of wildcards (natural disasters, terrorism, geopolitical flashpoints). This is what we discovered in relation to the Worldview Scenarios.

Nature

Climate Change

'… unless we free ourselves from a dependence on these fossil fuels and chart a new course on energy in this country, we are condemning future generations to global catastrophe.' *Barack Obama, politician*

The problem of climate change is one that we ignore at our own peril. Every continent is reporting that the volatility of climate change is increasing — warmer winters, wetter summers, melting icecaps, snap freezes, and unexpected heatwaves. Such are the exigencies of the global climate that this alone can frustrate the creation of an efficient, competitive society that enjoys the benefits of growing global wealth. How would a burgeoning middle class in Bangladesh create a bedrock for social development?

There may still be disputes about exactly how much we're contributing to the warming of the Earth's atmosphere and how much is naturally occurring, but there is hardly a scientist anywhere in the world who denies that our expanding and continued use of fossil fuels is pushing us in a highly dangerous direction — at least for the foreseeable future. Climate change is radically re-engineering attitudes and behaviours at a governmental, institutional, and individual level. Will we respond to this by unplugging and switching things off — the Earth Hour response? Or will science, as a result of our optimism in technological solutions, help us to solve whatever problems nature throws our way?

The pressure to reduce greenhouse-gas emissions is likely to become exacerbated over time. It is mind-boggling to imagine the potential impact of the global and national policies that may be put in place to deal with climate change. Can you imagine a world in which we cannot drive cars, travel by air, own mobile devices, use air-conditioning, or blast the central heating in winter? Or a world in which we *choose* not to do these things? However this influence unfolds, perhaps its greatest uncertainty is who will be the agents for change. Individual countries, particularly the mature Western democracies, question the wisdom of acting alone, fearing that it may reduce the competitive edge of their economies. The Asian tigers have a different view: you in the West have had a headstart, so why should we be restrained when our per capita GDP is so much lower than yours?

Energy costs will be a continuing problem, too. They are likely to increase in the medium term, and new energy regulations are probable in the longer term as we hunker down against shortages, or at least volatility, of supply. Nevertheless, by 2040 it is unlikely that our addiction to fossil fuels will have completely abated — and climate change certainly won't have disappeared.

Water

'Water, water everywhere / Nor any drop to drink.' *Samuel Taylor Coleridge, poet*

Scientists are now talking about 'peak water'. The idea is that we are approaching a point in global history when sustainable water management is no longer taken for granted, as climate change, salination, population growth, and other macro factors introduce restraints on water availability, quality, and equity. These factors are creating new approaches to water pricing, and to government incentives being made to water users for such acts as recycling, managing greywater, and conserving water. Peter Gleick, from the Pacific Institute in the United States, argues we are not going to run out of water, but that the restraints will become deeper at all levels: renewable water, non-renewable water, and ecological water.

Drought causes environmental and economic damage. The deluge experienced in parts of the world between 2010 and 2012 may be a water spike in a very long-term drought. Drought is pernicious: it results in soil erosion and loss of vegetation, reduced water quality, and an increased risk of fires and dust storms, as well as crop and stock losses. It is worth remembering that while energy and food are crucial, fresh water is even more so. Wars have been fought for less.

Energy

'We've embarked on the beginning of the last days of the age of oil.' *Mike Bowlin, former CEO of American oil company ARCO*

It was not until late in 2008 that the multinational oil industry publicly acknowledged the concept of 'peak oil' — a problem that had been on academic researchers' agendas since the 1970s. The topic, like any other that is interesting or important, has its supporters and dissidents, and it is worth noting that 'peak oil' generally refers to conventional reserves (so not tar sands, for instance). It's also important to consider some basic economics, namely that the amount of oil that's left in the ground depends upon what people will pay for it: the higher the price, the more incentive there will be for individuals and companies to get it out and to find new supplies. In addition, it is important to give due consideration to how oil use might change depending upon price.

By 2040, we may have solved some of the problems relating to oil or we may not have. The interesting point, perhaps, is not simply what might happen, but why so few people are engaging with this question presently. Are we in collective denial, or are we just doing what we often do, which is leaving things to the last minute and hoping for the best? How prepared are we for another, deeper oil crisis, and can we stop our economies from collapsing when it happens? Could it trigger the advent of global strife, of the kind not seen for the last 70 years, or will we make do and mend?

It seems clear that cheap oil (under US$100 per barrel) won't last. What will this mean for our economies and for our highly transport-dependent citizenry? Is the higher oil price that we experienced in 2008 (US$147 a barrel) the exception or the new rule? What do we think about the possibility of oil reaching US$500 a barrel some time in the next 20 or 30 years? There are certainly arguments supporting the idea that oil could cost US$300 a barrel within the next decade.

On the bright side, advances in clean technology are making inroads; but the big question is how quickly alternative energy sources can come onstream at economic prices. Perhaps someone will invent a new clean-energy solution that transforms society. Oil at US$30 a barrel in 2040, anyone? This thought should certainly be explored, but it would be a mistake to rely upon it.

Pandemics

'I don't think pandemics make us afraid of death; I think they make us afraid of oblivion.' *John Green, novelist*

Our growing physical connectivity as a result of air travel and migration does enable disease and pestilence to travel around the globe — and quickly, too. Whether we worry about avian flu, swine flu, HIV/AIDS, or as yet unknown diseases, many experts believe that it is more a question of when, rather than if, a truly serious pandemic emerges. If this were to happen, what would people do? Would they go to work, and would children go to school? Would anyone even go out? More specifically, what attitudes would people have to social and cultural products, such as money or books, that have been touched by other people? Does the fear of health pandemics itself make life untenable?

Of course, the definition of a pandemic is not restricted to physical diseases. It can embrace an epidemic of psychosomatic disorders — eating disorders, for example, or what we have coined 'globesity', which is an escalating problem worldwide. Or a pandemic could be purely mental, in the sense of being triggered by rapid technological change (again, see *Future Shock* by Alvin Toffler).

Society

Your Brain on Computers

'Every year the progress of advanced capitalist society makes our population consist of more and more isolates. This is because of the infrastructure of the economy, especially electronic communications.' *Mary Douglas, scientist*

If you were living in the United States in 2008, you were part of a nation that gobbled up 300 per cent more information than it was guzzling in 1960. Americans were spending, on average, around half a day engaged with 'media' (and if the television was on while they were working on their laptops, we can almost double that screen time). Recently, the CEO of Google, Eric Schmidt, said that we are now creating as much new information every two days as we created from year zero to 2003. Whether much of this information is useful is another question, of course, but it seems reasonable to assume that as we start to geo-tag more physical objects, and broadcast our whereabouts and what we see, this explosion of 'big data' will continue.

Regardless of definitions of what data is or whether it's useful, we are spending an extraordinary amount of time looking at screens of one type or another. Businesses and organisations will be pressed to create smart filtering systems so as to be able to surface above the noise. This non-stop connectivity and interaction also has other side effects. For instance, we are becoming addicted to new information. We feel bored and powerless without it. If we leave our phone at home, we feel naked. If our email goes down, we feel we can't do anything worthwhile, and if we don't receive updates from our friends, we feel alone. Indeed, communication in general feels impossible unless we are digitally connected.

One consequence of all this frantic activity may be a loss of concentration. There are just too many things, too much information, competing for our attention, and we are becoming distracted and disturbed as a result. We are becoming better at finding information quickly, but the excess of information, much of it worthless, fractures our thinking. Some argue that the human brain is wired to adapt, and that all this will sort itself out in the end. But while filtering excessive information may be possible, we may lose the capacity for deep, reflective analysis and originality. Moreover, the more we become connected digitally, the weaker our physical ties may become. The more we are in an Apple oblivion, personalising information and looking down at screens for hours on end, the less we will engage with family members in the same room, colleagues at work, or even strangers in the street. We may also become less alert to potential risks and opportunities because we will increasingly see only what is in our direct line of vision. It will be a global economy, but we will become a society of impulsive individuals, where loneliness is a crowded room with no wi-fi access or mobile reception.

Laptops Before Breakfast

'Electronic aids, particularly domestic computers, will help the inner migration, the opting out of reality. Reality is no longer going to be the stuff out there, but the stuff inside your head. It's going to be commercial and nasty at the same time.' *J.G. Ballard, author*

According to the Bercow Report, a UK government report on the speech, language, and communication needs of children, our addiction to technology could lead to a fragmentation of family life and could damage the way our society works. If you can find a house with more than one occupant, chances are that each individual will be in a room on their own, clicking or bashing away at something connected to a screen. And that's before anyone even gets out of bed.

In many households, the first and last action of each day is to check for emails, text messages, and Facebook updates. Moreover, an increasing number of what were once face-to-face encounters and communications are made digitally, even in individual households, either because that's become the most resonate way for families to communicate or because it's seen as quick and easy. For example, rather than telling someone in person that it's time to have breakfast or get out of the bath, more parents are sending messages, requests, and other communications via instant messaging, smartphones, and tablets.

The more accessible and affordable digital devices become, the less we have to do with each other. This trend toward 'digital isolation' is well documented. For example, a PEW Research Center study on internet usage in the United States found that people who use social networks are 30 per cent less likely to know their own neighbours. The same trend applies to families — the more family members are allowed to put themselves first and live in personalised bubbles of information and friendship, the more they will tend do so.

Researchers have also found that people who are nice to other people on Facebook are much more popular than those whose stance is critical. This research suggests, if nothing else, the dumbing-down power of the internet, which may be a great disappointment to those who see in its social democratisation a tool for radical change. Maybe Alexis de Tocqueville, the 19th-century French author of *Democracy in America*, got it right when he warned us of the 'tyranny of the majority'. We are in grave danger of losing deep and empathetic understanding of real needs and wants. We are also in danger of losing many subtle signals, such as body language, and we are at risk of breeding a generation of young people that are lazy, self-absorbed, narcissistic and, popularity aside, rude.

But then, what generation of young people isn't?

Ageing

'"You are old, Father William," the young man said ...' Lewis Carroll, novelist

The populations of Western democracies are ageing. Everywhere. Fast. The uncertainties that ageing populations bring with them are legion. Over the last decade we have documented emerging skill shortages in many fields, and they look as if they will deepen over time. Government interventions to offset the impacts of ageing on employment are under pressure because of the restrictions on migration — which is often for political and social reasons. In Australia, informal immigration is a hot topic, as the amount of media coverage on the incursions being made by 'boat people' shows. The labour market liberalisation that has been a feature of the European community brings with it, in a similar manner, social problems that governments would prefer to avoid.

The enduring impact of an ageing public is bringing into question the tensions that we are likely to see on the generational front. What might the political clout of the baby boomers be, as they stop work and enjoy long retirements? Will there be a return to the pre-JFK era in politics, when world rulers were all ancient (Adenauer, de Gaulle, Churchill, Mao, and Khrushchev) and the elder voters ruled the roost? Or will the grey brigade be happy to take a back seat and leave things up to the young?

Moreover, it's not just the speed with which most societies are ageing, but the scale of the problem. In the United Kingdom, for example, at the start of the 1900s there were about 100 people who reached the century landmark. In 1960, around 300 UK citizens reached the age of 100; in 2011, it was 12,000 people, and the forecast is for 90,000 centenarians in 2035. That's a lot of false teeth–friendly foods, memory-enhancing pills, and hip replacements. The implications for everything from savings to healthcare are staggering.

Urbanisation

'Why build these cities glorious if man unbuilded goes? In vain we build the world, unless the builder also grows.' *Edwin Markham, poet*

In his work on the urban revolution, Canadian innovator Jeb Brugmann identifies key features of the urbanisation of the planet — possibly the most significant of all of the influences changing our world. But we need to adjust our concept of a city, not just because they are getting bigger, but also because we are creating a new global system. Concern about the number of citizens is a second-order problem because we are forming a new geography for the human race, and the growth of urbanisation seems to be unstoppable. The big question for some is not *if* we are going to increase the world's population to more than nine billion by 2040, but just *how* we are going to do it. On the other hand, in praise of uncertainty are thinkers like James Lovelock, who suggest that the drive for population growth will be rebuffed by the systemic adjustments of, among other things, the biosphere, and the impacts of pandemics and warfare.

Brugmann also argues that, at a time of rising dependency on cities, we have forgotten the basics of urbanism. The current global economic woes seem to be connected to a new approach to creating cities, in which we construct commoditised buildings for increasingly transient consumer groups. The tensions we are witnessing stem from a growing lack of alignment between the capitalist interests of property developers and their stakeholders, and the realities of the economics of emerging urban regions. This was a major feature of the sub-prime mortgage disaster of 2007–2008 in the United States.

Another consequence of urbanisation is the deepening of the divide between the haves and the have-nots. Over 20 million people live in slum conditions in South Asia's five major conurbations: Delhi, Dhaka, Karachi, Kolkata, and Mumbai.

If there were further movement towards big cities in Australia, for instance, what would the consequences be for service provision in rural areas? Perhaps urban–rural splits will become the new class division of the 21st century. Some demographers expect the number of squatters to reach one billion globally by 2030. Although many Western democracies are experiencing static, if not declining, populations, will they get caught up in this global slumdog problem, or will they develop in splendid isolation? Imagine one million Indonesians deciding to move south to Australia or, in a stumbling Europe, the number of transient workers quadrupling from current levels. Impossible? Hardly. As a minor example, 10 per cent of Latvia's population has moved to another country since Latvia joined the European Union, in 2004.

Households

'Children now love luxury; they have bad manners, contempt for authority; they show disrespect for elders and love chatter in place of exercise. Children are now tyrants, not the servants of their households. They no longer rise when elders enter the room. They contradict their parents, chatter before company, gobble up dainties at the table, cross their legs, and tyrannise their teachers.'
Attributed to Socrates, philosopher

Australian households are getting smaller while houses are getting larger and, happily for Socrates, fewer households contain children. In 2000, the leading type of household consisted of a couple with children. By 2020, the dominant household type is likely to be either a couple without kids or an adult living alone. Divorce rates are booming, and the incidence of single-parent families is increasing dramatically. Same-sex marriage is being (slowly) ratified around the globe, and by 2040 it looks as if it will be universal.

A notable trend in family dynamics is 'extended adolescence'.

The period of transition between compulsory schooling and full-time employment has extended. Young people are delaying leaving the family home, marriage, home ownership, and family planning. With industry demanding ever-increasing levels of skilled labour, young people are pursuing post-compulsory education and training pathways prior to commencing full-time work. The gap year morphs into gap years (and hopefully not into a gap life!), prompting friends of ours to move to a smaller house as a way of moving their kids on to a life of independence.

Another significant trend is household fragmentation. Even if you can find a 'nuclear' family (given that, for example, 34 per cent of homes in the United Kingdom now contain only one person), chances are that you will also find four people in four different rooms doing four different things on four different screens.

Generational Change

'For over a thousand generations, the Jedi Knights were the guardians of peace and justice in the Old Republic. Before the dark times, before the Empire.'
Star Wars

It is interesting how fast things can change. The media — and many employers — were obsessed with complaining about Generation Y. Its members were arrogant, impatient, and in charge. But following the global financial crisis these concerns seem to have slipped away quietly. Will they come back? Are there any long-term differences in attitudes and behaviour between baby boomers, Gen X, Gen Y, and the Millennials, and how could these differences have an impact on us? Similarly, will Gen Y–led mobile apps and Web 2.0 be passing fads, or will they change the way we think, and our approaches to social activism?

The so-called Google generation is new, and we do not yet know what demands it will make on society or how much structure it will require in the way that information is sourced.

However, anecdotal evidence suggests that anyone born after Google was created has the potential to make Gen Y look like pussycats. Many children under 12 really are from another world.

In addition, self-directed learning, which is fast taking hold in our schools and universities, may produce self-directed people whose demands for political and social action might be different, too.

Multiculturalism

'It's just like when you've got some coffee that's too black, which means it's too strong. What do you do? You integrate it with cream, you make it weak. But if you pour too much cream in it, you won't even know you ever had coffee. It used to be hot, it becomes cool. It used to be strong, it becomes weak. It used to wake you up, now it puts you to sleep.' *Malcolm X*

The cultural diversity of the populations of Western democracies is a result of the history of migrations, which is itself the story of colonialism, slavery, sea and air travel, and our incessant curiosity to do things differently and to improve our lot. With the growth of multinational business, information and communications technology, and the disposable income to support leisure travel, we increasingly see ourselves as part of a global community. We seek to take advantage of what the wider world can offer, whether for employment, pleasure, or products and services at ever-cheaper prices.

The openness of these movements of people, both physically and virtually, comes at a price. Nation-states, while accepting their membership of these larger global and sub-global communities — the United Nations, the European Commission, ASEAN, and so on — become conflicted with the tension that the 'one-world' value systems pose for economic performance and cultural stability at the national level. Moreover, what are the long-term implications of increased immigration, or of immigrant baby boomers retiring to countries that do not speak English as a first language?

New Media

'The unnatural way of spreading ideas must be opposed by the natural one, which ... relies solely on the truth of the thoughts and the hearer's receptiveness for new truth.' *Albert Schweitzer, polymath*

A symbiotic relationship is rapidly emerging between mainstream or traditional media (newspapers, magazines, books, television, and radio) and social or new media (blogs, podcasts, and online social networks). All forms of media are starting to feed off each other. Are the downward trends for printed materials pre-determined, or will there be a push back against this?

Through shifts in format and technology, some media content is now user-controlled. The conjoining of the new media with the new consumer presents a powerful new paradigm. According to the late Steve Jobs, in 2008, 40 per cent of Americans read one book or less in a 12-month period (in the United Kingdom, the equivalent figure was 34 per cent). Playwright Tom Stoppard believes that children's love of reading is being swept away by a digital torrent. Words are being replaced by pictures and, especially, by the moving image, although this may change as we start to talk to machines and they start to answer back.

Facebook and Other Social Media

'If content is king, then conversation is queen.' *John Munsell, CEO of Bizzuka*

If Facebook were a country it would be the world's third largest, with 900+ million registered members. The so-called information superhighway has become the relationship superhighway. Who would have guessed that back in 2005?

According to some reports, Facebook attracts more visits in the United States than Google. But while Facebook may have the size in terms of page views, Google still has the influence, especially in the States. For now, Google is still the gatekeeper, the one referring users to other sites, although Facebook is gaining ground. So is it simply a matter of time before Facebook eclipses everything else in cyberspace?

One trend working against Facebook is privacy. Some folks are getting mad and quitting it because it makes too much information public and gives too much away to others, including sites such as Yelp, Pandora, and Microsoft, to name just a few. Most people don't even know this is happening, but the site's free service does come at a personal cost. Many mobile apps do much the same thing, although, again, few users realise it. While you can stop this from happening, it's time-consuming to do it. In the early days, before digital, information such as your home city, your photo, and the names of your friends was private by default, but you could sometimes make it public. Now sites such as Facebook have changed the rules so that, unless your interests and friends are to some degree made public, you cannot list them. Open and public is now increasingly the default setting.

Some people don't care about this. Online privacy is dead, they say. Or as Facebook themselves put it, this is just social norms catching up with new technology. Personally, we think you should be careful about who you share information with, and especially careful about putting information in the hands of people you don't wholly trust. Think about what you say where and to whom — because once it's out there you can't ever get it back.

Politics

Cyber Risk

'Video games are one step before a whole other virtual universe.' *Vin Diesel, film actor*

Is China a military threat to the United States, and to the West more generally? The answer is probably not, but perhaps only if we think of war in conventional terms. China is growing economically and militarily, but historically it has not been expansionist. Many of the scare-stories about a military threat have more to do with the Pentagon budget-building than reality. China has a plethora of internal problems, and its military power is not as impressive as you might imagine. The US military budget is between five and ten times the size of China's, and the sophistication of US military planning and equipment still exceeds China's in most areas. The United States is also more battle-ready and has more experience of actual combat. It's true that China has an ambition to one day be strong enough to take back Taiwan, possibly by force if necessary, but at the moment transitioning the economy and creating new jobs, housing, and infrastructure are far more important priorities for them.

While China is a huge country with a massive depth of resources, especially people, as Mike McConnell, a retired US admiral and former head of the US National Security Agency, puts it: 'We tend to think of everything about China as being multiplied by 1.3 billion. The Chinese leadership has to think of everything being divided by 1.3 billion.' So if China doesn't represent a conventional military or hard-power threat, where is it strong? The answer is in cyber war and the potential for digital disruption.

China has more internet users than the United States, and therefore a large hacker population. This means lots of potential cyber criminals and the scope for highly coordinated electronic spying, some of which is already undoubtedly directed at US military and defence engineering. But it's not just conventional targets that could be at risk: computer networks are not only used to control military assets, but everything from financial services to public utilities, and it's probably only a matter of time before something very big goes wrong. Moreover, with everyday life moving online and living 'in the cloud', the implications of cyber attacks (whether government-sponsored or not) are enormous. Everything from money and energy to transport, water, and health are at risk. In addition, China is not the only nation eavesdropping electronically. Russia, Israel, France, and Brazil are also known for using electronic espionage to acquire secrets for financial or political ends.

So what's next? The key message is that, in the West, all of our critical infrastructure is dependent on computer networks: our trains, planes, electricity, hospitals, pipelines, supply chains, banks, and stock exchanges. China is less of a threat than people in the West think, even in cyberspace; again, China's priority is domestic control and regime survival, and anything else is just icing on the cake. Furthermore, it is in China's interests to accommodate American interests, and vice versa, and both nations have a vested interest in developing secure data networks and financial stability. So, if there is a threat of a 9/11-style cyber attack, it is probably from someone or somewhere we don't expect.

Politics and the Media

'I think it's a terrible shame that politics has become show business.' *Sydney Pollack, film director and actor*

A new organising principle is emerging in politics. Politics used to be about Left and Right, but now identity and technology are shaping the landscape of political ideas, political parties, and political action. Media presence and exposure is an all-embracing requirement. New political movements are appearing and gaining strength, drawing their support from appeals to religion, race, language, and regional or national identity, and are using the community-building power of social media to create new channels for action. The rise of GetUp in Australia is an example of this new dynamic in action. So too, perhaps, are Anonymous and the Occupy movement.

This is all giving way to a new set of concerns associated with cultural values and with national, racial, and religious identities that do not comfortably fit within the traditional Left/Right paradigm. It suggests new fields of action for activists. Amid the political and media furore about Julian Assange and WikiLeaks is an upside: 'systems of interest', from governments to the Catholic Church and from corporations to trade unions, spend enormous amounts of energy on ring-fencing the boundaries of their world; WikiLeaks smashes the barriers and invites us in to have a peep at what is going on. The winner is the one big system that should be binding us all together. Democracy depends on ethics (how should we lead our lives?) and freedom of information (how well do others protect and promote our ethical interests?) But just what is the future of democracy, and how will technology influence that future?

The leak of vast amounts of confidential US data about Afghanistan highlights one downside of the information age: privacy is dead. Leaking confidential information is, of course, nothing new. What's different nowadays is just how easy it has become to steal data, and how quickly this data can be distributed. It is the speed, scope, and reach that's changed.

To some extent, we could argue that companies and institutions which keep things secret deserve everything they get, and it is in society's interest to make all decision-making public and accountable. This is probably a view held by WikiLeaks, but things are never so simple. For example, the leaking of thousands of secret US military documents would almost certainly put a number of individuals at risk in Afghanistan. Is that fair? Or what about if an individual hacked into a computer and downloaded a user's search history and threatened to make this public if a ransom were not paid. Is that ethical?

WikiLeaks itself is interesting for a number of reasons. Firstly, it is an example of open innovation, as anyone can submit information. Secondly, the organisation hosts its data in more than one country, making it difficult for a single government or institution to prevent material from being published, or to force the website to remove content. However, there are some serious concerns here beyond secrecy. To whom is an organisation like WikiLeaks accountable, and what happens when they get something wrong? Previously newspapers were the ones to leak information or expose wrongdoings, but when they got it wrong they could be forced to issue a retraction or be sued. Not so with WikiLeaks.

Takeaways from all of this? Firstly, expect the amount of confidential data to grow exponentially, but also expect leaks to become more frequent and more damaging. Secondly, expect the time that institutions have to react to leaks to shorten considerably. Thirdly, expect a battle between governments imposing more restrictions to prevent data abuse and individuals lobbying for more transparency and access to data that has an impact on their lives. Somewhere in the middle of this muddle will be commercial organisations that openly, and sometimes less openly, collect customer data.

Government

'It is hard to feel individually responsible with respect to the invisible processes of a huge and distant government.' *John W. Gardner, politician*

Government systems around the world are becoming more complex, with multiple centres of policy-making and regulation. Globalisation is also contributing to this complexity, with more standards being set in international forums. The challenge of managing complex intergovernmental systems requires a whole-of-system and whole-of-policy approach. Intergovernmental systems worldwide seem to be outmoded and inefficient, and there has been much speculation about the sustainability of the three tiers of government: national, state, and local. Meanwhile, new media is putting pressure on governments and providing forums to question their relevance in people's everyday lives, as traditional political debate in parliaments becomes marginalised compared to 50 years ago.

A big debate for the future will be about democratisation and governance. The democratisation that has been heralded by the internet is quite new. The 'equity' of the internet threatens to kill off privacy, copyright, and many other forms of ownership: elitism, unionism, cartels, political parties, and so on. And the open, bottom-up governance model that it thrives on makes closed policy-making bodies and all forms of patronage (as in, 'we do it just for you') unworkable. However, a government's role — to provide security for its citizenry and protection of its borders — sits unhappily in this new discourse, as the WikiLeaks case clearly shows. Globalisation is the enigma here: it accelerates the democratising movement on the one hand, while it increases the need for top-down security on the other.

Public/Private Partnerships

'I support public and private partnerships whenever appropriate in order to achieve our goal of a prosperous and vibrant downtown.' *Alan Autry, former mayor*

We have seen a shift away from direct service provision, where government assumes the dominant role in delivering services.

There is also a move towards partnerships with profit-seeking suppliers. For example, in the United States, federal contractors outnumbered federal employees by more that two to one, and contract federal jobs increased by more than 700,000 from 1999 to 2002.

While the idea of public/private partnerships is still strong, recent events in the United States and United Kingdom — for example, the nationalisation of banks — may indicate a shift of direction, towards state capitalism. Questions of work–life balance and free markets versus the public interest obviously have an impact on these ideas.

Economics

Consumer Preferences

'Apple does great products, but at the end of the day we think consumers want choice, consumers want openness.' *Rob Glaser, founder of RealNetworks*

Is the switch from price to value deepening as consumers change their buying patterns? Consumer behaviour might be the next big thing. For example, will consumers really make decisions that fly in the face of price, in favour of other criteria? Economic theory has been on the nose for some time — look at the way consumers respond to brands and to fashion. The psychology of choice is thus a more powerful force than price, and looks to be a key determinant of the future. As students of classical economics soon learn, the quantitative interplay of supply and demand as a price determinant is the exception, not the rule. Quality, in all its haziness, is a much more interesting variable. The economist Sir Robert Giffen identified goods that sold in greater numbers as the price rose — for example, French champagne and luxury cars. Consumers looking down the barrel of the recent financial crisis are beginning to link good citizenship with consumer choice, and to be motivated by their views about the future when it comes to their economic behaviour.

Innovation

'Resilience — if you think of it in terms of the Gold Rush, then you'd be pretty depressed right now because the last nugget of gold would be gone. But the good thing is, with innovation, there isn't a last nugget. Every new thing creates two new questions and two new opportunities.' *Jeff Bezos, founder of Amazon*

This topic will gain momentum as we seek design-based solutions to the complex challenges ahead. Transnational and multinational businesses will want to develop innovation practice on a global scale, but success is not a given. Governments will pursue innovation practice too, but with no guarantees that it can break free from the innovation-as-efficiency or innovation-as-productivity concepts, which do not necessarily generate any systemic change.

Protagonists of the smart-planet philosophy, which argues that we can succeed in solving the problems we face (such as climate change), are the great optimists of this idea. They face the sceptics on the other side. It's an interesting confrontation, as it does seem possible that both sides are wrong. The optimists may fail to see the role that business culture must play in enabling us to change things radically. Giving people in white coats piles of government money to 'get on with it' does not deliver innovation; it needs a business culture that welcomes and invests in creating the infrastructure for innovation to flourish. This includes the creation of financial resources and incentives for investment — an activity that in Australia, for example, is visibly absent. As for the sceptics, their error is in thinking that their worldview is adequate for engaging with a topic such as climate change. The road of denial leads to the palace of over-simplification and, as we learn — albeit bit by bit — the mantra, to borrow a phrase from Richard Bawden, is not the KISS principle ('keep it simple, stupid') but the KICK principle ('keep it complex, kid').

Crowdsourcing, Crowdfunding, and Microlending

'For solving a surprisingly large and varied number of problems, crowds are smarter than individuals.' *Michael Sharmer, writer*

The concept of crowdsourcing burst onto the scene in 2007 and 2008. Freelancer.com has over four million members offering services on just about any topic. We might bear in mind that the Chinese army has a mere 2.5 million members and Walmart employs a paltry two million.

Crowdsourcing provides users with immediate quotations for any job from a host of sources worldwide. It is essentially leveraging the differentials in wages between global economies. The Australian-founded company 99Designs provides website, print, logo, and other design services from its more than 100,000 members, and it is just one of several such examples. It is open to serious debate whether the quality offered by some of these services is better or worse, or whether pay and conditions for crowd workers is an improvement — but it's certainly a trend worth watching.

The latest crowd topic is crowdfunding, which is being used, among other things, by creative people to fund creative projects, and by charities to fund small infrastructure projects. Sites such as Pozible and Kickstarter are examples. Similar variations include organisations such as Kiva, a microlending site that allows individuals to provide seed funding to small-scale entrepreneurs, often from developing countries. What is significant about these developments is that they offer people without capital a way in — and to an environment that is not

100 per cent driven by cash. The transactions that take place on these sites often include providing capital in exchange for equity sharing, bartering, payment in kind, and so on.

Economic Growth

'Economic growth may one day turn out to be a curse rather than a good, and under no conditions can it either lead into freedom or constitute a proof for its existence.' *Hannah Arendt, historian*

What used to be the number-one goal is now the number-one dilemma: we now realise that the unfettered pursuit of economic growth, once so encouraged, may destroy the biosphere upon which all human life depends. Countries like Australia have ridden out the GFC particularly well, but they are almost certainly going to experience lower and more volatile growth rates and higher inflation in the near future.

The triple-bottom-line approach to evaluating business performance created a shift in views about business success, but pressure is mounting to see if there is a new economic currency in sight that is based on the commodification of things like happiness, sustainability, and social equity. Strategists talk about the restorative economy as another way of highlighting the need for these new values to be adopted. Whatever the future holds, economic growth is the mother of all dilemmas.

Jobs

'All paid jobs absorb and degrade the mind' *Aristotle, philosopher*

What does the future of work look like, in a general sense? We will probably see more open and collaborative ways of working. There will be a shift from tight and formal hierarchies to looser and more fluid networks. Alliances will increase. Job mobility will rise. There will be calls for greater flexibility and more personalised contracts. But the biggest battle is likely to fall along the commoditisation–customisation continuum. Can Western democracies compete with the commoditised low-price offerings from people in China and India — and, watch out, from Africa? Or has the horse already bolted?

What are the underlying influences that are changing the way we look at jobs? And what is the role of the nation-state in a global environment that frowns on protectionist domestic legislation? Most mature economies are facing a long-term skills shortage. This is caused by the lack of foresight in our social planning, an ageing society, falling fertility rates, and, perhaps, by the fact that highly skilled jobs (and workers) are becoming increasingly mobile. Short-term solutions include retraining, outsourcing, and immigration. They also include more casual work, more part-time work, more automation, and re-hiring of retirees. In 2040, will we see a return to vertical integration in business, as economic volatility creates some urgency to internalise tasks that were entrusted to third parties?

The Creative Economy

'As with anything creative, change is inevitable.' *Enya, singer*

The rise of the creative economy has been a function of the knowledge revolution. As Richard Florida has argued, the flowering of communications technology has brought together creatives from all walks of life to collaborate in a new world. Everybody is a writer these days; inside every tweet and SMS is a blog post just waiting to come out. And everybody has the prospect of mining revenue from their creative activities, however limiting their day-to-day work might be.

Western democracies are moving rapidly from post–Industrial Revolution manufacturing economies to knowledge-based economies, in which close to 40 per cent of people work with knowledge in some form. As we move from a manufacturing and service economy to a knowledge-based economy, there will be a demand for different sets of skills, and education will come under pressure from the business community to provide the 'right' sort of workers for future employment. Moreover, as low-skill and no-skill jobs move to developing nations like China (or become automated, thanks to developments in robotics and artificial intelligence) there will be a further shift. Creativity and innovation are the new mantras.

Ironically, Australia's recent 'economic miracle' as the star economy in the OECD flies in the face of the creative economy. It results from digging things out of the ground, rather than out of the mind. We should be careful not to assume that this is a temporary phase. There are plausible futures that will see a prolonged return to survival economics.

Culture

Popular Culture

'This is the culture you're raising your kids in. Don't be surprised if it blows up in your face.' *Marilyn Manson, musician*

The democratisation of the media is being driven by technology and is dramatically changing media literacy. Wiki pages, blogs, tweets, and, especially, mobile phones are the beginning of the most significant changes to media dynamics since the invention of the printing press.

Of course, a nation's culture is not the same as global culture — even if you are the United States — so we need to be circumspect as to the relationship between the two. Nevertheless, when we look at the impact of YouTube, in particular, we can view the world through a different lens from the truly local.

However, there is a big difference between YouTube as a

source of millions of videos and YouTube as a call to action. Info-glut tends to drown your capacity to make a difference in the world, as you are flooded by reasons for inaction. YouTube users collectively upload over 60 hours of videos every minute of every day, so to review just one day's content would take three years! Uploads are also limited to 15 minutes for most users. YouTube is thus doing for video media what tabloids did for news media: little bits of stuff; lots of it. Not too taxing on the brain cells, and who cares about what's missing?

Me or We?

'Always go to other people's funerals, otherwise they won't come to yours.'
Yogi Berra, athlete

Do we, in the Western world, have a set of shared values? We are told that we value respect for democracy, have a strong sense of justice, and believe in fairness, tolerance, and loyalty. However, increasing levels of individualism in our culture over the past 50 years and the growing disparity between rich and poor suggest that our egalitarian values centre more strongly on equality of opportunity than equality of outcomes. The American dream is essentially individualistic, as it focuses on personal performance as the creator of community outcomes, rather than the other way around. Free-market capitalism is the purest cultural expression of this point of view.

'Me-ism' is one of the most powerful contributions made by the new technologies. Don't be fooled: social media isn't that social after all. The more connected we are, the lonelier we become, and the more powerful the ego-centred worldviews that flow as a result.

Inward Focus

'The home ... is ... his castle and fortress, as well for his defence against injury and violence, as for his repose.' *Edward Coke, lawyer*

Australian social commentator Hugh Mackay has identified a trend in which we have abandoned a cosmic view of the world in favour of turning the focus inward to concentrate on things we control: backyards, home renovations, our children's schools, and our next holiday. Those of us who have been around for more than three minutes will have noticed that the concept of 'lifestyle', with its connotations of self-enjoyment and personal development, is very new. It's a step away from battening down the hatches and telling the rest of the world to go hang.

Consumerism

'The corruption of the American soul is consumerism.' *Ben Nicholson, artist*

Consumerism is a significant feature of Western culture, which has led academics Clive Hamilton and Richard Denniss to diagnose us as suffering from affluenza: they contend that we are obsessed with money and material things. We are — or at least were — in the grip of luxury fever, with our expectations for material wealth outstripping our means, resulting in growing levels of consumer dissatisfaction and debt.

The global financial problems of 2007–2008 have introduced new ideas onto the agenda, as citizens look to increase their wealth in a world that is becoming increasingly intolerant of bare-faced consumerism. This intolerance is not just social; it's also ecological. We are pushing our planet to a world that will be much less hospitable for us. Debating the minutiae of the science of change is far less important than embracing the ethics of it all. How do we continue to indulge our livestyles when the 'we' means everyone?

Technology

The Internet

'The American people and nations that censor the internet should understand that our government is committed to helping promote internet freedom.'
Hillary Clinton, politician

Much has been said and predicted about the phenomenal impact of the internet on our societies. The greatest uncertainties about the future of the internet are cyber security, including the reliability of access, and net neutrality. The optimistic suggestion that the internet will always be free, generative, and secure is contestable; we just don't know how this will turn out. Think, for a moment, about the sacrifice regarding human rights that was made following 9/11: our governments asked us to waive the right to a trial before incarceration in the name of homeland security. Will we be asked to make a similar trade when it comes to net neutrality? Will online anonymity be a fleeting stage and, if so, what happens when we all admit who we really are?

The other big change in the way that the internet operates is, as we have mentioned, the shift from information to relationships — from Google to Facebook. Web 2.0 is about cooperation and collaboration, and the internet itself is essentially turning into a giant conversation. In 2006, we ran a financial-services scenario project and not one executive in the room full of bankers had heard of a blog. Half a decade later, we are all trying to work out how the blogosphere might be catalogued and reviewed, and to find out what we need to do via social media to be noticed.

Mobile Telecommunications

'An iPod, a phone, and an internet mobile communicator ... these are not three separate devices! This is one device. And we are calling it iPhone! Today Apple is going to reinvent the phone. And here it is.' *Steve Jobs, co-founder of Apple*

The smartphone is the great success story of the last decade. Globally, we buy more of them than PCs, and Apple sold enough units in a recent financial quarter to give one to every single child born on the planet over the same period. Maybe the laptop is a soon-to-be-archived piece of technology after just 25 years. It is relevant that one of the world's fastest growing religions is Buddhism, as it seems to be the mobile-me version of belief systems. Catholicism and high Church of England are definitely mainframe products, and devotional Muslims are really more like communal cinema-goers than iPad users.

Around 80 per cent of people in Western democracies aged 16 years and over use a mobile phone. Across the world, in both rich and poor countries, mobile-phone sales are booming. Indeed, they are increasing at more than twice the rate of global GDP growth. India is attracting three million new phone-plan subscribers each month, and subscription rates in Western Europe are expected soon to reach a penetration of 96.8 per cent. Voice Over Internet Protocol (VOIP) — a technology that allows users to make phone calls over the internet through programs such as Skype — is also booming.

Biotechnology

'We have the means right now to live long enough to live forever.' *Ray Kurzweil, author*

Developments in biotechnology are changing our approaches to health, agriculture, industry, and the natural environment. In the health arena, biotechnology is increasing our capacity for predictive diagnostics, preventive interventions, and personalised healthcare. In primary production, we can use biotechnology to produce pharmaceutical proteins in livestock and plants. Industrial bio-processing technologies use microorganisms and enzymes for products such as detergents, and for some pharmaceuticals. We are at work on creating the capacity for large-scale bio-processing of energy derived from renewable products, such as woody biomass. This would be supported with bio-refineries that are analogous to today's petrochemical refineries.

The environmental scanning task is, in essence, a celebration of divergent thinking. We have gone out of our way to bathe in the waters of Babylon so as to give the future special possibilities that may transform the world we live in and change the way we think about ourselves as participants in it. Our next task is to give form and content to the future by creating scenarios to detail how it may turn out.

11

Building Scenario Worlds:

the third stage

Now we are finally ready to build our scenario worlds. This stage involves convergence. We take the fruits of our brainstorming about the external environment and mould them into several scenarios. There are two main process that we can use to do this, but whichever process we use, this stage is not about prediction or probability. It's about imagining alternative futures that are plausible, robust, and challenging. We also need to ensure that we have created very different futures, from the utopian to the dystopian, and from the incremental to the radical.

Narrowing the Influences

We started by narrowing down the 300 or so influences that we identified in Chapter 10 as having the potential to change the world. We're not going to drown you with an initial list of all 300 influences — we'll skip ahead to a shorter, refined list. We used the (I)NSPECT categories once more to both simplify and expand on our brainstorming, and to identify the relevant influences. The table on the next page is the result. Next to each influence we have also given details of the uncertainty that we want to examine.

The Worldview Scenarios Influence Table

INFLUENCE	WHAT WE WANT TO EXAMINE
Nature	
Climate change and the weather	Level of volatility
Polar ice-caps	Rate of melting
Fresh water	Availability, price, and quality
Oil and other natural resources	Scarcity and price
Pandemics	Incidence
Natural disasters	Impact of local events on global systems
Society	
Neurology	Impact of technology on
Reality	Physical versus virtual
Ageing	Impact on the economy and households
Fertility	Impact on labour supply
Urbanisation	Ubiquity and rate of growth
Households	Dynamics of living spaces
Family life	Nature (e.g. fragmented, nuclear, cohesive)
Generational change	Impact on the economy and society
Multiculturalism	Impact on society
Traditional media	Top-down versus bottom-up
Social media	Active versus passive
Attention spans	Level
Surveillance	Level
Measures of progress	Economic versus humanitarian
Politics	
Cyber security	Level of risk
Media	Impact
Government	Big versus small

Governance	Top-down versus bottom-up
Taxation	Level
Regulatory framework	Level (e.g. low/restorative/high)
Infrastructure	Public versus private provision
Values	Conservative versus liberal
Green politics	Level
Global trade	Free versus protectionist
Representative democracy	Relevance
Globalisation	Global versus local focus
Warfare	Tech-based versus physical

Economics

Consumer preferences	Price versus value
Innovation	Level
Crowdsourcing	Level
Crowdfunding	Level
Economic growth	Long boom versus collapse
The economy	Free market versus mixed and ethical
Jobs	Availability and type
The creative economy	Size
Money	Equitability, physical versus digital
Brand loyalty	Level
BRICs	Power base
PIIGS	Economic health
Capitalism 1	Autocratic versus free market
Capitalism 2	Individualistic versus communitarian
Capitalism 3	Ascendant versus in decline

Culture

Popular culture	Dynamics of participation
Individualism	Me versus we
Worldview	Global versus local

Consumerism	Active versus passive
US culture	Global dominance of
Literacy	Text-based versus visual
Spirituality	Growth
Privacy	Level
Leisure pursuits	Pleasure versus improvement
Maslow's hierarchy of needs	Survival and utility versus status and fun

Technology

Internet 1	Dependability
Internet 2	Level of neutrality
Internet 3	Access
Mobile	Level of convergence
Landline telephones	Amount
Cloud computing	Global versus local control
Optimism regarding technology	Level
Biotechnology	Organic versus radical
Technology pushback	Level of 'must have'
Nanotechnology	Impact

Our next task was to sort the list by ranking each of them by importance and level of uncertainty.

Before we did so, we once again reminded ourselves of the framing questions against which this sorting needs to be done: *What opportunities and challenges might we face in 2040, in terms of lifestyles that are socially, culturally, and ecologically desirable? What can we do to influence the future as it might unfold to promote more resilient and successful ways of living?*

Figure 12 on the next page shows how we charted the key influences, the critical uncertainties. In charting them, we could see the environmental conditions that are more likely to shape the relevant alternative futures out to 2040.

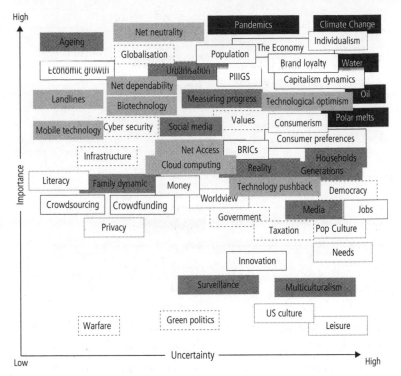

Figure 12. A chart showing the influences relevant to the Worldview Scenarios

Creating a Scenario Matrix

Remember the critical uncertainties we discussed in Chapter 8? When we used them in relation to the Worldview Scenarios, we created an impax chart, shown in Figure 13 on the following page.

We then created a series of matrices by selecting any pair of impaxes that we believed would be significant shapers of the future. We chose impaxes that were quite dissimilar to ensure that the relationship between the two was orthogonal — that is, that each was qualitatively different from the other.

After several days of play, we settled on the pair in Figure 14 on the following page: individualism versus collectivism (the prevailing level of emphasis on 'me' at one end of the continuum, and on 'we' or 'us' at the other), and whether society as a whole

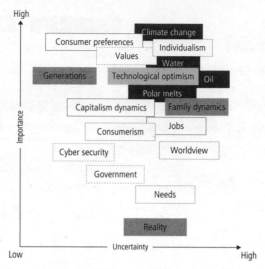

Figure 13. A chart showing the critical uncertainties relevant to the
Worldview Scenarios

felt optimistic or pessimistic about the present and the future
(optimism, primarily about climate change and economic
prospects, at one end, and pessimism at the other). We also
considered many other drivers — for example, societal attitudes
towards technology — but we felt that while they were uncertain,
they did not carry quite the level of impact or uncertainty
provided by either climate change or the economy.

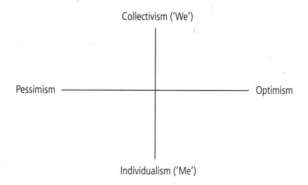

Figure 14. The Worldview Scenarios matrix

We choose this pair as a starting point because we know that we don't live in a two-variable world — however enamoured you may be of the two speed economy!

Then we enriched each world by going back to the larger group of impaxes and introducing each instrument, rather in the manner of *Peter and the Wolf*, until we had a veritable orchestra to create the music of our Worldview Scenarios.

It's important to name each of the four quadrants, or scenarios, represented on the matrix. After much discussion, we settled upon the following four names.

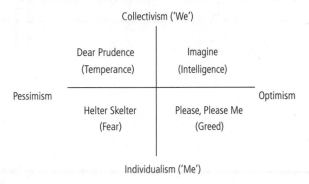

Collectivism ('We')

Dear Prudence (Temperance)	Imagine (Intelligence)

Pessimism ———————————————— Optimism

Helter Skelter (Fear)	Please, Please Me (Greed)

Individualism ('Me')

Figure 15. A matrix showing the names of the four futures in the Worldview Scenarios

This matrix was the foundation upon which the Worldview Scenarios stories were built. But before we wrote the stories, we had to enrich the worlds, imagining that we were living in each of them and ensuring that there were more than two characteristics to give each future its individual sex, colour, and movement. We have summarised our thinking about what it would be like to live in each of these futures in the table of scenario characteristics on the following four pages (pp. 290–293).

Armed with our matrix and the table, we were able to write the narratives to bring our worlds to life.

	IMAGINE	PLEASE PLEASE ME	DEAR PRUDENCE	HELTER SKELTER
Society	» smart » collaborative and open » reliant on technology » crowdsourcing is popular	» oriented towards the individual » hedonistic, narcissistic, and self-indulgent » competitive ('get rich or die trying') » culture of excess » economic inequality » decline of empathy	» ethical and responsible » sense of resilience » rebirth of communal living » people learning to live with less ('make do and mend') » culture of helping others	» high levels of disillusionment » survivalist mentality » self-sufficiency is increasing » self-centred attitude ('look after your own problems') » xenophobia » nostalgia » theft of fuel, food, and water a major problem
Economy	» undergoing a boom driven by investment in technology » productivity gains from automation » not immune to bubbles or volatility	» undergoing a long boom driven by BRIC/N11 income growth and consumer spending » free-market capitalist ideology	» has suffered a collapse » high inflation	» has largely collapsed » short-term volatility » little available credit
Environment	» positive attitude ('if we caused it, we can fix it') » increasing reliance on clean tech » growth of geoengineering	» reluctant attitude ('we'll deal with it if we have to') » threat of climate change seen as exaggerated	» acceptance of climate change ('we're in serious trouble') » sustainability goals » carbon tax and other 'green' regulation	» resource wars » constant problems due to extreme weather

	IMAGINE	PLEASE PLEASE ME	DEAR PRUDENCE	HELTER SKELTER
Politics	» e-government polling on key questions » online and mobile voting » public–private partnerships	» liberalism » tension between globalisation and localism » focus on human rights	» the rise of the 'third way' » longer-term focus » voter engagement	» national self-interest » culture of blame » distrust of politicians and government
Regulation	» geared to encouraging green investment	» minimal » subject to frequent abuses	» targets individual excess	» protectionist
Technology	» revered; seen as bringing order to chaos » high level of automation » advanced developments in AI, biology, robotics, and genetics » customised virtual realities	» coveted; seen as must-have » high levels of addiction » used to offset the effects of obesity and sedentary lifestyles	» technology regression » rationed	» blamed for causing problems; there is a Luddite backlash » active hostility to job-destroying automation
Personal relationships	» strong online social networks » large number of acquaintances » weak personal ties	» strong online social networks » fragmented personal relationships » loneliness and high rate of mental illness » little sense of community	» family rediscovered and embraced » close relationships with neighbours	» restricted to immediate family and near neighbours » many in single-person households » often more than one generation living under one roof in multiple-person households

	IMAGINE	PLEASE PLEASE ME	DEAR PRUDENCE	HELTER SKELTER
Work	» often internet-based and fast-paced » flexible: work from anywhere; many freelancers and project workers	» globalised » high pressure, low loyalty » youth in control » growth of concierge services and household outsourcing	» reduced hours to rebalance work and family time » usually based locally » little pressure and competition	» high unemployment » highly regulated conditions » resurgence of trades and manufacturing
Leisure activities	» shopping » virtual entertainment » online gaming » co-creating media content	» shopping » following celebrity gossip » eating and drinking	» do-it-yourself projects and crafts » community activities » reading	» gardening and home maintenance » do-it-yourself projects
Spending patterns and currencies	» mobile retail » e-money » peer-to-peer lending and borrowing	» impulsive spending » mobile purchasing » high levels of personal debt » income polarisation	» responsible and ethical spending » peer-to-peer lending » bartering » ethical savings and investments » more local purchasing	» cash » local bartering » personal savings » growth in black markets » pride in spending as little as possible

	IMAGINE	PLEASE PLEASE ME	DEAR PRUDENCE	HELTER SKELTER
Key needs	» utility » convenience: access to anything, anytime, from anywhere	» status » immediate access to new technologies » consumer goods » pleasure	» meaning and purpose » simplicity » information » reassurance and comfort	» protection » security » safety » comfort » value » face-to-face contact
Dominant or admired companies and organisations	» Google, Apple, Facebook, GE, IBM, Siemens, and other tech-based companies	» Ferrari, Vertu, Harrods, Louis Vuitton, Moët, and other luxury-goods companies » casinos	» Ben & Jerry's, John Lewis, Toms Shoes, Co-op Bank, and other cooperatives	» Fox News, *Daily Mail* » The British National Party, One Nation, the Zaitokukai, and other right wing political groups
Epitomised by	» Mark Zuckerberg	» Paris Hilton	» Al Gore	» Jean-Marie Le Pen
In a word	» Ingenuity	» Excess	» Hope	» Foreboding

12

Creating Transformational Strategies:

the fourth stage

Now let's turn our attention to the lessons that we can draw from the Worldview Scenarios, so that we might see how the scenarios-to-strategy process works in action, as we apply what we have learned from the future. This chapter involves taking the relevant elements of our scenario worlds and using them as the basis to formulate strategy.

Identifying the Strategic Domains

Our first step was to identify the strategic domains that are relevant to the framing questions. We needed to decide who the responder to the questions might be — would it be an individual, a family, or household unit? A village, town, or city? A country, a region, or the whole world? We decided to run with the national governments of democratic countries as the putative clients for our Worldview Scenarios.

As for the strategic domains, we imagined that they conformed to a typical grouping of government departments.

The Worldview Scenarios

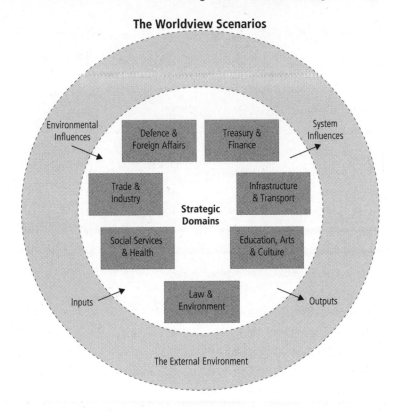

Figure 16. The seven strategic domains

Our next task was twofold: firstly, to generate a set of strategic implications for each scenario world and to move those implications into an actionable set of options. Secondly, once these actionable options were identified, we needed to assess their relevance and importance — ranking them as high (H), medium (M), or low (L) — to decide what we should focus our attention on. The strategic options table on the following page shows the outcome of these two steps.

Strategic Options Table

	Imagine	Please Please Me	Dear Prudence	Helter Skelter
Defence and Foreign Affairs				
Reduce immigration levels	M	H	M	H
Increase defence budget	M	M	L	H
Increase counterterrorism measures	M	H	L	H
Negotiate multilateral trade agreements	H	H	M	L
Focus on global disarmament	M	L	H	L
Global collaboration on human rights	H	M	H	L
Global focus in environmental action	H	M	H	L
Investment in global institutions	H	M	H	L
Global collaboration on climate change	H	M	H	L
Treasury and Finance				
Tighten central control of funding	L	M	L	H
Increase welfare spending	M	L	H	L
Corporatise all aspects of government funding	M	H	L	M
Encourage 'not for profit' organisations	M	M	H	L
Increase personal taxation levels	L	L	H	H
Focus on higher productivity	H	M	M	H
Focus on non-economic performance measures	H	L	H	L
Increase participation rate in the economy	M	M	H	M
Infrastructure and Transport				
Reduce new investment levels	M	M	M	H
Shorten payback periods	M	L	L	H
Encourage private investment	H	H	M	H
Ramp up public expenditure	H	H	M	L
Focus on increasing productivity	H	M	M	M
Inhibit the use of motor cars	L	L	H	M
Education, Arts, and Culture				
Broaden the role of schools at the local level	M	L	H	L

Reduce funding for education, particularly for universities	L	M	L	H
Emphasise business skills for educational leaders	H	H	H	M
Reduce staffing in all sectors	L	M	M	H
Develop skills training	H	H	H	M
Invest in multicultural capital	H	M	H	L
Increase private education	M	H	L	M

Law and the Environment

Invest in alternative energy	H	M	H	H
Strengthen corporations law to encourage private investment	H	H	M	M
Strengthen social-responsibility provisions in corporations law	H	L	H	L
Emphasise global environmental policy goals versus local goals	H	M	H	L
Introduce more individual rights and social-justice legislation	H	M	H	L
Value the non-commercial aspects of the environment	H	M	H	L

Social Services and Health

Increase mental health budgets	H	M	L	H
Focus on pastoral care	H	M	H	L
Ramp up use of technology in health services	H	M	M	L
Provide for the ageing population	H	M	H	M
Introduce personal-identity digital tracking	M	L	M	H
Increase policing	L	H	L	H
Introduce mandatory detention	L	M	L	H
Invest in welfare programs	M	M	H	L
Build refugee centres at home	H	L	M	L
Encourage private healthcare	M	H	M	H
Focus on sustainable population growth	H	M	H	H
Promote social inclusion	H	M	H	M
Promote population increases	M	M	L	L

Trade and Industry				
Build tariff walls and trade protection devices	L	L	L	H
Focus on bilateral trade agreements	L	L	M	H
Build in-house training capabilities	H	M	M	L
Fund innovative technology from the public purse	H	L	M	L
Focus on team-building	H	M	H	L
Invest in cloud computing	H	H	M	L
Focus on innovation	H	M	H	L

Deciding on the Strategic Outcomes

The scenario worlds represent the macro environment. We can draw a link between this macro environment (the global context for the future of the planet) and the meso environment (the national environment in which our governments are operating). In doing so, we might also begin to see how the strategies are relevant in the micro-context of our community. After all, we don't live everywhere in our nation-state. Ideally, an individual would look at the broad brushstrokes of our scenario worlds and imagine what life might be like in their area if the characteristics of the external environment were as we present them. These meso narratives make it easier to identify the scenarios' strategic implications for an individual and for their community, and to see how the diversity between communities in that country would need to be taken into account by the relevant ministerial department when it was assessing options for action.

Let's look at the strategic outcomes for national governments on a scenario-by-scenario basis. We've presented these as if we have attended four different meetings, all involving national governments, in 2040.

Imagine
Moon Hub POD104
2 April 2040

The idea of hologram conferences on the Moon was a brainwave because it reduced the opportunities for cyber hackers, with their rogue bots, to trash the whole process. Secure hubs such as Moon Hub POD104 are impregnable because their data shields are located in the Moon's atmosphere, so as to create a parallel network to those on Earth. The piping from one network to the other is also secure. This technology allows the ministers from all of the nations in the Global Intelligence Alliance (GIA) to gather together 'hologrammatically', and to form policy initiatives that will help humanity through the next phase in our determination to design our way through every wicked problem that providence wants to throw at us.

Many of the geo-economic and political roles of the United Nations and the G7 have been absorbed by the GIA. The novelty of the technology ministers from around the world framing policies in the Virtual Intelligence Parliament has now been replaced by our deep admiration of the technology-led innovations brought into being by the GIA. The geeks have indeed inherited the Earth!

The defence and foreign-affairs policies of nations have been transformed by cyber travel, and hologram-based business meetings have become the flavour of the month as peak oil cuts in. The concept of physical migration from country to country is very low on the agenda, as 'deliverables' are replaced by the virtual world. The technology ministers are doing a great job in promoting the virtues of the virtual. And following the merger of Google and Apple to create the Goople Corporation (now headquartered in Beijing), the introduction of the pea-Pod (the personal environmental audit device) was a brilliant adjunct to the plethora of mobile devices on the market.

Broadening the shareholder base of Goople to involve millions of people improves the chances that its development will be transparent and accountable, too.

The centrepiece of the policy discussions is global collaboration on climate change. Policies should not simply be based on mitigating climate risk, but also on systemic intervention to change the conditions that are increasing climate-change volatility. This involves developing further sources of renewable energy using the low-energy systems of solar and wind power, and increasing individuals' responsibilities to monitor and mitigate their net carbon footprints. The ministers cleverly also agreed to use the climate-change platform as a means of seeking new agreements on other environmental initiatives and on improving the status of human rights on a global scale.

The next major policy focus is to continue to build the metrics for assessing progress on a broader basis than traditional economic performance measures. The days of GDP-itis are long gone. But policy-makers worldwide have noted that we have to replace GDP with a quantitative metric or metrics; if we can't figure it then it won't figure. The Global Progress Quotient (GPQ) is planned for launch in 2045. It will be made up of five metrics: economic growth, happiness, health, environmental sustainability, and audience participation in the arts and culture. The benefit of the new metric is to enshrine in national governments the valuing of non-commercial aspects of their countries and the ability to compare their performance with others.

The GIA has dealt with the problem of funding global technology initiatives through the creation of the Cybertek Global, a risk-based stock market located at Moon Hub POD111. Investors are restricted to the treasury and finance departments of national governments, and the recipients of the funds are technology innovators worldwide.

Another major initiative is the Little Car Project. As the world population has grown to nine billion and average GDP for the increasing number of 'haves' is rising, the demand for car ownership is growing at an alarming 25 per cent per annum. The technology ministers are collaborating to do for car transport what Sony did for music and Nokia did for telephony: make it personal, small, and cheap. Visions for personal transportation devices have been legion since Leonardo invented the helicopter in 1493. The technology breakthrough has been the Cybertek-funded development of air tech, to provide the safety cushion for a car you literally put on like an overcoat.

Urban development is another priority for the GIA. The integration of agribusiness into city life, prompted by population growth and rural drift to the cities, is working well. Vertical farms are commonplace as well, as are the more mundane backyard vegetable boxes.

One of the more difficult aspects of the GIA's work has been its attempts to develop a whole-planet cultural platform — what used to be called multiculturalism. The truth about national policies is that they were usually monoculturalism in disguise: whether you were engaging with the American dream, British savoir faire, the Chinese diaspora, or Aussie egalitarianism, the resulting worldviews were always ethnocentric. The ministers agree that a new approach is needed, and they will set up a task force that excludes the traditional world powers in order to report on how a different balance might be achieved.

Technology skills training is an ever-present agenda item, and all countries agree that it requires more emphasis — and certainly agree that it is more important than defence budgets. Another priority is the development of leadership and business skills for technology innovators, and the ministers agree to put together a draft course outline for this, for online delivery in local languages, and to be backed up by physical seminars and workshops.

Voluntary corporate social responsibility, the old non-performing chestnut from way back when, will finally be abandoned with the adoption of the GIA directive on national corporations law. GIA Directive 101 is simple enough: nation-states are asked to adopt a new obligation — for companies to place social responsibility above their responsibilities to shareholders and for that social responsibility to be global, not just local.

Of course, not everything in the techno-global garden is lovely. The ministers recognise the need for the dramatic expansion of social and health services in member countries to deal with what has become branded as 'nerdophobia' — anxiety over the amount of hours spent online. This 'inner warfare' is a larger problem than conventional conflict and terrorism, although at the physical level the three billion 'have-nots' continue to threaten global stability. The ageing population is an enduring problem but, cleverly, the ministers have increased the funding of technology for at-home community care, which is an effective way to do two things at once: empower people and reduce costs.

Before the meeting breaks up, the Indian Minister of Technology requests that the GIA's next funding directive should means-test national contributions, based on per capita GDP indexed to 2036. The ensuing vote is carried unanimously. We are truly somewhere different!

Please Please Me
Tory Party Annual Congress
Harrogate, Northern England
September 2040

Prime Minister Preeta Pataudi makes her way to the rostrum to outline the new policies on which her cabinet will be working, in preparation for the upcoming opening of parliament. Her party has been re-elected for a record fourth time since 2019, with the opposing parties in disarray and unable to offer an alternative in the wake of a long period of prosperity.

'Colleagues, it is a great pleasure for me to present to you today the outline strategies and policies on which your party has been working following the general election in July for the state opening of parliament this coming November.

'As in our last government, the economy is the centrepiece of our strategic focus, with our commitment to the operation of the market as the key to the continuation of the prosperous times we have enjoyed in recent years.' [applause]

'We will continue still further the corporatisation and privatisation of the public sector. We have long since abandoned the idea of the mixed economy. Every pound that we can move from the public to the private purse is a nail in the coffin of socialism. And every public employee we can encourage to join the private sector is equally effective in maintaining a free open-labour market.

'Free-market economics enables us to introduce still further reductions in the rates of personal taxation and the raising of their thresholds. We have underlined that every adult citizen's personal and family responsibility for wealth, education, health, and welfare management is at the heart of our policies. Everywhere you look we are encouraging investment, savings, and self-help, so we are doing everything we can to keep the economic-growth fires burning. Economic growth is the prime measure of our success. Productivity gains mean as much to our government as economic growth because they liberate existing resources to do more for the economy. And as you know, friends, in our book, more is … more!' [much applause]

'We are continuing to build business skills in all sectors, and the government is particularly pleased to be introducing corporate responsibility into public education at primary and secondary level. Budgetary control will remain in Whitehall, but every school is now encouraged to govern the spending of their budget and make their own decisions about staffing levels, infrastructure costs, and day-to-day disbursements.

'Education at the tertiary level continues to provide us with the problem of how to ensure we get value for money from research. Consequently, as with schools, we are furthering the philosophy of central budgetary control, combined with increased local autonomy on how to spend it. We are going to provide bonus payments at all levels of education to institutions that are successful in their productivity growth, and in their business and management skills. Private education will also be encouraged, so as to offer choice to parents and students who can afford to pay their own way. Lastly in this sector is the introduction of a new vocational training scheme to help us become more self-sufficient at skills development.

'In foreign affairs, we maintain our total support for GCU as a global currency and will continue to resist the pressures for the political unification of Europe. Our decision to leave the European Commission in 2024 still looks good, even 15 years later. It's a fact of life that in the first phase of globalisation (1990 to 2010), leaders were mistaken in thinking that globalisation was about nations, when it was clear that it is about corporations. It was the economic demise of Spain, Greece, and Italy that confirmed the message being promoted so successfully by Apple, Google, Amazon, and the like. And when the Chinese began their concerted drive to invest their trillions of US dollars in overseas corporations, the writing was on the regional economic wall.

'You may remember that, apart from the euro disaster, the incentive for leaving the European Commission was to regain control of our borders. A crowded island like ours cannot offer open access to foreigners for any reason, European Commission or no European Commission. We will continue to keep immigration levels low, but will offset this by developing our growing number of multilateral trade relationships and agreements. This will include some work on climate change but, as for the last decade or so, the global community will only be able to work on voluntary climate-change control, on topics agreed to by key nations worldwide. We won't be first among unequals.' *[much applause]*

'The Attorney-general is designing a new approach to corporations law that will encourage private investment by reducing the red tape for investments in public infrastructure such as roads and rail. The no-tax capital-asset program will expand these incentives by giving investors 100 per cent tax relief for schemes in which they match public investment on a pound-for-pound basis. The investment focus for the scheme is initially on the next round of renewable energy projects, on road-transport systems, and on the health-sector technology program I announced in May. Of particular interest is the project to extend the high-speed rail network in Scotland, Wales, and Northern Ireland, and I think this will be extended to continental Europe, and onwards to Africa and the Middle East.

'I am also pleased to announce that the Home Secretary will increase prison facilities. He has successfully demonstrated the need for extra policing, given that the riots that were sporadic during the first part of this century are now persistent in marginalised urban communities. With the Foreign Secretary, he is also increasing investment in counter-terrorism, as a security measure hard on its heels, and we will also be putting money into our defence budget, with a focus on European security once more. Since the dismantling of the Commonwealth after the passing of King Charles III, increased provision has also been made, however, for our growing relationships with India and China — who, between them, seem to own half of anything you like to think about!' *[laughter]* 'This will also continue.

'The market mechanisms that we believe are at the heart of a free world democracy may not always deliver the goods, and we recognise the need for intervention — particularly in health, where we have never been able to solve the gap between demand and supply. We are therefore increasing the safety net for young and old with the introduction of the developmental healthcare subsidy, which will be used to augment the normal health budgets in the public sector. It will be funded by the lottery scheme. We know that population growth will continue to decline as more wealthy people defer child-rearing even later than we have so far experienced, and the less well-off forego the marginal expenses associated with family development.

'On the industrial front, the government will continue to expand its investment in information and communications technologies — an integral part of our participation in globalisation. With regard to the other technologies — genetics, robotics, and nanotechnology — we will be happy to be a fast follower rather than a leader, and will allow the Indian and US software giants to lead the way.

'That, party members, just about wraps everything I want to say today, other than to note that this is the 100th anniversary of the Battle of Britain. My illustrious predecessor Sir Winston Churchill was the shining light in the darkness that shrouded the Europe of yesteryear. He showed us the importance of self-reliance, honour, and courage, whatever the challenges that confront us. Let us remember him as we venture forth into the exciting future that lies ahead.'

Dear Prudence

Parliament House
Canberra, Central Australian Region
3 May 2040

The Australian Treasurer is delivering her 2040–2041 budget on 3 May 2040, with her budget speech this evening in the House of Representatives at around 7.30 p.m. AEST. Budget material has been made available to approved members of media organisations in a secure area in Parliament House. The lock-up started at 1.30 p.m. and will finish when the Treasurer begins her budget speech.

The ABC political correspondent, Sandy Bull, looks gingerly at the budget pack he's just collected from the document area, wondering what goodies are in store for the citizens of Australia over the next 12 months. Time was, he thinks, when the long boom of annual surpluses would mean a friendly budget that incentivised the rich and did its best not to penalise the poor. But those days are long gone. Who'd have thought that the Earth Hour movement, from the days when he was a hedonistic student at the University of Sydney, would have morphed into the Earth Year movement, in which the evangelical posturing of environmentalists and the born-again fraternity have turned Australia into a paradise for do-gooders, and where the message is 'turn off and tune out'?

The Treasurer's party, the National Labor Party, is a coalition between the old Labor Party and the Nationals, the latter having eventually had enough of the Liberals. It was a surprising coalition to begin with, but it proved to unite working people from the Australian bush and the fast-growing cities, helping to create an ecologically sustainable future following the flood debacle of 2028.

Although the centre of their attention is Australia as a nation, the politicians know full well that global cooperation is essential to combat such things as pandemics, climate change, and dramatic population growth. No surprise, then, when the opening budget materials relate to our contribution to global action on human rights and environmental action (including on climate change, but also on tackling biodiversity and on energy conservation).

A new topic is the need to spend less on global disarmament: it is a rational way of freeing up funds. We've long since realised that Australia is not defendable, so why spend money trying to pretend it is? Big tick.

The reinvention of the idea of a mixed economy has been working well. So the introduction of measures to pump up welfare spending — particularly on community care for the aged, and on child support — reflects the new focus of a government that sanctifies self-reliance for working people, maximises labour-force participation, and frowns upon 'voluntary' unemployment (of those people who could not be bothered). Dole rates are stingy and are moving further behind.

A new round of incentives for not-for-profit organisations underlines still further the emphasis on the public good. The Treasurer is to confirm, also, the new section to be established in the Department of the Prime Minister and Cabinet, the Common Weal Unit, which will develop progress indicators on a whole-of-government basis. These include: gross national happiness (comprising indicators for adult mental health, crime rates, child delinquency, suicides, and divorce rates), the employment churn, emigration levels, gender equality, health expenditure, population growth, birth rates, educational performance, employment, age demographics, multicultural performance, and religious participation.

The government will also announce a new department that combines the roads section of the old Department of Transport with sport, recreation, and personal health. The focus is to introduce policies to further inhibit the use of motorcars while encouraging people to walk, use bicycles, and participate in sports and recreation outdoors.

Skills training is to be expanded by the introduction of a tax bonus for qualifying trainees, with increased bonuses for courses relating to agriculture and manufacturing — those 'orphaned' industry sectors that are now critical to the country's survival in the age of austerity. As for mainstream education, all institutions are being asked to expand the local and social aspects of their roles by ensuring that buildings and technology assets are available 24/7 for community activities — including, of course, continuing and further education. Principals and vice-chancellors are now required to be asset managers as well as teachers and researchers, and to introduce new asset-management supervisory boards that include personnel from the local business and council communities. This broadening of their roles is seen as an important component in the government's social inclusion policies. In a parallel development, the Treasurer indicates that hospitals will also widen their role with pastoral-care facilities, and with bridgeheads into local communities and establishments.

Although technology is no longer seen as the answer to all of our problems, the Treasurer surprises Sandy when she reveals a new section in the trade and industry department, to be called the Inproductivity Unit. 'Inproductivity' is the new phenomenon that brings together two staples from the past — innovation and productivity. Innovation is no longer the province of people in white coats in academic or remote government organisations, thinking about new products or services with little practical experience of how businesses work; far from it. New innovation funding is to be directed at product and systems enhancement of existing technologies, with the aim of increasing output and performance, and lowering operational running, with payback timeframes of no more than 24 months.

So far so good, thinks Sandy. But then he comes to the bombshell, the policy initiative that will make the headlines of his report — and, indeed, those of every other Australian media reporter. The government is at long last going to put in motion a referendum on whether Australia should become a republic. How long has this been a-coming? There'll be no funny business this time, trying to link whether we become a republic with fears about how we elect our president; no, it will be a straight-out yes or no referendum, with the implementation details to be worked out later if the required double majority is achieved in parliament and in the Australian states.

The government argument in favour of a republic is far less nationalistic than it is practical. The link with the United Kingdom costs precious money, with no tangible benefits now that we are living in a backs-against-the-wall world. The Australian community, with its newfound focus on self-reliance and local performance, has no need of any global relationships that are not delivering to the economic bottom line. Nor is there justification in expenditures on pomp and ceremony or on redundant roles like that of the Governor-General. All money and effort has to be productive. No wonder the Protestant religions are where the action is these days — and the rising interest in Amish and Quaker belief systems are a sign of the times, too.

Just as the Treasurer begins her speech, Sandy sends his report and analysis to his boss, and waits for the call to go into the studio.

Helter Skelter

The White House
Washington, DC
January 2040

Re-elected Republican president Roberto Martinez surveys the scene and introduces the purpose of the strategy meeting: to review the next triennial budget, for the period 2041–2044. He explains how we have come to this position of extreme isolationism in the United States. The collapse of the US dollar as a world currency started it all, in the wake of the abandonment of the Euro. Add to that internal strife in China, created by a non-empowered but wealthy and upwardly mobile working class, and the recipe was at hand for a US retreat from its role as world banker, trans-everything business leader, global policeman, and cultural leader. (It is no surprise that foreign films in any language were excluded from the 2037 Oscars.)

The Secretary of State, responsible for the Department of Defense, begins by outlining their plans. The focus of the government's long-term policy is to continue the reduction of expenditures in all theatres of global trade and cooperation; and as for warfare and policing, there will be only a skeletal physical military presence in Europe and Asia. Nevertheless, he wants to maintain and modestly increase the US contribution to the United Nations' budget. Budget increases will also be required to strengthen the government's counter-terrorism activities, which include a significant rise in the number of soldiers policing the US-Mexico border — which now includes a five-mile 'no-man's-land' ribbon along most of its length.

The Secretary goes on to explain that the Department of Homeland Security will also require significant increases in funding for the intensified surveillance at ports, airports, and railway stations, and for the recently opened Department of Cyber Intelligence and Warfare Monitoring, which is attached to Homeland Security. The departments covering employment, housing, and urban development are inevitably caught up in the whole security kerfuffle. And immigration levels are to be drastically reduced, so as to provide the existing population with better access to the dwindling job market and to social services that have been under the gun from a funding point of view.

The Treasurer is up next. He explains that aspects of current policies for government departments, particularly the focus on small government, will be maintained. Inevitably, taxation levels will go up for those lucky enough to be in work so as to maintain the provision of social service, albeit around 10 per cent below its current levels. The big focus in government is increasing productivity, as the Treasury trials a new econometric tool, the

MARAVE, that will compare the productivity of each dollar invested at the margin with the average contribution of all dollars invested in the activity under review.

The government will further centralise the control of public expenditure and increase the corporatisation of government bodies nationally. Corporatisation is the only sensible way to offer some degree of decentralisation; what must be avoided is control of the public purse by small-town bureaucrats who know nothing about the national interest and can't see the wood for the trees.

Belt-tightening policies are widespread across government. The departmental heads of transportation, housing, and urban development each request reduced budget levels for the public purse and for the switch to private funding and more public-private partnerships. Transportation also introduces a five-step plan to inhibit the use of motor cars by a combination of levies (the Californian congestion tax of 2028, much vilified at the time, having now been adopted federally) and increased taxation on fossil fuels — ironically, made more palatable as a result of the price of crude, now at US$330 a barrel. The department argues for the need to switch to renewables, which are now cheaper to produce than dirty energy.

The departments of commerce and agriculture are unified on the strengthening of US tariff walls and a legion of trade protection devices. Trade relationships are now exclusively bilateral; the theme is 'you scratch my back and I'll scratch yours'. As with Treasury, the central domestic policy is about increasing productivity, but with new investment to focus on the applications of existing technologies, rather than on innovating new ones.

The Secretary for Education spoke next. The reduced-funding strategy is key to the departmental approach to the Budget, and will be implemented by swinging staff cuts across the board. The only exception is in the area of skills training. In view of the national policy to restrict immigration, and of the Buy American campaign, building skills is very important. Funding for skills training will be made for universities by cutting academic research funding and switching funds to vocational education. IT-based productivity gains are stressed, with the introduction of national curricula to be taught online at secondary and tertiary levels. Building private education is also a key part of the strategy, as the integration of preschool and primary education services within gated communities is catching on.

The departments of justice, the environment, and energy endorse the Treasury's approach to renewables, placing emphasis on the need to attract further private investment into the sector. This will be promoted by tax concessions of 150 per cent for renewables being developed inside the United States, and tariffs on all imported energies. The justice department is also contributing to the work being done in homeland security, cyber surveillance, and warfare monitoring by drawing up a revised bill of rights that sacrifices aspects of precious individual rights (in particular, the right to a fair trial, the right to bear arms, the right of free speech, and the right to publish) in favour of the need to make national security as watertight as possible — both in the physical world and in cyberspace. Visa restrictions are also set to become more strict, in accordance with the new security protocol.

On the health and human services front, the departmental secretary surprises delegates with her budget increases for mental-health services — but she explains that in the 'age of the battler', which is on us now, anxiety and stress are on a rapid upward curve. Budget increases will also be needed to provide for an ageing population, as labour-force participation rates have been declining and are expected to decline further over the next triennium. Private healthcare is to be encouraged, with tax rebates for participants who sign up for premium-approved packages. And new measures will discourage population growth (despite the ageing economy). These include reducing tax exemptions and other benefits for minors, and the introduction of a bedroom-window tax on all dwellings with more than three bedrooms, as defined by US building codes.

Personal identity tracking, which has been the cause of so much unrest in the past, is now accepted as one of those inevitable evils created by the times we live in. The trials of this using barcode technology are looking solid, and linking tracking to the mandatory process for registering new births will be effective. The full implementation is to be budgeted for in 2041. Meanwhile, policing budgets will be increased by 20 per cent over the budget period and, with the reintroduction of mandatory detention, prison facilities will be increased by 25 per cent.

Despite the tough measures being introduced by all departments, the secretary ended on a more optimistic note by announcing the Community Enhancement Fund. This will provide resources for community-building at the local level, focusing on schools and public libraries as the hubs for networking and social activities.

President Martinez thanks the secretaries and their senior managers for their input. The policy proposals are now ready to go to Cabinet. He reminds the departmental heads that, in addition to the policies for tackling a bleak external environment, there is a need to take policy initiatives that will help the nation to emerge from recession and depression, gloom and doom. To this end, he announces the creation of a Foresight Policy Unit within Cabinet, and asks the team to recommend who might be its inaugural head.

Linking the Future to the Present

Playtime is over. We have built four very different futures from the database of influences that are affecting the future. We have imagined what it might be like to live in those worlds by creating scenario stories based on the key characteristics of each. And we have looked at the policies a typical national government might employ in 2040 in response to any of these turbulent external environments in which they are trying to best serve their citizens.

So what now? What does our foresight suggest we might be doing? Benedetto Croce, the idealist Italian philosopher, said 'all history is contemporary history'. And so it is with foresight; all futures are contemporary futures. If we turn to the second of the framing questions, we begin to see why. It asks us: what can we do to influence the future as it might unfold to promote more resilient and successful ways of living? This is the invitation to act generatively by influencing the influencers; to try and change the world as it changes, rather than respond to it as if we are its victims.

With one last leap, let us imagine we are today visiting the oracle at Delphi, and her answer to this framing question is not informed by divine prescience, but based on the intelligence that the four scenarios bring. What would she have to say to us?

'The inequalities in your world today — inequalities such as wealth, status, opportunity, gender, ethnicity, access to education, technology, life expectation, and political representation — are conspiring to make the nation-state, particularly in an age of globalisation, a less stable institution for the management of human affairs than it might otherwise be. They are also reducing individuals' capacity to embrace the sense of community that is necessary if you are to tackle the challenges that you are facing in the future. Your Please Please Me future is based on the grip that inequalities have in the world today, inequalities that may be among the driving forces behind the activities of organisations such as al-Qaeda.

'There are nevertheless many things that you can do today to soften the harsh realities that otherwise might bedevil you. Policies are required to reduce global migrations. You do not live on 'one planet'; nor is it a one-size-fits-all universe. Local communities, with traditions based on their own cultures and a strong capacity for self-regulation, are much more resilient than anonymous urban societies, where there is less connective tissue between people and a reduced sense of responsibility towards others. Highly necessary counter-terrorism and counter-crime measures might be best supplemented at a global as well as a national level, but it is a priority for all citizens to feel safe in their own communities.

'In almost all futures, there is strong demand for action on the ecologies of climate change, biodiversity, and energy creation. Futures like Helter Skelter, which lack concerted systemic intervention on these topics, are dystopic and to be averted at all costs. Alternative energy is the most important of the global challenges because its need is not dependent on other factors. Natural resources are finite, and if you argue this is not so you are in denial. The timing and nature of resource depletion is of course an uncertainty, but the demand for environmentally friendly alternatives is clear.

'Many of you want to see some expansion of the public good as you go forwards, but one of the lessons from the future is that the public sector is always under pressure to perform efficiently. The attractiveness of free market–based regulatory systems will continue undaunted. Increasing private equity is essential, wherever the world takes you. Even though education, transport, and health will require public funding, the futures suggest that the spirit of the market is a necessary adjunct for them, so their managers need to be performance-focused and imbued with a business ethic in the way that they approach their jobs. A natural corollary to the so-called corporatisation of the public sector is an understated need to "socialise" corporate activity. This means that typical provisions of corporate law, placing pre-eminence on the fiduciary responsibilities of directors to their shareholders, has to be supplemented, if not superseded, by the responsibilities of corporations to the community.

'The topic that has received an almost unqualified tick in all of your futures is increasing productivity. Innovation, a common bedfellow, is not as universal a need as "making more out of less". Global population growth, pandemics aside, will reach at least nine billion by 2040, and without a global economy that recycles, repurposes, resaves, renews — and, indeed, rejoices in this — the slippery road to perdition is nigh. In the focus on productivity, care must be taken to balance its growth with an equitable impact upon citizens. Not all growth is beneficial, much as not all movement is forward. Fully costing externalities in the economies of the future will go some way to achieving the correct focus.

'The role of technology in the future is ambivalent. The Imagine future suggests that you can fix all problems with technology, but this optimism is absent in at least half of the futures you have created. You would be well served to see technology as a necessary but not sufficient condition for a resilient and successful Earth — and be prepared for the technology push back that emerges in Dear Prudence.

'Population growth is a topic like the ocean tide. It is relentless, and cannot be denied. Although population growth is a global problem, there are no global regulatory frameworks to manage it. If the agent of control is the nation-state, it raises questions around democracy and the freedom to procreate quickly. Cynics argue that the price for unrestricted growth is the pandemic, but nobody would wish a pandemic on anyone else. Perhaps declining fertility rates will solve this problem for you over time, but for now this is your major dilemma as you head towards 2040.'

These, then, are some of the conclusions for the world today that we have drawn from our interrogation of the future. We invite you to think about what you might have learned from our work with the Worldview Scenarios, and to ponder the implications for you and the people you associate with daily.

Fore-gone Conclusions

Much of what you have read may be proved wrong in time, but it is not offered to be right. As for some of the detail, it is irrelevant. The point, if you haven't picked this up already, is not to predict accurately everything that will happen in the future, but rather to engage in deeper conversations about what's happening right now, and to discuss why this might be the case and where such developments may lead. It is about thinking deeply and considering various alternatives, which in turn make our thinking more open, more agile, and more resilient.

One pattern that appears to be emerging from the daily deluge of instant judgement and shallow commentary is that change is itself changing. It appears that more things are becoming connected, which is not only acting as an accelerant to change, but is also creating more systemic volatility. In short, the shocks will become more frequent and more severe. Moreover, technological change appears to be accelerating rapidly too, as new attitudes and behaviours appear, and old attitudes and behaviours disappear, with much greater velocity.

The result of all of this is that we are living in a world where getting 'back to normal' seems a distant possibility. Hence the need to develop thinking that is more rigorous so that we can cope with all of the above, and unearth new opportunities and identify new risks. But we can't do this if we are constantly running from one emergency to the next, always on call, with a smartphone clamped to our heads, never thinking more than a few days or weeks ahead. We need to take time out; we need to schedule an appointment to think about where we are going and consider at length whether this is somewhere we really want to go.

The endemic short-termism that plagues every aspect of life today can be mitigated by the realisation that all short-term decision-making benefits from the long view. Indeed, all decisions that ignore the long view are the worse for it. Foresight reveals the true path to resilience today.

Much of the value of scenario planning is experiential: you really do have to be there through the scenario-building process for it to change how you think. Nevertheless, we do sincerely hope that we have opened a window in your mind and that you will now reject, or at least question, fatalism, in favour of taking control. Every individual's job, after all, should be to leave the world in a better shape than we came to it, and to do this we will always need to change it.

Well, it appears as though we have come to the end of our brief journey into the future, at least for the time being. At the beginning of this book we commented that throughout history people have been curious about what the future might look like. Alongside questions about the universe, God, and intelligent life on other planets, conversations concerning what's next for us individually and collectively are universally fascinating. Perhaps this is because these questions link to other questions about meaning, purpose, and direction — which, in turn, tracks back to why we are here and how we should live (the universe again, and perhaps God again, too).

Scenarios are usually commissioned by and connected to sober-suited commercial or government interests, but they are at their most fascinating and involving when they spill over and rub up against deliberations about the human condition. You can't really say this in front of most sober-suited people. But quite often they discover this for themselves when they engage with scenarios, and they are changed forever in terms of how they think about themselves and the organisations with whom they work.

Of course, scenarios are primarily used to test the resilience of various strategies and assumptions, and they do this in spades. But they can also be useful for unlocking a more philosophical discussion about where individuals and institutions currently stand and what, or where, they would like to be, and be like, in the future. Maybe this is why scenarios are so powerful. Done well, they tap into a universal desire to think freely. They liberate our imaginations and give us permission to think differently and to dream new dreams about building a better world: to really think deeply about how things are now, and ask why; to think about how things could one day be, and ask why not.

Scenario planning and other foresight methodologies also open a window on the most perplexing philosophical puzzle: it is only by living our lives that we learn how to live the life already lived.

It doesn't take an army to change the world. All it requires is an individual who has the courage to begin asking questions, and who starts to tell stories about how things might change.

Epilogue:

strategic shocks — ten game-changers for 2040

Just when you thought it was safe to relax, here are a handful of radical ideas that could turn your world upside-down. In scenario parlance, these are the wildcards — events that may seem unlikely, but would have a huge impact if they were ever to occur.

A Second American Civil War

Don't say we weren't warned! Bruce (The Boss) Springsteen's 'Wrecking Ball' anthem, stating that 'we take care of our own', and the Occupy Wall Street movement of 2011 hinted at what was coming.

The nascent failure of US capitalism to deliver the American dream has created the great divide. In the blue corner: the Tea Party traditionalists and the do-what-is-good-for-me Democrats. In the red corner: everyone else, including many Republicans, who have been persistently marginalised and exploited to pay for the extraordinary US global debt and the failure of 'small' government to protect its citizens against natural phenomena such as hurricanes, flooding, and the hell-bent erosion of the country's natural assets. This has lead to what is effectively a Balkanisation of the United States.

Children Born Today Need Never Die

The science of cryogenics has been frozen out by the dramatic inventions in bio-engineering. Stem-cell research and the advances in the human genome mean that we can now renew our bodies again and again: replacing ageing tissue and faulty organs, repairing trauma sites, and even substituting brain cells. And the ability to use the technology to alter the way we look or even our gender whenever we want has given new meaning to our life experiences. Rites of passage are swamped by the ennui of eternity, and the concept of romantic love is swept away by the mantra of manipulation.

Oil Hits US$500 a Barrel

Oil has, as we thought it might, risen sharply to US$300 a barrel in 2035. Unfortunately, alternative energy didn't save us; it was always going to be too little, too late. Traditional fuels were also hounded by problems, not least of which was their link to carbon — so, no saving grace from natural gas, coal, and other fossil fuels. Conservation seemed to be the only solution; doing more with less fuelled the focus on productivity and the need to change lifestyles as best we could.

But then a black bird flew in from the Middle East. This was not on the wings of conventional concerns about OPEC-style control of oil supply. Nor was it about the political stability of the Saudi royal family, or even the entrenched 'Al-Qaeda question'. No, it was when Israeli rockets rained on Tehran in 2039 and forced the closure of the Strait of Hormuz, between Oman and Iran, which carried a third of the sea-traded oil.

Bird-flu Pandemic Kills 500 Million Worldwide

It started innocuously enough. Well, not really, as nobody had been inoculated against this strain of bird flu. We learned later that the fatal event was an illegal cockfight in the Canary Islands, of all places, where local canaries were being pitched against saffron finches from the Amazon. One of the bird owners became contaminated after receiving scratches from both species. And the incubation period — well, it was a lightning 48 hours.

Of course, all of this needed something else. Unfortunately the carrier was a big rock 'n' roll fan, and hopped on a plane immediately after the fight to join 100,000 young kids at Shea Stadium, where an ageing Lady Gaga was performing on her Really Gaga tour. The rest, as they say, is history.

The Moon Becomes a Colony of China

This is a reprise of the Moon landings of almost 80 years ago. Space Race Two has been between Russia and China. It burst into life when the Russian space agency, Roskosmos, announced a manned mission to the Moon in 2035. The United States had long given away any interest in Moon landings, but the Chinese took up the challenge. Their Long March programme was more than a wish to lead the world in the science of manned space travel; it was also a push to lead the world in extraterrestrial colonisation. Peak oil and peak everything makes the search for new sources of raw materials — and, indeed, new materials — a critical requirement. Get in first and the cosmos is your oyster.

On 1 April 2040, Zai Zigzag in Shenzhou 21 blasted off from Jiuquan Space Launch Center in Inner Mongolia with his crew of 11; and just seven hours and 24 minutes later, the five yellow stars on the Chinese national flag were fluttering in the Moon breeze at the top of Mons Huygens. Earth's satellite is now a colony of the Chinese.

Louis XX Crowned King of France

The collapse of the European Union after 60 years of trying, and the disappearance of the euro as a currency, had every European looking back to whence they had come. And none more so than the French, whose fervent and, at times, chauvinistic national pride had forever made them outsiders to Germany's view of a united Europe, and the major anti-US cultural force. With the renaissance of the franc (although this time in mercifully smaller denominations) came a groundswell of nostalgia, and the idea of re-establishing the French monarchy. The website www.ancestry.net.fr suddenly became the focus for frantic research to confirm that Louis XX, born in 1974 and now 65 years old, was indeed the rightful heir to the throne. And on a bloodless Bastille Day of 14 July 2040 in the cathedral of Notre Dame, the coronation of Louis Alphonse de Bourbon, Duke of Anjou, took place. *Plus ça change plus c'est la meme chose* ...

The Internet Collapses

While everyone is waiting for a devastating physical or cyber attack on the internet, users start to abandon it in droves, due to serious problems. These do not involve spyware and viruses or hackers and trolls, but rather the government and corporate takeover of what was once a free worldwide web. Governments start to impose censorship, which effectively turns the internet into a series of regional intranets, while large corporations lock down much of the content, which results in the internet losing much of its free, open, and generative nature.

Hollywood Movies Plummet

For the first time in movie history, the Oscar nominations for best movie, best director, and best actor (male and female) failed to include one Hollywood movie. The Global Oscars, as they are now called, have long since been open in all categories, but the demise of Hollywood still comes as a surprise. Who would have thought that English-language movie production would now be centred in Chinawood, the film-making centre outside Tianjin, which has been servicing co-productions between the United States and China since 2012?

Water is the New Oil

Urbanisation, along with rising incomes, means that attitudes and behaviours relating to consumption change significantly. The result is that that half of the world's population ends up living in highly water-stressed regions. China, India, parts of Africa, and numerous other rapidly developing economies all suffer from severe water shortages and problems with water quality, which puts a brake on economic growth and triggers widespread social unrest.

Energy Becomes Almost Free

Breakthroughs in new technologies, ranging from synthetic biology and fusion technology to nanotechnology, lead to incredible gains in terms of energy production and supply. Moreover, developments in artificial intelligence, robotics, and intelligent systems create productivity gains that are totally unexpected and solve many of the problems related to societal ageing.

And now, we'll leave you with a final caution from Ian McEwan's great scenario-puzzle novel *Enduring Love*:

> Can you blame me for hating you for the things you allow to fill your mind — satellites, nano-technologies, genetic engineering, bio computers, hydrogen engines. It's all shopping. You buy it all, you're a cheerleader for it, an adman hired to talk up other people's stuff ... [There's] not a word about the real things like love and faith.

References and Useful Sources

Bawden, Richard and Freeman, Oliver, *Scenario Planning as an Experiential Exercise in Social, Reflexive and Transformational Learning*, Richmond, Sydney, 2007.

Brockman, Max, *What's Next: dispatches on the future of science,* Quercus, London, 2009.

Brugmann, Jeb, *Welcome to the Urban Revolution: how cities are changing the world,* Bloomsbury Press, New York, 2011.

Canto, Christophe and Faliu, Odile, *The History of the Future: images of the 21st century,* Flammarion, Paris, 1993.

Chakravorti, Bhaskar, *The Slow Pace of Fast Change: bringing innovations to market in a connected world,* Harvard Business School Press, Cambridge, 2003.

Forster, E.M., *Aspects of the Novel,* E. Arnold, London, 1927.

Freeman, Oliver, *Building Scenario Worlds,* Richmond Reports, Sydney, 2004.

——, 'Embracing Uncertainty: using scenarios to create strategy for alternative futures', paper given at 'Book: the international conference on the future of the book', Cairns Convention Centre, 2003.

——, 'People, Scenarios and Innovation', in *Inside the Innovation Matrix: finding the hidden human dimensions,* Australian Business Foundation, Sydney, 2008.

——, 'The Publisher in the New World if Only I Had Known That: the publishing world', *Publishing Studies,* no. 1, Spring 1995, pp. 37–42.

——, 'An Australian Perspective on the Future of Book Publishing', *Logos,* vol. 23, issue 3, Autumn 2012, page numbers not available.

Freeman, Oliver and Pattinson, Hugh, 'Exploring Client Scenarios Associated with Scenario Planning', *Futures*, vol. 42, issue 4, pp. 304–312.

Friedman, George, *The Next 100 Years: a forecast for the 21st century*, Black Inc, Melbourne, 2009.

Friedman, Thomas L., *The World is Flat: a brief history of the twenty-first century*, Farrar, Straus and Giroux, New York, 2005.

Gardner, Dan, *Future Babble: why expert predictions fail — and why we believe them anyway*, Scribe Publications, Melbourne, 2011.

Garreau, Joel, *Radical Evolution: the promise and peril of enhancing our minds, our bodies — and what it means to be human*, Doubleday, New York, 2005.

Gershenfeld, Neil, *When Things Start to Think*, Henry Holt and Company, New York, 1999.

Gladwell, Malcolm, *The Tipping Point: how little things can make a big difference*, Little, Brown and Company, Boston, 2000.

Greenfield, Susan, *Tomorrow's People: How 21st-century technology is changing the way we think and feel*, Penguin Books, London, 2004.

Jones, Tim and Dewing, Caroline, *Future Agenda: the world in 2020*, Infinite Ideas, 2010.

Kaku, Michio, *Physics of the Future: how science will shape human destiny and our daily lives by the year 2100*, Allen Lane, London, 2011.

Kunstler, James Howard, *The Long Emergency: surviving the end of oil, climate change, and other converging catastrophes of the twenty-first century*, Atlantic Monthly Press, New York, 2005.

McRae, Hamish, *The World in 2020: power, culture and prosperity*, Harper Collins, London, 1995.

Midgley, Gerald, *Systemic Intervention: philosophy, methodology and practice*, Kluwer Academic/Plenum Press, New York, 2000.

Milo, Paul, *Your Flying Car Awaits: robot butlers, lunar vacations, and other dead-wrong predictions of the twentieth century*, Harper Perennial, New York, 2009.

Naisbitt, John, *Mind Set!: reset your thinking and see the future*, Collins Business, New York, 2006.

Neville, Richard, *Footprints of the Future: handbook for the third millennium*, Richmond, Sydney, 2002.

Ogilvy, James A., *Creating Better Futures: scenario planning as a tool for a better tomorrow*, Oxford University Press, New York, 2002.

Pattern, Chris, *What Next?: surviving the twenty-first century*, Penguin Books, London, 2009.

Penn, Mark and Zalesne, E. Kinney, *Microtrends: the small forces behind tomorrow's big changes*, Allen Lane, London, 2007.

Saul, John Ralston, *The Collapse of Globalism: and the reinvention of the world*, Penguin Books, London and New York, 2005.

Schwartz, Peter, *The Art of the Long View: paths to strategic insight for yourself and your company*, Richmond, Sydney, 2002.

Seidensticker, Bob, *Future Hype: the myths of technology change*, Berrett-Koehler Publishers, San Francisco, 2006.

Shapiro, Robert, *Futurecast 2020: a global vision of tomorrow*, Profile Books, London, 2008.

Siemens, 'Horizons 2020 — A Glimpse of Things to Come', *Pictures of the Future*, Fall 2004, www.siemens.com/horizons2020.

Smith, Laurence C., *The World in 2050: four forces shaping civilization's northern future*, Plume Books, New York, 2011.

Stevenson, Mark, *An Optimist's Tour of the Future*, Profile, London, 2011.

Surowiecki, James, *The Wisdom of Crowds*, Doubleday, New York, 2004.

Toffler, Alvin, *Future Shock*, Pan Books, London, 1971.

Turney, Jon, *The Rough Guide to the Future*, Rough Guides, London, 2010.

van der Heijden, Kees, *Scenarios: the art of strategic conversation*, John Wiley & Sons, Oxford, 1996.

van der Heijden, Kees, et al., *The Sixth Sense: accelerating organizational learning with scenarios*, John Wiley & Sons, Chichester, 2002.

van Santen, Rutger; Khoe, Djan; and Vermeer, Bram, *2030: technology that will change the world*, Oxford University Press, New York, 2010.

Watson, Richard, *Future Files: a history of the next 50 years*, Scribe Publications, Melbourne, 2007.

——, *Future Minds: how the digital age is changing our minds, why this matters and what we can do about it*, Nicholas Brealey, London, 2010.

Weber, Steven, *The Success of Open Source*, Harvard University Press, Cambridge, 2004.

Zittrain, Jonathan, *The Future of the Internet: and how to stop it*, Penguin Books, London, 2008.

Acknowledgements

We would first like to thank our many clients, who have allowed us to help them in the challenge of embracing the uncertainties of the future and in improving the quality of their strategic planning.

Our scenarios about the future are built on a methodology, the foundation of which was provided by our work with Global Business Network in San Francisco, where Peter Schwartz, Napier Collyns, Stewart Brand, Kees van der Heijden, Jay Ogilvy, and Lawrence Wilkinson were inspiring mentors. Our spin on the Shell approach to scenario work, the scenario-planning QUEST, was developed with our consulting colleagues — in particular Richard Bawden and Melanie Williams.

In terms of our own development as futurists, there are many people to thank — fellow consultants, outstanding thinkers, academics, writers, and the people who have worked with us on the nuts and bolts of the day-to-day administration of our projects. In any order, all hail: Richard Neville, Richard Bawden, George Burt, Susan Oliver, Hugh Pattinson, Keith Suter, Anita Kelleher, Ross Dawson, Tom Brigstocke, Richard Slaughter, Kylie Gillon, Stewart Clegg, Peter Lazar, John Trudgian, Charles Handy, Theodore Zeldin, Douglas Slater, Alan Sekers, Wayde Bull,

Alexandra Berthold, Greg Rippon, Hardin Tibbs, Bob Frater, Howard Dare, Peter Wallman, John Loty, Michael Hollingworth, Kristen Hansen, Gill Coutts, Roger West, Georgia Freeman, Roy Green, Clare Hallifax, Bernard Lloyd, James Cowan, Michael Killalea, Adam Kahane, Bronwyn Jones, Louis van der Merwe, Ian Dunlop, Gerald Harris, Geraldene Callanan, Andrew Campion, Lisa Coles, Simon Marks-Isaacs, Richard Hames, John Thackara, Narelle Kennedy, Howard Dare, Jack McLoone, Kate Delaney, Scott Martin, Richard Eckersley, Carmelita Emperado, Andrew Crosthwaite, Stuart Henshall, Noah Raford, Rhonda Evans, Ewan McEoin, and Barbara Heinzen.